MOUNTAIN WATER AND RIVER GOLD

& MOUNTAIN WATER RIVER GOLD

Stories of Gold Mining in the Alexandra District

John McCraw

Square One Press
P. O. Box 2143, Dunedin, New Zealand
www.book.co.nz

Book Design, Trevor Reeves
Cover Illustration (painting), Judith Wolfe

Published by Square One Press, P. O. Box 2143, Dunedin, New Zealand. Phone 03 455-3117, Fax: 03 456 1053
Email: treeves@es.co.nz

ISBN 0 908562 04 7

Internet catalogue:
The Book Company of New Zealand:
http://www.book.co.nz

Book Design, Trevor Reeves.
Cover Ilustration, Judith Wolfe. (arts site: www.arts.org.nz)

Produced by Mediaprint Services Limited,
P. O. Box 2143, Dunedin, New Zealand.
Printed by Otago University Print, Dunedin.

CONTENTS

ILLUSTRATIONS

PREFACE

The gold mining era was the most important period in the 150 year history of Central Otago. It was during this period that the region was populated, towns established, roads formed and the water races constructed that were ready- made for the irrigation which was to be the prosperity of the district after the gold had gone.

Alluvial gold mining and water are inseparable. The lone miner, squatting beside a stream with his gold pan, uses the water to swirl away the sand and so leave behind a few specks of the heavy yellow metal. Another miner bails water from the stream into his cradle, which he vigorously rocks as the water finds its way tortuously through the device, leaving the heavy gold to be trapped on mats and riffles as the sand is washed through. Men pooled their resources to construct, with difficulty and ingenuity, long and expensive water races to bring water from distant streams to their claims. There it was used to wash sand and gravel through sluices where the gold was trapped.

Later water, under pressure, was directed from nozzles to break up compacted gravel before it was washed into the sluices. Later still water, under even higher pressure, was used work elevators that sucked sand and gold out of deep mines. And water was necessary to keep the giant gold dredges afloat in their ponds and to wash the never-ending stream of gravel and sand, brought up by their groaning chains of buckets, through the screens and over the gold-saving tables.

So the efforts to obtain water and bring it to the claims became as important as mining the gold itself. Water became a valuable chattel which was owned through 'water rights' and which could be bought and sold and squabbled over in endless litigation in the Wardens' Courts. The remains of water races, flumes and dams scattered throughout the district are as significant to the history of the mining era as the remains of the mines themselves.

People, of course, needed water for 'domestic purposes.' But in a proclaimed Mining District, as was Central Otago, mining was paramount and the Mining Act ruled that water was to be used for mining only. No provision was made for water to be supplied to towns. But in the semi-arid environment of Central Otago a reliable water supply was as vital to the towns as it was to the miners. So constant confrontations took place between townspeople and powerful mining concerns who had the legal advantage, and the water.

Interest in the fascinating history of Central Otago is growing apace. Perhaps one reason is the increasing popularity of genealogy, with its chance of discovering that an ancestor followed an exotic pioneering occupation such as gold mining, coach driving or running a goldfields pub. Newcomers are curious about the unique landscape and ubiquitous scars of early gold mining visible on every side. Yet other people see commercial opportunities in conducting ever-increasing groups of visitors to points of interest.

Whatever the reasons may be, the interest is leading to an increasing demand for accurate information about the history of the region. Central Otago is fortunate in that there has been a large number of books and booklets published in the past. Classics such as Pyke's History of Early Gold Discoveries in Otago or Gilkison's Early Days in Central Otago were written by men with personal experience of the early mining days. Others such as Hearn and Hargreave's The Speculators' Dream and the Otago Centennial series are the result of painstaking academic research of early records. Others again are based on anecdotes passed down from the pioneers.

This book consists of a selection of historical essays, each of which deals with a separate incident or aspect of the gold mining days. It was intended that incidents from the whole of Central Otago might be recorded but it quickly became obvious that so much material was available that it would be necessary to restrict the present study to the southern end of the Manuherikia Valley and, in particular, to the district around Alexandra and Clyde. Further volumes in preparation will extend the scope of the study both in subject matter and in geographical coverage.

ACKNOWLEDGEMENTS

Although much information is available, it is often not easily accessible. The prime source of information is in the Record Books of the Wardens' Courts and in the bundles of Applications made to the Court which are held in the Regional Office of the National Archives in Dunedin. Each bundle, tied with tape, consists of the applications made to a Court over one year and may easily exceed 100. It is laborious work unfolding each fragile application, scanning it, noting its contents and carefully refolding it. And yet here is where the accurate information is concealed.

The task was made much easier by the knowledge and willing cooperation of the Chief Archivist, Peter Miller and his staff.

It was a relief to turn to a perusal of the goldfields newspapers such as the Dunstan Times;, the Alexandra Herald, and the early issues of the Otago Daily Times and the Otago Witness with its weekly page on mining. The comments of the mining correspondents put flesh on the bare skeleton of the Court Applications. Many issues are on microfilm and my thanks are due to the staff of the Interloan Department of the University of Waikato Library for their patience over many years in arranging a constant supply of reels of microfilm from the Alexander Turnbull Library.

But many issues of goldfields newspapers are not yet microfilmed and these were consulted in that treasure house of Otago: the Hocken Library. Again the knowledge and cooperation, far beyond the call of duty, of the Reference Librarian, David McDonald. is gratefully acknowledged.

People in Alexandra and Clyde contributed. Many who told me stories of the early days are no longer with us—the late Glad McArthur, Geoff and Alex Taylor and George Govan. Other were recorded on early tapes, thanks to the New Zealand Broadcasting Service and to Les Thomson of Alexandra.

Others who have provided information or logistic support include Ernie King, David Blewett, Graeme Anderson, Jerry Sanders, Rowland Lopdell. John Wilson and John Breen.

Helena Heydelaar, the former Manager, and Cheryl Grubb the present Manager and Elaine Gough of Alexandra's William Bodkin Museum have been very generous with photographs from the extensive

Museum collection. The members of the Alexandra Historical Society have been most helpful and in particular Joan Stevens has spent much time in obtaining information and in trying to find answers to difficult questions.

Thanks are due to the University of Waikato, particularly the Department of Earth Sciences, Campus Photography and the Library, for steady support over the years. Finally grateful acknowledgment is made to Dr David McCraw for field companionship, field assistance and editing and to Jean King for skilled proof reading.

1.

DISCOVERING THE DUNSTAN

Henry Stebbing[1] and his mates were unlucky—they only just missed discovering the Dunstan Goldfield. In mid-August 1862 they had found payable gold at the confluence of the Manuherikia and Clutha Rivers less than 200 metres downstream from the end of the main street of the present town of Alexandra. The place is now known as Prospectors Point.

Stebbing's party packed up and began the 80 kilometre journey back to Gabriels Gully, where gold had been discovered the previous year, to report their find to Major Croker, Commissioner of the Tuapeka Goldfield.

Stebbing couldn't know, even as his party struggled down through the rugged gorges of the Clutha River on the afternoon of Friday, 15 August 1862, that two other prospectors, Hartley and Reilly, were already heaving heavy bags up on to the counter of Dunedin's Gold Receiver.[2] Little wonder the bags, roughly sewn from bits of moleskin trousers and canvas, made a substantial thump as they hit the wooden table-top—they contained 87 lbs (32.5 kg) of gold.

Stebbing reported-in three days later and so missed any chance of a reward for discovering a new goldfield. As a consolation he was granted an enlarged 'prospector's claim' in recognition of his discovery.

Horatio Hartley and Christopher Reilly were not the first to find gold in what would become known as the Dunstan district. John Buchanan, a member of Alexander Garvie's surveying party, had found gold in the Clutha River several years before. In his account of the expedition Garvie had said:

> It was found in the Clutha river above the junction of the Manuherikia, and in the Tuapeka stream, in sufficient quantities to make it probable that it would pay to work if set about in a proper manner, with some wholesale system of washing, such as sluicing. Specks were also found in the Manuherikia. . . [3]

This information was buried in an official report which, for some reason, was not published until 18 months after the expedition had taken place. Even then the newspapers did not pick it up and, under the circumstances, it is not surprising that there was no reaction from the population.

16

In 1861 there was another discovery. M. W. McCrae had led a prospecting party across Otago from the Shag River valley to Lake Wanaka. On the way he found gold in the Manor Burn and predicted that a payable goldfield existed in its headwaters. Above the Manuherikia River junction the party found gold along the Clutha River, not only in surface gravels on both banks but also in a hole sunk to a depth of several feet. This, unfortunately, had to be abandoned through lack of supporting timber and pumping gear. McCrae wrote:

> I am, however, of the opinion that deep sinking exists in this part of the country, which would remunerate miners well if timber was easily obtained.[4]

Even though this report was addressed to the Superintendent of the Province it was not 'laid on the table' of the Provincial Council and so was apparently ignored.

No one, however, could ignore 87 lbs of gold. Saturday's *Otago Daily Times* broke the news of the men's arrival in town with their gold but could only speculate as to its origin. Hartley and Reilly had made it quite clear to the astonished Gold Receiver that they would not disclose the whereabouts of their discovery until some financial incentive was forthcoming. The newspaper made a wild guess that it came from Mt Watkins, 36 kilometres north of Dunedin, purely on the grounds that two strange men were reported as having visited the nearby township of Waikouaiti for stores.

Vincent Pyke, the newly appointed Secretary to the Goldfields Department, carefully examined the contents of the prospectors' bags and concluded that the thin flakes of scaly gold had been subject to pounding by boulders in some large stream. From his knowledge of other reports of gold from the interior, he was sure this gold came, not from Mt Watkin, but from some river bed in the interior.

So while interviewing the men on the Saturday morning about a proposed reward in return for their disclosure of the location, Pyke[5] caused the pair some consternation by suggesting the gold came from near Lake Wanaka. When Reilly got up to walk out, muttering about having their brains picked, the Secretary knew his guess was close to the mark. Pyke told them if they left the room he would go straight to the place where they got the gold and that would be the end of any reward. Pyke was bluffing, but the two prospectors were not to know he had never been further into the interior than Tuapeka, and they disclosed the location. Negotiations went on during the following Monday and finally they were promised a reward of £2,000 if 16,000 oz of gold were brought down to Dunedin within three months.[6]

The Announcement

The town was in a state of great tension and mounting excitement during that weekend with rumours growing by the hour. When, finally, Tuesday's paper[7] disclosed, in headlines unusually large for the time, that the gold had come from a rugged gorge of the Clutha River far to the west, the place went mad. The turmoil engendered as frantic preparations were made by hundreds of men for an immediate start for the new goldfield, has been well documented.[8]

The news reached the miners at Gabriels Gully that same Tuesday evening, just the day after Stebbing had proudly, but belatedly, announced the finding of his new goldfield to Major Crocker. Repeated warnings by the *Otago Daily Times* that the new goldfield was more than 160 kilometres away across rugged, snow-covered country where supplies were non-existent went largely unheeded. Perhaps the paper had good reason for discouraging the frenetic exodus that was developing. It announced it had to increase its price to 6d. because compositors' wages had had to be increased fifty percent—presumably to try to stop them joining the gold rush. By Wednesday morning, 20 August, the Rush was under way both from Dunedin and from the Tuapeka Goldfield.

Waiting for News
It was four or five days' ride or about a week's hard tramp from Dunedin to the new diggings. This meant that it would be about 10 days before word could be expected from those who had reached the Dunstan. While it waited, the local newspaper was hard pressed to find news to match the excitement in the town. Over the next week or so the paper repeated Hartley and Reilly's story several times and discussed at length a suitable name for the new diggings. It came up with 'Hartley.' Then it discussed what little was known about the various routes to the new goldfield and wrote several columns about the possibility of a shipping service up the Clutha River. Then it reopened the discussion about the name for the new diggings and, deciding that 'Hartley' was unfair to Reilly, toyed with 'Cairnmuir' but fortunately, came up with 'Dunstan' instead. So from 23 August 1862 the new discovery was known as the 'Dunstan Diggings.' [9]

Hartley and Reilly's Story
Once more the newspaper went over the Hartley and Reilly story but this time managed to extract some interesting details from the two prospectors. They had worked their way up the Clutha River from the vicinity of Beaumont, they said, and in the gorge some miles below the junction with the Manuherikia River, they began to get prospects. They thought these would return an ounce a day with a cradle and it encouraged them to push further up the river. With a gold pan borrowed from a sheep station to replace their own which had been broken, as had their shovel, Hartley and Reilly followed the river up into the gorge where it cut through the Dunstan Mountains.

They prospected along the western bank until, about three kilometres below the junction with the Kawarau River, they struck good gold at a place they named 'Reillys Beach.' Here they obtained about 40 oz for a week's work. Further up the river, on the other side, they could see parallel rock bars running out into the river similar to those where Hartley had obtained good gold on the Fraser River back in British Columbia.

With their provisions exhausted and their gear damaged Hartley and Reilly had to go out to Waikouaiti for supplies, but they then returned to the rock bars they had seen on the eastern side of the gorge. Here,

Figure 1.1. This 1956 photograph looks down the Cromwell Gorge (Dunstan Gorge of the miners) from a point a few kilometres below Cromwell. It shows the highway and railway with orchards on the left and in the distance. There is evidence of goldmining along the river bank on the right. All of these features are now inundated by Lake Dunstan.

at a beach they named 'Hartleys Beach,' immediately beneath the future site of the Cromwell brewery, they struck it rich. Helped by the fact that the river was at its lowest level since settlement began, they collected, from the shallow wash behind the rock bars, not less than 12 oz (0.37 kg) of gold a day. It was the recognition that these rock bars acted as natural traps for gold that led to their success. But it must be remembered they were prospecting and not mining, so they were not confined to a 30 ft (9 m) square claim as later miners would be. They were free to roam over a wide area collecting only the richest accumulations of gold.

Choice of Routes

It was estimated by the *Otago Daily Times* that by 25 August, only six days after the announcement of the discovery, 2,000 men were on their way to the new diggings. Again the paper warned of the total lack of provisions in the interior and added a new warning of the dangers of snow on the inland routes. It gave point to its warning by relating the story of two miners crossing the Lammerlaw Ranges from the Tuapeka diggings who were lost in a snowstorm for four days. They were fortunate to escape with only the loss of toes from frostbite.

The most popular route for the hordes leaving Dunedin for the new El Dorado was by way of the Shag Valley and the Maniototo Plains. This was a relatively easy, if lengthy, route once Waikouaiti had been reached. The easiest and quickest way to do this was by sea. A procession of steamers was soon leaving Dunedin, each crowded with hopeful miners who were to find landing on the open beach at Waikouaiti was an interesting experience. Boats manned with Maori oarsmen came alongside and each headed for the beach loaded to the gunwales. On reaching the surf passengers were met by muscular Maori women standing up to their waists in the swirling water. Each hoisted a surprised man on to her back and for the price of one shilling conveyed him, more or less dry, to the beach.

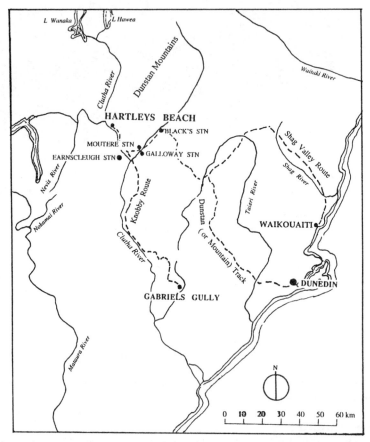

Figure 1. 2. Hartleys Beach in the Dunstan (Cromwell) Gorge was the scene of the major gold discovery in August 1862. Miners rushed to the Dunstan discovery from Dunedin and from Gabriels Gully.

At Waikouaiti Johnny Jones's store did a roaring trade outfitting men with whatever food they could carry and with the tools that the more experienced miners told the new chums they would need. When loaded up with even minimal mining gear, few men could carry, in addition, more than four or five day's food, with the result that most arrived at the diggings just as their food ran out.

In spite of warnings by runholders, many would-be miners tried to take the Mountain Track that was reputed to be the shortest route to the new diggings. It began at West Taieri and headed west over the Barewood Plateau and then began to climb over the Rock and Pillar Range. This 57 kilometre section was not only arduous but also downright dangerous, as for more than eight kilometres it lay at an altitude of about 1,000 metres. Snow lay heavily on the ground and there was no shelter from the icy wind. Many wisely turned back on this stage of the track.

Those who had left from Gabriels Gully had a head start of at least two days on the Dunedin contingent and they made the most of it. Their route involved much scrambling up and down steep ridges, an easy stretch along the terraces that flanked the Clutha River and then a long climb up to the summit ridge of the Knobby Range. Here again snow and cold winds were the order of the day but finally the tired travellers could descend to the confluence of the Clutha and Manuherikia Rivers. Now they were within sight of their objective and, with the crossing of the Manuherikia River, the worst of the journey was behind them.

News at Last
At last the waiting was over. On 1 September the Dunedin newspaper published the first reports from the diggings. Two miners, George Graham and John Williams, had arrived back in town on the afternoon of 31 August and told how they had reached the Dunstan on 25

Figure 1. 3. Hartleys Beach in the Cromwell Gorge in 1865. It was among the rock bars on the right that Hartley and Reilly gathered 87 pounds weight of gold in August 1862 and so precipitated the Dunstan Gold Rush.

August and found only about a dozen miners there. As the pair had no cradle and had exhausted their food, they left after two days and made a quick trip back to town, meeting on the way hundreds of men heading in the opposite direction.

Also to hand was the first report of Jackson Keddell,[10] who signed himself 'Sub-Inspector of Constabulary in charge of the Clutha Gold Fields'. Keddell, formerly the officer-in-charge of the gold escort from the Tuapeka Goldfield, had left Dunedin with Hartley on Saturday, 23 August and arrived at Shennan's Moutere Station late on the following Tuesday. Next day the pair went up the Dunstan Gorge but were met by hundreds of disgruntled miners who had arrived over the last two days but could not see any ground suitable for mining. They were used to the flat valley floor at Gabriels Gully where they could dig a hole and strike gold-bearing 'wash' a metre or so below the surface. Where were they supposed to start digging here? All they could see was a rough, boulder strewn gorge with precipitous walls and a wide, swiftly flowing river.

There were mutterings and threats of violence towards Hartley— 'Throw him into the river,' came from the back of the crowd. Hartley, backed by Keddell, no doubt with his hand on the hilt of his sword, patiently explained that here the gold was under the beach sand and trapped behind the rock bars running out into the water. He took a shovel and pan and, luckily, was able to demonstrate to the astonished assemblage that there was ample gold available.

Figure 1. 4. Captain Jackson Keddell arrived at the Dunstan as Constable in Charge only a few days after the first miners. He acted as Commissioner of the Goldfield for some time before being officially appointed. After serving in the Land Wars and as Goldfield Warden on the Coromandel Peninsula he returned to the Dunstan in 1880 as Warden.

Keddell estimated that by 28 August there were some 2,000 miners on the field and, in spite of all the warnings, only a few had sufficient provisions. In fact, he thought that because of lack of suitable tools and shortage of food, fewer than 100 men were actually at work.

Among the throng of new arrivals who tramped over the Knobby Range from Gabriels Gully were Sarah and Lewis Cameron accompanied by their two sons, George aged six and Lewis, a baby of 16 months. According to one account they arrived on 27 August, a day after Keddell himself. It is almost certain that Mrs Cameron was the first woman on the Dunstan Goldfield.

Some miners were already starving and many had to start a forced march back to the nearest store, either at Gabriels or Waikouaiti, for supplies. It was not until drays with provisions began to arrive from Waikouaiti, the first on 30 August, that the food shortage was relieved.

Keddell seemed to be exactly the right man for the very difficult job he had been given. Without 'back-up' to rely on, his handling of hundreds of testy men relied on a nice mixture of diplomacy and bluff, overlaid with an air of authority and knowledge which was respected by the miners. His settling of disputes at Hartleys Beach was an example. Early arrivals naturally made for this spot and promptly occupied every metre of the beaches by pegging out 'creek or river claims.' With everyone of them a 'goldfields lawyer,' they pointed to the prevailing regulations by which claims in the beds of creeks or rivers could be up to 50 ft (15 m) long and embrace the full width of the river, including both banks, instead of the usual 30 ft by 30 ft (9 m by 9 m).

Not to be outdone, Keddell drew the miners attention to the fact that they had read only that part of the regulation which suited them. The regulation went on to say, he pointed out, that such claims had to be registered and before this could be done, notice in writing (on the form prescribed) had to be given to the warden (in this case, Keddell), and the same notice displayed for 14 days. Then, if there were no objections, the warden would register the claim and work could go ahead. But Keddell pointed out that such registration would only be given where it was intended to divert the stream or river. Needless to say, that was the end of talk about river claims.

Within a few days things had settled down. Every metre of the river beaches was taken up from the junction of the Kawarau River down through the Dunstan Gorge and into the gorge below the Manuherikia River junction. Those miners who had a cradle were reclaiming at least an ounce of gold per man per day. A large number were camped about the mouth of the Manuherikia River and for 3 kilometres or so up this river the beaches were occcupied with busy miners. One township (later to become Clyde) had sprung up at Coal Point at the mouth of the Dunstan Gorge. Another was established 3 kilometres further down the river, at Muttontown, where sheep were killed for meat for the miners and where the Earnscleugh Station boat provided the only means of crossing the river. Although large numbers of disillusioned, disappointed and hungry men had left to return to Dunedin or to their hastily abandoned claims at other gold fields, about 3,000 remained. Food was extremely dear because of the high freight rates but starvation was no longer a threat. For a couple of weeks life along the river beaches was busy and productive, but then things started to go wrong.

The Rising River
On Saturday 20 September, in the face of a steady, strong north-west wind, everything changed. The river began to rise as snow in the back country melted and by Monday all the beach claims were under water. The pale sea-green river became an angry, swirling mass of muddy, turgid water and rose 3 metres so quickly that many miners were forced to flee, leaving behind tents and mining gear. Many piles of valuable 'wash,' carefully stacked above what was assumed to be high water level, were swept away. On the advice from old hands, who predicted the river level would not fall again until the following winter, disappointed miners abandoned the river beaches and set out to search for other sources of gold.

The Dispersal
In some ways the flooding simply speeded up the inevitable need for miners to look elsewhere for gold. From a point 12 kilometres up the Kawarau River to about 10 kilometres below the Manuherikia junction, men were panning and cradling, but the easily obtained gold in the limited area of the river beaches was nearly exhausted.

Some had already been poking about with prospecting dishes in tributary streams but now, in the face of the rising river, a swarm of out-of-work miners descended on the surrounding countryside. Reports of gold discoveries soon came in thick and fast. Up the Manuherikia River, which had not been subjected to serious flooding, gold at shallow depths was reported from near the mouth of Springvale Creek. There was gold, too, in another tributary, the Manor Burn, and rich gold was found near Stebbing's original discovery at the junction of the Manuherikia and Clutha Rivers. But all of these finds were eclipsed by reports of fabulous quantities of gold in the valleys of streams falling from the Old Man Range on the western side of the Clutha River.

The Gullies
It was a miner named Conroy who, on 1 October 1862, reported rich gold in the gully that, later, was to be named after him[11] and at the same time Hill and party discovered gold in Butchers, the neighbouring gully to the south. Within a few days 400 miners were at work in these gullies, with Conroys proving to be one of the richest streams in New Zealand. Two German miners, working there, brought in 50 lbs (18 kg) of gold for a few days work.

They were heady times. Each day brought fresh reports of discoveries, and the miners, reinforced by some of the 4,000 immigrants who had arrived in Dunedin from Australia during the last eight days of September, swarmed over the land like rabbits. Gold was found in Obelisk Creek and its near neighbours, at a place that was first called Speargrass Flat, later Bald Hill Flat and much later still, Fruitlands. In late November, Blackman and party discovered gold in two streams that combined to flow into the Fraser River. The locality is known to this day as 'Blackmans' and the two streams are Omeo Creek and Coal Creek. For a short time interest was diverted to Potters Gully, in the Nevis Valley and then to the Cardrona River near Lake Wanaka. Soon however, the attractions of Conroys and its neighbouring gullies, drew most of the miners back.

This was the pattern of the hour—excited miners rushing from one discovery to another. If the new field did not yield more gold, or more easily recovered gold, they gave it away and either rushed on to the next discovery or streamed back to the field they knew. Gone was the depression caused by the flooding of river claims. No one was interested in mere ounces of gold any more—the talk was all of pounds weight. And the main method of recovery was still the gold pan and cradle.

Those mining in the gullies were convinced that somewhere at the head of each stream was a 'mother lode' which supplied the gold, and the search for this mythical source took the miners higher and higher up the ranges. They did not discover a mother lode but they did find gold at very high levels. In early November two separate rushes took place high up near the summit of the Old Man Range. One, on 11 November by Davis and party, was to the basin at the headwaters of the Fraser River. The other, in the same week, was by a large crowd who rushed right over the Old Man Range to Campbell Creek where rich gold had been discovered at an elevation of 1,200 m. Although this locality, where the best-known diggings was Potters No 2[12], lay in the headwaters of the East Branch of the Waikaia River, which flows southwards to the Mataura River, the miners looked to the Dunstan for their supplies. In early December gold was discovered at high elevation in Merediths Gully and McLennans Gully, now known as Omeo and Coal Creeks respectively. By the end of 1862 miners were at work in some 10 or 12 gullies along the face of the Old Man Range.

Their success was reflected in the gold won. The first gold escort left the Dunstan township on Tuesday 23 September with over 6,000 oz of gold; a second left the goldfields a fortnight later with another 6,200 oz. There would have been more but the buyers ran out of cash to purchase the gold. The third escort in November took 13,000 oz. But the Dunstan Rush was over. Things began to settle down in December and as the newspaper said:

> After a storm generally comes a calm, and so it has been in mining matters here. During the last two days we have not had a single instance of a discovery of great importance taking place.[13]

Not all of the gold came from the gullies of course, but it was the gully discoveries, together with discoveries in the lower reaches of the Manuherikia River and its tributaries, which encouraged the growth of a settlement at the junction of the rivers. Although the fantastic early returns from these localities quickly diminished, steady, continued production ensured the success of the township—the township which at first was called Manuherikia but within a year was to be christened 'Alexandra.'

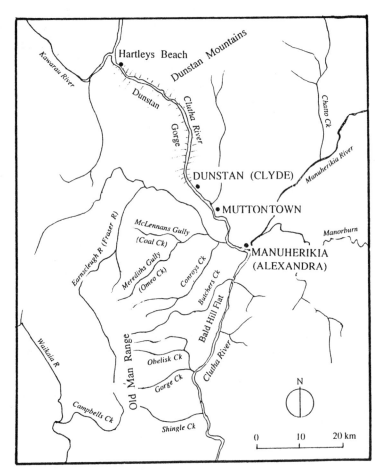

Figure 1. 5. Map of Alexandra district showing places connected with early gold discoveries.

NOTES

1. We don't know much about Stebbing. He is described as a 'Government prospector' who led one of three prospecting parties sent out by the Provincial Government. He is mentioned again in late 1862 as having just returned from a journey from Otago into Westland.

2. *Otago Daily Times* 16 August 1862. The report said that the gold was deposited at the Treasury. This was later corrected to the 'Office of the Gold Receiver.'

3. Garvie, *Otago Provincial Gazette* 22 September 1859, p. 279.

4. Appendix to Votes and Proceedings of the Provincial Council Session XIII p. xv.

5. Pyke, 1887, p. 69.

6. The £2,000 was the amount of the Gold Tax (at 2s. 6d. per oz) on the 16,000 oz.

7. *Otago Daily Times* 19 August 1862. The decision about the reward was made on Saturday so there seems little reason why the announcement could not have been made in Monday's newspaper. Perhaps some administrative matters needed attending to on the Monday before the announcement could be made.

8. For example Pyke, 1887 p. 74

9. As the new gold discovery was in the gorge of the Clutha River at the western end of the Dunstan Mountains (named by surveyor/explorer J. T. Thomson), the gorge was

referred to as the 'Dunstan Gorge.'

10. Only the Superintendent of the Province could proclaim a Goldfield and he was visiting Wellington, so the Dunstan Goldfield was not proclaimed until 23 September. Until that time Keddell acted not only as a police officer but also, without legal status, as Goldfield's Commissioner. He was fomally appointed Commissioner on 1 October, Justice of the Peace and Resident Magistrate on 21 October and Judge of the Wardens' Court on 2 December 1862.

11. To the miner a 'gully' was a small, narrow valley where mining took place. Generally, but not always, a stream ran through it. The gully was usually named after the original discoverer of gold. Mining activities were not confined to the bed of the stream but included any alluvial flood plains on either side and the lower side slopes of the gully. Modern map makers have almost everywhere replaced the miners' 'Gully' with 'Creek.' Exceptions are Conroys Gully and Butchers Gully.

12. Not to be confused with the Potters Gully, later called 'Potters No 1,' which is a tributary of the Nevis River. The prospector, John L. Potter, had a hand in the discovery of gold at both localities.

13. *Otago Daily Times* 5 December 1862.

DUNSTAN GOLD RUSH

Chronology of First 12 Weeks

August 1862

10 Sunday	Hartley and Reilly leave Dunstan Gorge for Dunedin.
14 Thursday	Hartley and Reilly arrive in Dunedin via the Mountain track.
15 Friday	Hartley and Reilly deposit 87lbs of gold.
16 Saturday	First report of find published.
18 Monday	Location revealed and reward claimed.
19 Tuesday	Report in *Otago Daily Times*; reaches Gabriels Gully in evening.
20 Wednesday	Duntan Rush leaves Gabriels Gully and Dunedin.
23 Saturday	Captain Keddell leavesDunedin for Dunstan.
25 Monday	Only a dozen miners in the Dunstan Gorge.
27 Wednesday	Keddell arrives at Shennan's Moutere Station.
28 Thursday	Keddell inspects diggings. All the 2,000 miners are from Gabriels. Keddell and Hartley face angry miners who can't find gold.
29 Friday	Gold discovery reported in Moa Creek, a tributary of the Nokomai River which is a tributary of the Mataura River.
30 Saturday	Population 3,000 miners. First dray with food arrives.

September 1862

1 Monday	Keddell's first report published.
4 Thursday	Several drays arrive from Waikouaiti.
9 Tuesday	Hill arrives to set up river ferries.]
11 Thursday	Keddell reports miners 6 miles below Manuherikia River junction. Population decreased to 2,000. Two townships established, one at Coal Point (Clyde) and the other 2 miles downriver at Muttontown.
20 Saturday	River rises 10ft.
21 Sunday	Claims flooded. Dunstan Gorge abandoned.

October 1862

2	Gold discovery reported in 8-Mile Gully by Conroy
3	Gold discovery reported in Butchers Gully
15	Gold discovery reported in Potters Gully, Nevis Valley.

November 1862

12	Gold discovery Cardrona River.
20	Gold discovery Campbells Creek west side Old Man Range.
21	Gold discovery at Arrow River reported.

Figure 1. 6. Chronology of the Dunstan Gold Rush.

2.

JUNCTION TOWNSHIP

To the weary miners rushing from Gabriels Gully to the new gold discovery in the Dunstan Gorge,[1] the junction of the Manuherikia and Clutha Rivers was a convenient place to camp. After a long hard day tramping over the Knobby Range and the plunge through the cold waters of the Manuherikia River, most were glad to make camp on the narrow river flat at the foot of the high bank overlooking the confluence.

It was a good camp site. There was ample scrub for warming fires, and river water for the billy was only a couple of metres below. For most, however, the camp was just a brief resting-place before beginning the last stage of their journey to the diggings. But some, who had already found gold in the nearby beach sands, decided to stay on and soon the low flood plain was covered with tents. Once wagons arrived with supplies, a store and the inevitable grog-shop were set up and a settlement was soon taking shape.

Figure 2. 1. Previous page: The tent village of Manuherikia (the future Alexandra) at the confluence of the Clutha (on left) and Manuherikia Rivers sketched by Lysaght from the Teviot track in December, 1862. Many of the structures are on a low river terrace subsequently destroyed by floods. Frenchmans Point (before it was destroyed by mining) on left of junction and Prospectors Point on right.
Above: From about the same viewpoint today.

Three weeks later, when hundreds of miners were displaced from the Clutha River beaches by the rising river, the population of the junction camp increased rapidly and space was soon at a premium. As still more miners arrived, newcomers had to camp higher up the bank and finally spread out on to the terrace above. There, tents were pitched along the tracks leading to the Dunstan and to the newly established police camp.

The setting up of canvas-roofed stores and hotels marked the transition from a camp to a township.[2] It was at first referred to as the 'Lower Township' to distinguish it from the 'Upper Township' (now Clyde) established at the mouth of the Dunstan Gorge. Sometimes it was called the 'Lower Junction,' but from the end of September 1862 despatches sent to the Dunedin newspapers were headed 'Manuherikia.'[3]

Land of Terraces

Those who settled on the higher level (referred to here as the 'town terrace' to distinguish it from several other terraces which will be mentioned), found themselves at the southern end of a gravelly, tussock-covered plain. There was a steep drop to the Clutha River on the west and south, and a rocky ridge on the east that hindered easy access to the Manuherikia River. Later they would find that this ridge, with one notable gap, ran up the side of the Manuherikia River for nearly two kilometres. Looking northwards the settlers could see, about a kilometre away, a break in the otherwise smooth plain. A rise of 5-6 metres marked a steep scarp that cut across from the rocky ridge to the banks of the Clutha River. The scarp was, not unnaturally, designated 'The Terrace' and has remained so ever since. A century later a street formed along the edge of the scarp was named 'Royal Terrace.'

The Terrace separated the town terrace from a slightly higher plain, soon to be known as Dunstan Flat, which stretched along the river some eight kilometres to the entrance to the Dunstan Gorge. This sandy wilderness, up to two kilometres wide, was bounded on the west by the Clutha River and on the east by the impressive 75-metre scarp of an even higher terrace.

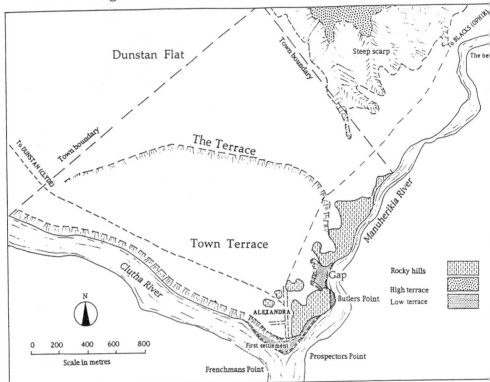

Figure 2. 2. Physical features of Alexandra and vicinity. Although the first settlement took place on a low terrace at the confluence of the rivers, the main township was quickly established on the higher terrace (the 'town terrace'). A low scarp, cutting across the plain north of the township, separates a higher level which is still referred to as 'The Terrace.' Further north, another much higher terrace (top right) forms a backdrop to the town. A discontinuous line of rocky hills runs along the north-westen bank of the Manuherikia River.

Need for Water

Those who settled on the town terrace faced an immediate inconvenience; they found themselves some distance from readily available water. No streams crossed the terrace for many kilometres and ground water was far below reach. The infrequent rain showers were quite incapable of reliably providing even the small amount of household water deemed adequate in those days. The new town would prove to have the lowest rainfall in New Zealand.[4] Domestic water could only be obtained by a scramble down steep banks to the rivers flowing 20 to 25 metres below and, as the township continued to grow, a more convenient supply of water became of some concern.

Not surprisingly, someone saw there was a ready market for river water delivered to the door. Soon the jog trotting of the water-cart horses became a familiar sound in the township. At 1s. a barrel for those living close to the river and 1s. 6d. for those farther away, we are told that it cost those households which could afford the service about 5s. a week for water. From necessity this trade was to persist, off and on, for the next forty-odd years.

Alexandra's summer heat, winter frosts, shortage of water, and dust raised by the nor'westers which howled out of the Dunstan Gorge, were apparently all regarded as small inconveniences when there was gold to be won. The township grew apace as discoveries were made at Conroys Gully and neighbouring gullies, at the Manor Burn, at Frenchmans Point and at Butchers Point. In August 1867, the township was proclaimed a Borough and a mayor and council were elected.

In spite of pressure from the townspeople, a year was to go by before the council was able to turn its attention to the provision of a convenient and reliable supply of water for the township. It was not to know that the struggle to provide the town with a 'supply of pure water for domestic purposes' was to continue for a hundred years, and some would say is still continuing. Water supply was a topic that would be discussed at almost every council meeting for the next century. It would be the cause of councillors almost coming to blows, of mayors resigning, of numerous court cases and of never-ending worry and frustration for council and citizens alike. All of this with the largest river in New Zealand flowing within a hundred metres of the council meeting room! But then, this was no ordinary river.

For one thing there was the difficulty and expense of raising the water the 30 metres or so from the river up to the level of the town. This was exacerbated, as many miners had found to their cost, by a water level that fluctuated widely. When the warm nor'westerly wind began melting the winter snow on the ranges, the river could rise 10 metres overnight. This made it virtually impossible to maintain any sort of intake structure for pumps or water races. The problems of utilising the Clutha River were just too difficult for the Borough Council of the time.

There was another problem, too, which concerned the council. In this dry goldfield, water was almost as valuable as the gold and the council knew that it would have to compete with the gold miners for a supply. In this competition the miners held the advantage, as this was a 'Mining District,' which meant that mining had priority in the use of water. In fact the Mining Act of the time did not recognise 'domestic purposes' as a legitimate use of water. Another difficulty was that the council could not hold a 'water right', as this was granted only to those holding a Miner's Right, and only an individual could hold such a Right.

But the townspeople were not the only ones who needed water—it was equally essential for the gold miners.

NOTES

1. Now called the Cromwell Gorge.
2. The lowest terrace was inundated in the 1863 flood and most buildings were moved to the town terrace above. The lowest terrace itself was completely swept away in the 'Old Man Flood' of 1878.
3. It was only after the marriage of the Prince of Wales to Princess Alexandra in mid-1863, that the name 'Alexandra' was adopted.
4. Annual rainfall is about 325 mm (13 inches) at Alexandra.

3.

CONROYS
– THE GOLDEN GULLY

Who was Conroy? Did Tod Symons, the Central Otago poet, have a factual basis for his poignant poem, *Red Conroy's Rose*, which tells of 'Red' Conroy dying on the Old Man Range in the dreadful snowstorms of August 1863? We really know little about the man.Even his first name is ucertain.[1] Presumably, like others, he had been denied access to his beach claim on the banks of the Clutha River by the flood which swept down the river on 20 September 1862, and was forced to prospect the surrounding countryside. Whoever Conroy was, his name lives on in the gully and the creek where he discovered gold on 1 October 1862.

Figure 3. 1. Looking up Conroys Creek towards a cloud-capped Old Man Range. Old gold workings in the left foreground are in Chapmans Gully. The orchards in the middle ground now occupy the Lower and Middle Basins of Conroys Gully. Conroys Creek flows out through the Lower Gorge at the right corner of the photograph.

33

Conroy turned up at Commisioner Keddell's[2] tent in Dunstan township (now Clyde) on Saturday, 4 October to announce his find and producing 16 dwt (25 gm) of rough gold. He asked to be granted a 'prospector's claim,'[3] the usual reward for discovering a new gold field. Accompanied by Conroy, the Commissioner set out to inspect the site of the new discovery.

The two men crossed the Clutha River, probably at Muttontown, and walked down Earnscleugh Flat, eventually coming to the lower reaches of what would later be called Conroys Creek. Keddell would note that the stream issued from a very narrow gorge before flowing for nearly two kilometres across the southern end of Earnscleugh Flat to join the

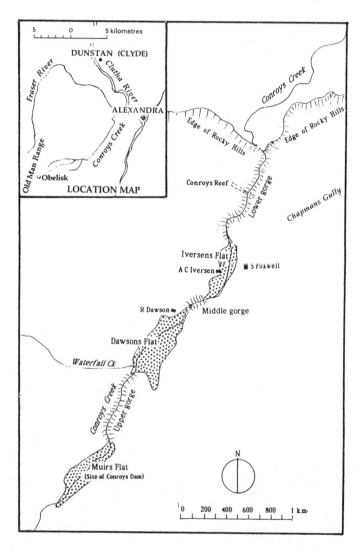

Figure 3. 2. Locality map and detailed map of Conroys Gully.

Fraser River. Skirting this 900 metre-long, impassable gorge, with its vertical rock walls 15-20 metres high and only a few metres apart, the pair came out into a small basin floored by an alluvial plain of about six hectares in area.

Miners were working along the creek here but the two pressed on and, after bypassing another very short gorge, Keddell found himself in a larger basin with a floor area of about eight hectares. Here was the main scene of activity, for this was where Conroy had discovered his gold and tentatively pegged out his 'prospector's claim.' Scores of miners were already working along the creek which issued from yet another narrow gorge at the head of this basin. Later Keddell would walk further up the valley and, above this upper gorge, find himself in yet a third basin (now inundated by the reservoir behind Conroys Dam) of about the same area as the last. From here he could see several steep torrents falling from the eastern slopes of the Old Man Range and joining about three kilometres upvalley to form the principal stream. He noted there was scrub suitable for firewood all along the creek with a particularly extensive cover in the headwaters.

Back in the middle basin,[4] Conroy explained to the Commissioner that he had sunk 11 holes, ranging in depth from 1.5 to 3.5 metres, into the alluvium bordering the stream. In six of these shafts he managed to reach 'bottom' and from five of these he obtained the 16 dwt of gold from 16 pans of wash.

Those familiar with mining at Gabriels Gully and in Victoria, should have found Conroys Gully[5] more to their liking than the beaches of the Clutha River. But many of the 100 or so miners who had arrived soon after the discovery reported poor returns, complained about the amount of water that they had to contend with, and left for more lucrative fields.

The Golden Lead

Those who persevered, however, were amply rewarded when it was found that there was rich gold in a narrow 'lead' at a depth of less than two metres. This lead ran more or less parallel to the existing stream and almost certainly marked the buried bed of a former stream.

By the end of October, fantastic returns were being reported from those fortunate to be 'on the gold.' One miner and his mate, who had dropped on to the rich lead near the stream, washed out 60 oz of rough, waterworn gold in eight days. Another party of four each brought in 9 lbs (3.3 kg) of gold for three week's work, while another two were said to have brought in 50 lbs (18 kg). Yet another party was reported to have banked 100 oz for a few day's labour, and another reported 14 oz from a single panning. There were even unconfirmed reports of a rich pocket of almost pure gold yielding no less than 200 oz from one pan. It must have been difficult to handle a pan containing such weight. So rich was the ground, the miners no longer bothered to refer to pennyweights and ounces—the talk was of pounds weight of gold per week and nothing less was regarded as a satisfactory return. A newspaper reporter who recorded these returns, and authenticated them, was worried that his Dunedin readers would not believe them:

> . . . individual returns from [Conroys Gully] have seemed almost so fabulous as not to have been credited at the distance. It is here that parties have reckoned their returns by the half-hundredweight . . . [6]

Little wonder that miners who had earlier deserted the diggings, swarmed back into the gully. By the beginning of November 1862, four hundred men were said to be at work and fortunes were being made.[7] Mining at Conroys Gully was fairly hard work because a great deal of material had to be moved by manual means. But, on the other hand, no elaborate equipment was required—only a pick, shovel and pan or cradle. Certainly, there was no large river to rise and flood the claims,[8] but water from the stream did seep through the porous gravels into the diggings in large quantities, necessitating constant bailing. Nevertheless, the golden lead was worked out quite quickly and many miners then joined rushes to other localities that promised high returns.

Those who remained behind soon found the gold in Conroys Gully was not confined to the narrow lead. Payable returns could be obtained everywhere from the alluvium on the floor of the basins—not the fabulous harvest of the 'golden gutter' certainly, but steady returns of three pennyweight (dwt), or so, to the pan. Miners who were satisfied with these modest returns spread along the gully until, at the end of 1862, almost every available square metre of ground in the three basins was being worked.

The method of gold winning was by 'paddocking.' Each miner chose what he considered a likely spot on the floor of the gully and pegged out a claim 30 ft by 30 ft (9 m by 9 m). Then a hole was excavated, perhaps a couple of metres or so square, in one corner of the claim. The soil and underlying gravel—'shingle,' as the miner called it—was not auriferous, so was heaped up beside the hole which, at a depth of less than two metres, reached the 'wash-dirt' or 'wash.' This generally consisted of a layer of sand 5 cms to 30 cms thick lying on the 'bottom' of pinkish clay. It was this wash that contained the gold which, in Conroys Gully, could be so coarse that pieces 'as thick as, and half the size of half a crown' [9] were easily visible in the sand. A couple of shovels of wash would be quickly but carefully placed in a gold pan and it is easy to imagine the excitement as the pan was taken down to the stream. Here it was swirled about with just its lip under water. As the sand was washed away, and the larger pebbles thrown out by hand, the gold, perhaps as much as would fill a teaspoon, became clearly visible heaped up in the bottom angle of the tilted pan. The larger pieces could easily be lifted out and dropped with a satisfying 'clink' into the miner's gold tin.

When all of the wash had been removed and processed, another paddock would be opened and the soil and gravel thrown into the initial worked-out excavation. When the whole claim had been 'paddocked,' the miner would gather up his tools and head for greener pastures, leaving his claim as a desert of bare gravel with a pit at one end where he finished work and a pile of gravel at the other end where he had commenced.

The area available for mining in Conroys Gully was too small to sustain a crowd of miners for long and soon the men began to drift away. Some moved further up the valley in their seach for the mythical 'mother lode' or into tributaries such as Aldinga Creek, but others rushed to neighbouring gullies where fresh discoveries were being reported almost daily. Others again went further afield, to the Arrow and Shotover Rivers.

Settlers
Some of those who decided to stay included James Muir, who worked in the upper basin, Richard Dawson in the middle basin and Andreas Iversen and Stephen Foxwell in the lower basin. There was John Bennett too, who later became interested in the quartz reef at Conroys, and Robert Scott, a builder of water races. They all applied for Residential Areas near their claims and Iversen and Dawson built houses, substantial for the times, after they married[10] As regulations changed, larger claims were allowed and these two miners eventually ended up with extensive claims. Dawson, for example, had a claim of six acres (2.4 h) and employed six men.[11] These large workings used the system of 'ground sluicing' where water, brought to the claim by races from higher up the creek, was used to flush the 'wash' through sluices where the gold was trapped. These sluices consisted at first of a trench lined with flat stones which caught the gold, but later wooden sluice-boxes with wooden or iron ripples set across the flow, were used.

Well maintained tail races were necessary to get rid of the 'tailings' after they had passed through the sluices, and at one stage Iversen was forced to lower the bed of the creek for part of the length of the lower gorge to gain sufficient fall for his tail-race. This entailed much expensive work with blasting powder. The Dawson and Iversen claims, in particular, averaged a return of about £8 a week for each man employed.

Fruitgrowing
Mrs Dawson, who had arrived in Manuherikia village in January 1863 and married Richard Dawson a year later, set out to make a garden around the house while her husband continued mining. According to her descendants,[12] Mrs Dawson was offered a bundle of one dozen fruit trees and two nut trees by William Theyers, the storekeeper in Alexandra, for the price of the freight. The trees had been sent out from Britain consigned to Galloway Station, and for some reason the station manager refused to accept them. Billy Theyers was keen to get rid of them to anyone who would pay the freight charges.

Mrs Dawson shared the bundle, and the freight, with her neighbour, Andreas C. Iversen, and her trees were planted in a corner of the garden. So began one of the most famous stone-fruit orchards in Central Otago. In the mid-1870s the orchards were expanded when William Fraser, owner of Earnscleugh Run in which Conroys Gully was included, offered to release two 40 acre (16 h) blocks from the run so

Dawson and Iversen could each lease the land from the Crown. In 1875 the two were importing apricot trees from Victoria, and as they began to bear fruit, the men devoted less time to mining.

Figure 3. 3. Dawson's orchard in 1903. Much of the land under fruit trees had been mined and was reclaimed with soil carried in from the hillsides. The high wall was built as a windbreak to protect the house and garden from the cold winds sweeping down from the Old Man Range.

These two men set about reclaiming the stony, pitted ground left by the miners. Heaps of shingle were levelled and the raw gravel covered by hundreds of cubic metres of soil carted in from adjacent hillsides. Slowly the flood plain of Conroys Creek was returned to something resembling its natural state before mining commenced. The planting of fruit trees kept pace with the reclamation and today almost the whole of the floors of the middle and lower basins of Conroys Gully are in prosperous, stone-fruit orchards.

The Chinese
Meanwhile, during the late 1870s Chinese miners began to work in the gully in increasing numbers. They brought with them a reputation for recovering profitable gold from ground already worked over and Conroys Gully was no exception. In fact, in October 1873 it was reported, but not verified, that they had recovered a gold nugget weighing about 12oz—the largest so far found in the district. In May 1881 the Chinese bought James Muir's claim in the upper basin for £40 and, from the unworked ground where his house and garden had stood, they came upon a rich patch of 400oz. They also procured a large amount of gold from a claim Richard Dawson had sold to them in

1879 for £80. Dawson was gradually giving up mining as he devoted more of his time to his orchard. Iversen, who had decided in 1882 to move out of Conroys Gully to a much larger property on Earnscleugh Flat, sold his claim and leased his garden.

By and large relationships between the Chinese miners and the European settlers in Conroys Gully was amicable, but there were one or two incidents which showed that there was some lack of trust between the two groups, and that they continued to 'keep an eye' on each other.

Some time after the sale, Richard Dawson claimed that You Chow and party were not entitled to an Extended Claim, recently awarded them by the Warden's Court, as the claim had not been marked out according to the regulations. Furthermore, the Chinese party, which had other claims, was now holding, in total, more area than it was entitled to under the regulation which granted one acre to each holder of a Miner's Right. Although we no longer have the full story, it is likely that the Chinese miners had pegged out part of the land that Dawson was using, or intended to use, for his orchard.

The Chinese were defended in the Warden's Court by James Rivers, a prominent merchant in Alexandra and one with strong financial interest in a number of mining claims. Rivers admitted that the claim was not marked out strictly in conformity with the Mining Act but pointed out it was, nevertheless, a genuine claim and that allowance should be made for the defendants' lack of English and their difficulty in understanding the fine print of the regulations. The party, Rivers said, had more than a sufficient number of Miner's Rights between

Figure 3. 4. Pioneer miners and fruitgrowers of Conroys Gully.
Left: Richard Dawson. **Right:** Andreas C. Iversen.

them to satisfy the requirements.

Nevertheless the warden ruled that it appeared that the claim under dispute had been acquired, not for immediate working, but as a standby for some future time. This was not allowed, so he cancelled the licence. This meant that the ground was now available for anyone who cared to mark out a claim in the approved manner.

As soon as the decision was announced there was an immediate exodus from the courtroom by both parties with the intention of racing each other out to Conroys to re-mark the disputed ground. The Chinese, who had anticipated that the verdict might go against them, had set up a simple signalling system with the help of friends stationed at intervals on high points along the 6 kilometres from the courthouse to Conroys Gully. A pre-arranged wave of the arms was all that was required to set the re-marking in progress and it was completed before Dawson's lads had finished saddling up their horses.

Richard Dawson, however, did better later in the same court session. Ah Tong and party applied for the cancellation of the licence for a tail race which, the Chinese claimed, Dawson had not used for some months. However, it was pointed out that when Dawson had sold the claim it was agreed that the tail race and its surrounding land would revert back to Dawson once the Chinese had worked out the claim. The warden supported Dawson who retained the tail race.

These battles in the Warden's Court were frequent and part of the mining tradition. They often took place between miners who, outside the courtroom, were the best of friends. It was almost as if the fortnightly court was part of the entertainment scene of the time. But there were also incidents brought to Court which showed that blatant racism towards the Chinese was only thinly veneered by tolerance.

Dawson and Iversen each held a water right from lower reaches of Conroys Creek for one 'head' [14] of water but their rights were of lower priority than the right to three heads held by William Noble and Craven Paget which they drew from the headwaters of the creek. Noble and Paget were supposed, by law, to allow two heads to flow down the creek at all times 'for general use' before they could draw their allocation. The Chinese buyers of Dawson's and Iversen's claims clearly understood the position about the water rights when they took over.

During a dry season in 1889, some years after the sale, Noble and Paget were diverting all of the water from the creek into their race so that none flowed down the creek. The Chinese miners applied to the Warden's Court to force Noble and Paget to release the two heads of water as they were supposed to do. Noble and Paget objected to the application. The warden compromised and ordered that *one* head should at all times flow down the creek. We do not now know his reasons for this decision but there were plenty of precedents, based mainly on the assumption that the creek would 'make' water through seepage over the several kilometres between intakes of the two races.

A letter [15] in the *Dunstan Times* from 'Miner' criticised this decision, pointing out that the claims were sold with the clear understanding that two heads of water would be available, and the warden should

40

have stuck to the letter of the law and forced Noble and Paget to release the full two heads. 'Miner' implied that the decision was influenced by the fact that Chinese were involved. Furthermore, the writer pointed out, it was not as if Noble and Paget needed the extra water for themselves, as they had promptly sold it to Chinese in the neighbouring Butchers Gully.

For his pains 'Miner,' who was quickly identified as James Rivers, was accused of being 'pro-Chinese' because of his frequent role as advocate for Chinese miners in various hearings before the Wardens' Court. Although the fuss died down, the Chinese miners of Conroys did not get the water they were entitled to.

Final Days of Mining

By 1889 the newspapers were reporting that alluvial mining on the floor of Conroys Gully was over. A few Chinese miners continued to work in some tributary streams such as Aldinga Creek, and work on the Conroy quartz reef which had begun in 1870 continued off and on until about 1908. A large sluicing claim in the wall of Conroys Gully, just south of the intersection of Chapman and Conroys Roads, was begun by Michael McCarthy in 1890 and persisted under various owners until the Great War.

Gold is still pouring out of Conroys Gully, not in the form of soft, heavy, yellow metal but in thousands of fruit cases filled with peaches, apricots and, above all, the famous Dawson cherries.

NOTES

1.Tod Symons, 1978: p18. Symons' story is perhaps supported by the published list of unclaimed mail for August 1863 which includes 'Henry Conroy' and the following month 'R. H. Conroy.'
2. *Otago Daily Times* 14 October 1862. Keddell had been officially appointed Commissioner of the Dunstan Gold Field on 1 October 1862.
3. .A 'Prospector's claim' was twice the area of an 'ordinary claim' and was granted as a reward for discovery of, and as an incentive to search for, new gold diggings. To qualify the prospector had to produce evidence that payable gold existed and the new diggings had to be a distance of several miles from existing diggings.
4. The upper, middle and lower basin were later to be known as Muir Flat (now largely submerged by Conroys Dam), Dawsons Flat and Iversens Flat, respectively.
5. 'Conroys Gully' strictly refers only to the two-kilometre stretch of the valley that contains the three basins. The final stretch of the stream across Earnscleugh Flat and also the branches high up on the Old Man Range were prospected and some mining done but these locations were referred to not as Conroys Gully but as 'Conroys Creek.' Similarly 'Butchers Gully' refers only to the basin, where there was much mining, above the lowest gorge.
6. *Otago Daily Times* 9 December 1862. A hundredweight was 112 lbs (42 kg).
7. *Otago Daily Times* 5 November and 8 December 1862.
8. Miners in these early days were not to know that this creek, like most of those in Central Otago, was subject to occasional disastrous flash floods, or 'cloudbursts,' as they were called.
9. A half-crown of the time was about 32 mm in diameter and about 2 mm thick.
10. The Dawsons built their house in 1864 and were unlikely to have built without some sort of title. It is likely that they were granted a Residence Area of half an acre (0.2h) but no record of this can be found. According to records of the Wardens Court, Dawson and Iversen were each granted a Residence Area of 1 acre (0.4h) on 25 May, 1869. According to McArthur, 1992 p. 127. Dawson's house was reputed to be 'the first real house built on the Dunstan Goldfield.' According to A. Don (1931) at least one

stone hut had been built previously.

11. McArthur, G. H. 1992 p. 87.
12. Johnston G, 1992 p. 26-27.
13. *Otago Daily Times* 25 May 1881.
14. A 'head' of water, short for 'Government sluice-head,' was equivalent to one cubic foot of water passing a point in one second (a cusec). Water was measured by passing it through a gauge box constructed in such a way that it standardised the rate of flow so 'head' then became, in effect, a quantity of water.
15. *Otago Daily Times* 12 June 1889.

4.
MOVING THE RIVERS

While the miners toiled in the gullies, 'paddocking' gravels two to three metres deep to reach the few centimetres of rich wash on the 'bottom,' their eyes kept turning to the big river still swollen with the waters of melting snows. As they worked, they remembered the easy gold obtained from the sandy beaches when the river was low. If only they could lower the river level, they reasoned, or better still, get rid of the water altogether, then surely it would be only a matter of shovelling the gold into sacks.

Pipe Dreams

A "Special Reporter" of the *Otago Daily Times* suggested[1] several schemes for exposing more of the Clutha River beaches. He worked out that it would be quite economic, in terms of gold recovered, to cut an outlet for Lake Wakatipu through the old moraine at Kingston. The flow of the existing outlet, the Kawarau River, could thus be halved, and this in turn would reduce the flow of the Clutha River by a quarter and expose large areas of auriferous beach sands.[2] He also suggested deepening the outlet of the lake at Kawarau Falls so the lake level would be lowered, and then temporarily blocking it again during the low flow of winter. It would take about six weeks, he thought, for the lake to fill and overflow the dam during which time the flow of Kawarau and the Clutha Rivers would be much reduced.[3]

The same author went on to describe even more ambitious schemes. Anticipating events by 130 years, he suggested damming the Clutha River at Clyde. The river would be diverted along the Dunstan Flat and into the Manuherikia River just above Alexandra thus dewatering about 12 kilometres of its bed. The only difficulty he foresaw was finding a suitable dam foundation in the gravel of the riverbanks. But when he went on to suggest it was within the available engineering skills to dig a new course for the Clutha River through to Roxburgh and so dewater some 50 kilometres of its course, he entered the realm of science fiction. He did allow this scheme would require some very heavy cuttings (about 300 metres deep, through solid rock) and in the end the amount of gold recovered might not pay the expenses!

Wing Dams

At a much more practical level, wing dams became the fashion. First used on the Manuherikia River during the spring of 1862, the system was extended to the Clutha itself during the autumn of 1863. As the frosts set in and the river level began to drop, it became practicable, in shallow reaches, to expose part of the river bed by damming out the river water. Formed from layers of sandbags or from other materials, set at an angle downstream, the dams reached out into the current until the increasing depth of water made further lengthening too difficult. The line of the dam was then turned back towards the shore to isolate a triangular- or crescent-shaped piece of river bed. A Californian pump, driven by a paddle wheel set in the river current, removed the water and any that might leak through the dam. Such dams were temporary affairs at best and were generally destroyed by the next flood in the river.

A WING DAM

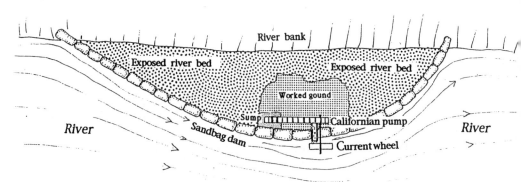

Figure 4. 1. Wing dams were built out from the banks to hold back the waters of rivers or streams and so expose a small part of th bed for gold mining. The dams were built from sandbags, stones cemented with clay, canvas attached to pegs driven into the river bed, and so on. Californian pumps were used to pump out the claim and then to take care of water which leaked through the dam and the gravel floor.
Upper: A wing dam. A small internal dam to the right is keeping the working area clear of accumulated water.
Lower: A plan of a wing dam.

More ambitious schemes involved the complete diversion of streams. Although it was beyond the resources of even large companies to attempt to completely dam and divert the full flow of the Clutha River[4] itself, its tributaries were more easily tackled. Narrow gravel necks separating swinging curves could be sluiced through. Where the necks were of solid rock, tunnels could be blasted through, as was done in several places in the Shotover Valley. It became common practice to divert smaller streams such as Conroys and Butchers Creeks for short distances so that the exposed bed could be worked.

Manuherikia Diversions

It was on 31 October 1862, only two months after the initial discovery of gold, that a co-operating party of 27 miners, under the direction of John C. Chapple, began work on a major diversion of the Manuherikia River.[5] About two kilometres[6] above Alexandra the river formed a very distinct loop, which shows up clearly on early maps. It was planned to cut a new channel across the neck of the bend, a distance of about 275 metres, and so dewater more than 400 metres of the original riverbed. It was not very difficult to do this, as all it required was a dam of sandbags across the river and a small ditch excavated along the new course. Once water began to follow the ditch the miners could stand back and let river erosion rapidly enlarge the cut until it was taking the full flow of the river.

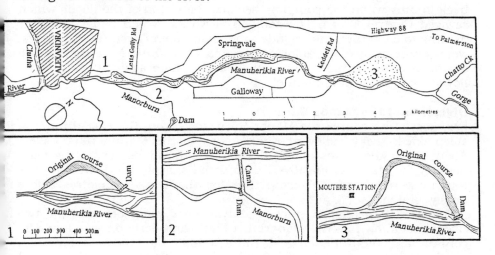

Figure 4. 2 The diversion of the water of large streams to expose their beds was a major undertaking. The location map on the left shows three major stream diversions (numbered) in the Manuherikia Valley with enlargements of each on the right.

Each of the men subscribed money to buy a certain number of bags. The storekeepers of the township, with an eye on increased trade if the scheme were successful, also agreed to contribute.[7] The diversion was accomplished by mid-November.

Two parties, one calling itself the Manuherikia Gold Mining Company and the other the Grand Junction Gold Mining Company,[8] staked out claims along the stretch of more or less dry river bed and within a couple of weeks 'ground sluicing' (see next chapter) was under way.

It was found, contrary to expectations, that the exposed river bed was not paved with gold, which was, in fact, very patchy. Furthermore, some difficulty was encountered getting rid of the tailings because of a bar of solid rock just below the surface at the bottom end of the claim. It took a week's hard work to cut a channel through it. The river still

45

follows the diversion and the old, worked-over course remains as a swampy channel.

Meanwhile Chapple, who seemed to be a born organiser, applied for another stretch of the Manuherikia River for a much more ambitious diversion. This was just upstream from Shennan's station,[9] about ten kilometres above Alexandra, where it was planned to cut across the neck of a large bend. This time he organised the Nil Desperandum Gold Mining Company, consisting of no fewer than nine groups of miners, each of six men. The diversion, as before, would be carried out on a co-operative basis and then each group would stake out a claim on the dry riverbed.

The first sod of the diversion was turned on 23 February 1863 amid much toasting and general jollification,[10] but there was a major set back in July when the company became the victim of the floods which ravaged Central Otago. The company's works, which had taken four months to construct and included the main dam of over 700 sandbags, were swept away with a loss estimated at £400[11]. Nevertheless the diversion was eventually accomplished and, here again, the river still flows through the new channel.

Diversion of the Manor Burn
For most of its course the Manor Burn flows from the east through a steep-sided, rocky valley at right angles to the Manuherikia Valley. About three kilometres above Alexandra it debouches on to the flood plain of the Manuherikia River, then turns sharply south-west to flow roughly parallel with the main river for about two kilometres before finally joining it.

The triangular-shaped tract of alluvial flood plain between the two rivers was known as the Manorburn Flat[12] and early on was found to contain large quantities of gold. Unfortunately the land was low-lying, poorly drained and subject to flooding from both streams. The gravels were porous and prospecting holes immediately filled with water. So plans were made to divert the Manor Burn along a more direct course to the river and so drain the Flat. The work involved digging a ditch about a kilometre long, two metres wide at the top and half a metre wide at the bottom.[13] This time it was not so easy to use the eroding power of the stream as the diversion was across the flood plain rather than downstream, as had been the case with the other large diversions. This meant that the new channel had to be dug progressively deeper as it moved away from the Manor Burn before finally shallowing again as it approached the Manuherikia River.

The ditch was finished in the later part of June 1864 but Mr Coates, the Mining Surveyor, declared that it was too shallow by some 35 cms and refused to pass the work[14] The men 'with much reluctance' turned to and deepened it and Coates finally certified that the work had been properly performed.[15]

From this time on the Flat supported a large population of miners and it was not until the dredges moved through in the late 1890s that the diversion was destroyed and the Manor Burn returned to its original course.

The Californian Pump

Even though the gold-bearing wash in dewatered riverbeds, or in flood plains, was generally not far below the surface and could be reached by shallow excavations, there remained the difficulty of inflowing water. As fast as a hole was excavated it filled with water seeping through the porous gravels. Bailing by bucket, and syphons of various kinds, were tried but the most successful device was the ingenious Californian pump.[16]

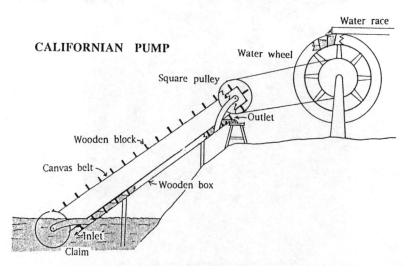

Figure 4. 3. The Californian pump was a version of a chain-pump but was made from wood and canvas so could be built and repaired from materials easily obtained on the gold fields. Small ones were turned by hand but large pumps were worked by current-wheels set in a stream or river or driven by water wheels supplied from a high-level water race.

The Californian pump was essentially a chain pump. It consisted of an endless belt of canvas (sometimes leather) on one side of which were securely fastened regularly-spaced blocks of wood of such a size that they neatly fitted the inside dimensions of a long, wooden, open-ended box. At either end of the box were rollers around which the belt passed. Turning the upper roller, after the lower end of the box was immersed in the flooded claim, caused water to pour out of the upper end into a receiving ditch.

The wooden blocks were usually of the order of 250 mm wide by 75 mm high and the total length of the pump from centre to centre of the upper and lower rollers was generally not more than 10 metres, but at least one pump at Prospectors Point was more than twice that length. Another set of twin pumps at Kaniere on the West Coast[17] worked in boxes 450 mm by 325 mm.

The speed of the belt ensured that most of the water trapped in the box above each block reached the top end of the box before it all leaked round the edges of the blocks. Obviously the tighter the fit of the wooden blocks in the box the more efficient the pump, but this had to be balanced against the extra wear on both the blocks and the box, especially if the pump was working in water with a high content of sand or gravel.

Figure 4. 4. A small Californian pump at work. The largest recorded pump was 21 metres long and required supporting, in the centre, by cables. The pumps were used not only for draining claims but also for supplying water for separating gold from the wash dirt.

The attractions of the pump were that it could be home-made from simple and readily available materials, and repair and maintenance work, although probably a constant task, were relatively simple.

Although the first small pumps were turned by hand, it was not long before water wheels of various kinds were in use. Those who built wing dams on the Clutha River thought they could make use of the powerful current to turn current-wheels. They soon found that the rapid rising and falling of the river not only made wing damming very difficult but meant that the current-wheels had to be mounted on floating pontoons. This led to difficulties in transmitting the power to the pumps fixed on land. Things were easier in the Manuherikia Valley where controlled water could be diverted into a channel in which the wheel was placed.

Large pumps required more power than paddle wheels driven by river current could provide. It was necessary to bring water from mountain streams for long distances by water races and use it to drive overshot water wheels. The discovery, in June 1864, of the very rich ground at Frenchmans Point, on the banks of the Clutha River opposite Alexandra, led to the assembly of the greatest mass of mining machinery seen in the district. Water was brought from the upper reaches of Conroys Creek in a long water race and used to turn water wheels. The wheels were situated above the claims so that long rope belts had to be used to connect the wheels to the drums of the Californian pumps with consequent great loss of power.[18]

A year later the Hit or Miss claim at Frenchmans Point installed a water wheel described as one of the largest and most perfectly constructed in the district up to that time. It was 4.2 metres in diameter and 70 cms wide divided into 64 buckets. Fed by two heads of water it was said to develop seven horsepower. From a drum 2 metres in diameter it drove a Californian pump 14.2 metres long with a bore 20 cms by 7 cms. The pump was so long that its length had to be supported by braces on the principle of a suspension bridge. When driven at full speed the pump gave an almost uninterrupted stream of water.[19]

The Californian pump held sway during the early days of gold mining at the Dunstan and its characteristic flop-flop sound echoed up and down the rivers. It was not very efficient, however, and it was gradually replaced by other devices among which were elevators consisting of a chain of steel buckets worked by water wheels. The great advance came with the introduction of hydraulic elevating which used the power of water pressure to suck water, gravel and, hopefully, gold from far below river level.

NOTES

1. 'Our Gold Fields ' *Otago Daily Times* 16 August 1864.
2. There is an old channel through the moraine that dams the south end of Lake Wakatipu but its floor is about 40 metres above present lake level. A canal, to provide an effective outlet for the present lake, would not only require an excavation up to 45 metres deep but would also have to extend more than 20 kilometres down the valley of the Mataura River.
3. This foreshadowed the scheme that was put into effect some 40 years later when an elaborate dam, with gates that could be raised and lowered, was built at the falls. Great expectations came to nothing when the gates were closed but the water level of the river did not fall appreciably—it was largely maintained by the inflow of large tributaries such as the Shotover, Arrow and Nevis Rivers.
4. At a point above Cromwell, where the Clutha River was split into two by an island, an ambitious scheme was attempted by the Nil Desperandum Company (a different company from the one with the same name which diverted the Manuherikia River). An elaborate and expensive dam was built across one branch from the riverbank to the island with the intention of exposing the bed of the branch. Unfortunately the dam was destroyed by a flood soon after completion and before any gold was recovered .
5. *Otago Daily Times* 20 November 1862.
6. This was the distance from Alexandra township (the intersection of Tarbert and Limerick Streets) of the time. 'The Bend' is less than a kilometre upstream from the

present town boundary.

7.. *Otago Daily Times* 26 November 1862.

8. It is believed that the Grand Junction was a branch of the Manuherikia Company.

9. At this time the headquarters of Shennan's Moutere Station was on the western bank of the Manuherikia River off the present Keddell Rd at Springvale.

10. *Otago Daily Times* 10 March 1863.

11. ibid 18 August 1863.

12. The name of the stream is given as two words on maps but when used as an adjective as in 'Manorburn Flat' or 'Manorburn Dam' it is apparently written as one word.

13. *Otago Daily Times* 21 June 1864.

14. Perhaps the work was subsidised by the Provincial Council.

15. *Otago Daily Times* 1 July 1864.

16. Although the idea was imported from California, the device is similar to that used for centuries in China for lifting irrigation water (Ng J. 1993 p. 167. Note 77).

17. May, P. R. 1962 p. 235.

18. *Otago Daily Times* 1 July 1864.

19. ibid 26 June 1865.

5.

TAKING WATER TO THE GOLD

The Big Water Races

Labour-intensive methods of mining such as cradling and panning, predominant during the first months of the Rush, were only profitable on the river beaches and in stream gravels where gold was abundant and easily obtained at shallow depths. As the search spread further afield, miners soon realised that gold was not confined to the river and stream beds. The extensive gravel terraces which flanked the Clutha and Manuherikia Rivers, the pockets of ancient gravels high up on the hills, and the patches of white quartz sand that lay on the schist rock around the edges of the big Central Otago valleys, all proved to be gold-bearing. All of these deposits were above, sometimes far above, river level. Although there were attempts to transport the gold-bearing 'wash' down to water by various means, it was soon realised that the deposits were not sufficiently rich to justify the labour and expense involved in this method of mining.

Those miners who had had experience on the Victorian goldfields knew the answer: bring water to the gold-bearing deposits by water races and wash large quantities of the material through sluices to catch the gold. And they were not slow to adopt the method in Central Otago. Only a little over a month after the first arrivals at the Dunstan, a group mining the high banks of the Clutha River opposite Clyde had constructed a water race to bring water from the Fraser River about two kilometres away.[1]

Constructing water races from distant streams to these higher-level deposits was, however, generally beyond the resources of individuals. But it was not long before enterprising men reasoned that by pooling their capital and labour it would be feasible to construct even very long races. Then the high-level gravels could be worked profitably, although they might contain only small amounts of gold. Groups formed were variously designated as a 'Company,' 'Syndicate' or 'Partnership' but all were comprised of miners who had agreed to work together, pool

51

their resources and share any profits.

Before any water could be diverted from a stream by a water race, however, there were procedures to be followed. Most important, a 'Water-Right' had to be obtained.

Water Rights

A 'water right' was one of the 'mining privileges' extended to miners under the Mining Act of 1858[2] and its many subsequent amendments. Granted by Wardens' Courts on the principle of 'first in time, first in right' or 'first in, first served,' a water right allowed the holder to take a certain quantity of water, measured in 'Government sluice-heads'[3] (or, more commonly, just 'heads') from a stream. But several water rights from the same stream were often granted to different people and so the total quantity allocated was often far in excess of the stream's normal flow. Then the matter of 'prior rights' became of utmost importance. The holder of a prior, or superior, right was entitled to water before others with inferior rights.

Central Otago streams, because of their mountain origins, have abundant water for only a few months in the spring when winter snow on the ranges is melting. Once the snow has melted the stream flow becomes erratic and depends on rainfall on the hills. Streams often rise again slightly in the late autumn as the summer heat dies away and run-off increases. As winter approaches, however, heavy frosts on the mountains causes the soil to freeze, moisture is locked up and stream flow is greatly reduced again.

Generally there was sufficient water for all water right holders during the spring, but as summer wore on and the flows diminished, those with inferior rights began to lose out and eventually even those with the prior rights could find themselves short of water. Water rights, especially superior rights, were valuable commodities which were jealously guarded and bought and sold for large sums. Disputes over water provided much work for the Wardens' Courts. And no doubt many acts of blatant stealing of water were settled by other, more direct methods.

Early versions of the Mining Act made it clear that if you were granted a water right then you had to use it for mining and for mining only. If you did not use the water, or used it for other purposes, then it was likely to be taken from you and would be made available to others who were eagerly awaiting just such an opportunity. The Act specified, for instance, that if you did not use your water for a month then the water right was liable to forfeiture—'use it or lose it'. There were many battles in the Wardens' Courts when those who held inferior rights to water accused the superior right holder of not using the water for some time and therefore becoming liable to forfeiture. If the court decreed that a right was forfeited, then the inferior right holder stepped up the pecking order and could well become the superior right holder.

Construction of Water Races

Building a long water race was a major undertaking. In places the race might traverse hillsides so steep that its outer walls had to be supported by carefully built stone walls; it might cross unstable country where the water had to be carried in wooden (later sheet-iron) fluming; it might cling to sheer cliffs where fluming had to be supported by iron rods sunk into holes in the solid rock and it might cross deep gullies by means of 'siphons.' [4] Water was also carried across large gullies, and even across the Clutha River, in canvas hoses slung beneath wire ropes.

Figure 5. 1. Difficulties in building water races.

    (a): (p.53, top) On steep hillsides races had to be supported by stone walls. Long lengths of high stone walling were required before this race was clear of the gorge of Little Valley Creek.

    (b): (p.53, lower) Wooden (later sheet metal) fluming was used to convey water races around cliffs or through very rough country. Fluming in Butchers Creek gorge.

    (c): (above) Large gullies were crossed by carrying the water in pipes which ran down one side of the gully, across the stream and up the other side. The resulting U-shaped structure was called a 'siphon' (more accurately an 'inverted siphon.') This is one limb of the siphon that crossed Butchers Creek. Note also the fluming.

Some race builders used their water in their own mines but companies were also formed solely to construct races and then sell the water. These large races often took several years to build and employed scores of men, which meant that much capital had to be outlaid before there was any prospect of a return. When the race was finally finished, the company hoped to recoup its original investment, cover running costs, and make a continuing profit. Because of shortages of water at the stream intake, damage to the race, or simply overselling, miners often did not get their full quota of water. This could lead to protracted court proceedings and often, heavy damages were awarded against the race owners.

Continual maintenance of long races was expensive but very necessary. Men had to be constantly on patrol to clear slips, which fell into the water, blocked the flow and so caused the race to overflow and wash away the walls. Frost could cause the race to freeze over and, when it thawed, floating ice would cause blockages leading to overflows and washouts. Then there was the major annual exercise of cleaning the race. Silt was constantly brought in with the water or was washed into the race by run-off from the adjacent hillsides. In addition the vegetation which grew luxuriantly in the nutrient-rich water greatly impeded the flow. Water had to be shut off and the race drained to allow men to remove the vegetation and accumulations of silt.

There was considerable loss of water along the length of the race. Evaporation, leaks caused by the walls of the race slumping away, and seepage into porous soils or through open joints in rock, accounted for the loss of as much as two thirds of the water. In particular, the races running across the broad terraces, which are such a feature of the Central Otago valleys, suffered greatly from water escaping into the porous gravels, and much effort went into 'sealing the race' to try to prevent this loss.

Water was subject to poaching. Often it was only a householder bucketing out water or perhaps poking a small diameter pipe through the race wall to provide water for domestic use or for stock, but sometimes the theft was much more blatant and serious. It was not unknown for a large part of the water to be diverted and to be used in some other mine for several days before the theft was discovered.

When the race finally delivered its water, or what remained of it, to the claim, it was used for sluicing.

Sluicing

At first 'ground sluicing' was adopted because it was simple and inexpensive. All that was required was a long 'sluice' or ditch in which flat stones ('pavers') were laid on the bottom. Gold-bearing gravel was shovelled into the water stream that flowed through the sluice and the

Figure 5. 2. Ground sluicing. Water from a race is flowing down the face of the mine and washing material into and through the sluice (lower left) which is a ditch lined with flat stones.

gold was trapped under the edges of the flat stones. At intervals the stones were lifted and the accumulated gold and sand washed, broomed or shovelled into a cradle or pan for final separation. Later, wooden troughs ('sluice boxes') were installed at the end of the ground sluice, and after the stones were lifted, the ditch was flushed out and the gold caught by bars of wood or metal in the sluice boxes. As timber became more readily available, long wooden sluice boxes completely replaced the stone-lined ground sluice.

A variation was 'hill-sluicing' in which the water race was brought to a point above the claim and then allowed to pour over the face of the excavation. This stream of water eroded the face and at the same time washed the eroded material through the sluice ditch. A good deal of labour with the shovel was saved by this method.

It wasn't long before 'hydraulic sluicing' was being practised. In this method water, under pressure, was forced through nozzles giving powerful jets which were used to break down a face of compacted gravel and then wash the loosened material through the sluices.

Figure 5. 3. Hydraulic Sluicing. High pressure water from a nozzle (rear) is dislodging gravel and gold-bearing sand and washing it through the sluice boxes in the foreground. The sluice boxes are designed to trap the gold.

To obtain the necessary pressure, the water race had to terminate in a pond or dam situated on higher ground well above the mine. Water was led down to the floor of the claim through canvas hose or, later, a pipeline, or 'pressure pipe' as it was called, to the nozzles.

Hydraulic Elevating
About 1880 the hydraulic elevator was introduced. This was a device which allowed gravel, sand and hopefully gold, to be sucked up from a deep mine and spewed out into gold-saving sluice boxes at such a level that the waste material—the tailings—could be disposed of by gravity.

The elevator was a vertical pipe up which a high pressure jet of water was directed through a restriction and the resulting suction carried the 'wash', already loosened by other sluice nozzles, up the pipe accompanied by a continuous, thunderous roar. This method enabled wash lying below stream level to be successfully recovered.

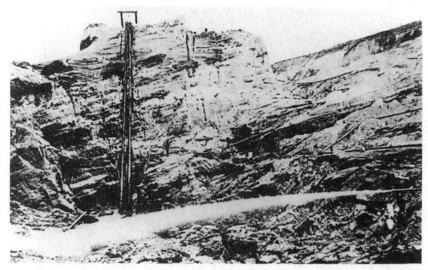

Figure 5. 4. Hydraulic Elevating. Where mines were deep and tailings could not be disposed of, a hydraulic elevator was used to lift the loosened sediments out of the mine. High-pressure water from the nozzle (foreground) is washing gold-bearing material into the inlet of the elevator (background). This device used a high-pressure water jet which, directed up the vertical pipe, sucked the material up and discharged it into sluice boxes.

Race Building Frenzy
Much of the alluvial mining activity in the district was centred on the gravel deposits flanking the rivers and in particular the extensive terraces on both sides of the Clutha River between Alexandra and Clyde. Sluicing was the only practical method available to deal with the great thicknesses of relatively barren gravel overlying the gold-rich 'wash' at the base, and the necessary water had to be brought to the claims by water races. So, beginning in 1863, water race building became the fashion of the hour, and all substantial streams in the surrounding hills were tapped. Within a few years, long water races, converging on Alexandra like the spokes of a wheel on to a hub, were bringing large quantities of water to the river terraces.

SOME LARGE RACES
A catalogue of all the races constructed in the vicinity of Alexandra and Clyde would now be impossible to achieve, given the sparsity of records for the earliest years, and besides, would be hopelessly tedious. Instead, a selection of races is chosen to give some idea of the

immense labour and cost involved in these enterprises. Most are described more fully in other chapters.

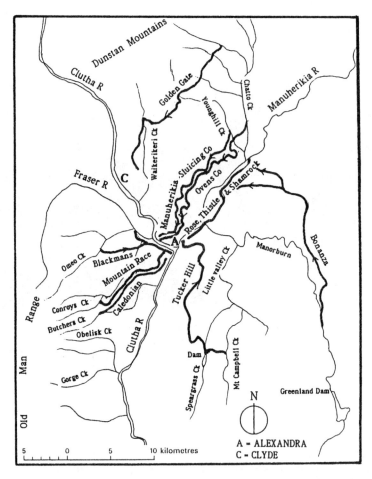

Figure 5. 5. Map showing the longest water races around Alexandra

Beginning in the north, and proceeding clockwise, the main races were:-

Golden Gate: McNally, Hastie and six men toiled for four years from 1872 to build a race along the foothills of the Dunstan Mountains. It was intended to convey water from Leahys Creek, a tributary of Chatto Creek, to the Clyde Commonage and the banks of the Clutha River near the Dunstan Hospital. The most difficult stretch, which took nearly three years to complete, was the crossing of the Waikerikeri Gorge where the race had to be supported on high stone walls. The partners began sluicing at Connews Gully at the Waikerikeri Diggings in 1876. A public company, the Golden Gate Mining Company (Ltd), was formed in 1878 with Borthwick R. Baird of Cromwell as the

58

principal shareholder. It was finally wound up in July, 1899.

Manuherikia Ground Sluicing Company (Drummey's): Between December 1863 and September 1864 Jeremiah Drummey and 11 others, working on behalf of the Manuherikia Ground Sluicing Company, constructed a race, about 40 kilometres long, which drew water from Younghill and Leahys Creeks—tributaries of Chatto Creek.[5] It terminated on the hillside near the present town boundary where it supplied water to the company's claim on the banks of the Manuherikia River.

Later the race was extended along the Terrace to Coal Point and another branch was taken across Dunstan Flat to the banks of the Clutha River near Muttontown Point.

Much of the race was enlarged and incorporated into the Manuherikia Irrigation Scheme race built during the Great War.

Ovens Water Race Company: Constructed between January 1864 and October 1865 to carry water from the main stream of Chatto Creek to Bedford Butler's rich claim at Golden Point on the Manuherikia River just above its confluence with the Clutha. For much of its more than 30 kilometre length the race ran closely parallel to, and a few metres below, Drummey's race until it reached Brennans Gully (now Letts Gully). Here water was allowed to cascade down to the floor of the gully where it was picked up again by the race.[6] In this 'drop,' as it was called, the race lost about 40 metres in elevation.

A branch race (which became the main race when the race to Golden Point was abandoned) was taken along the edge of the Terrace to Coal Point on the Clutha River. When the company was sold in 1867 the new owners opened up a claim on the banks of the Clutha River close to the township with a branch race extending southwards from the Terrace along the river bank. In late 1869, a small dam, which was to become the first Borough reservoir, was built on this extension. This dam lasted well into the twentieth century and was known during the later part of its life as 'Halpine's dam' because a family of that name lived nearby. Another branch race made use of an earlier race running through the gorge of the Manuherikia River below the present 'railway' bridge. It crossed the river in a flume just upstream from the Shaky Bridge, and then along to Prospectors Point where the company operated a claim.

In January 1873 the Alexandra Borough Council bought the race and, as the 'Borough race,' it supplied the town with water for the next 30 years. It was sold to the Government in 1922 and still exists as part of the Manuherikia Irrigation Scheme

Rose, Thistle and Shamrock: A company was formed by J. C. Chapple in 1864 to construct a race to the Tucker Hill diggings from an intake in the gorge of the Manuherikia River above the confluence of Chatto Creek. Owing to a miscalculation the race was built at too low a level to reach the claim and water was sold to miners around the Manor Burn. The race, in its 10 kilometre length, involved many rock cuttings, at least one tunnel, and very extensive lengths of fluming, but particularly noteworthy was the huge wooden viaduct built to carry the water across the Manor Burn.

Ida Valley Water Race Company: In 1865 a company began to build a race from the upper reaches of the Manor Burn, intending to supply 20 heads of water to Blacks No. 1 and Blacks No.3 diggings.[7] The Company failed and was taken over in 1867 by the Manuherikia Water Race Company which brought the water, from the completed part of the race, down Dip Creek and into the Rose Thistle and Shamrock race (which it had also taken over) and so supplied claims along the lower course of the Manor Burn. Later the water was used to develop Hansen's claim on the high terrace near Galloway Station, and another branch supplied Blackwell's claim overlooking the mouth of Chatto Creek. The Alexandra Bonanza Gold Dredging and Sluicing Company bought the main race in 1899, enlarged it to carry 40 heads, and built a dam in the headwaters of the Manor Burn at Greenland swamp. The work was completed in 1902 but the company went into liquidation in April 1903.[8]

The Government bought the race and dam in 1906 and shortly afterwards extended the race along the foot of the Crawford Hills. This race, whose name was changed from 'Bonanza' to 'Alexandra' in September 1906 still exists as an important part of the Galloway Irrigation Scheme

Tucker Hill: In 1891 Tom Jackson and George Campbell began to extend an existing race from Speargrass Creek, a tributary of the Manor Burn, through some 28 kilometres of very difficult country, to their claim at Tucker Hill diggings, just across the Manuherikia River from Alexandra. It took them three years to reach the crest of the ridge overlooking the diggings. Finally, the water was brought down the steep frontal slope in a series of waterfalls and then picked up by a race that terminated 30 metres above the mine workings.

The claim and race were taken over by James Rivers who extended the head of the race 10 kilometres to Mt Campbell Creek. In 1903 he built a large dam in Speargrass Creek. Water from the race and dam was used as Alexandra's water supply from 1903 until 1909.

Caledonian: Started in August 1866 by Andrew Wood and his party, to bring six heads of water from Butchers Creek to their lucrative Caledonian mine at Halfmile Beach on the Clutha River. Many small gullies were used to guide the water down from the hills and the race finally terminated above Woods's claim in a small dam in Tubmans Gully—a side branch of Halfmile Gully. Later owners included Michael Kett, George McNeill and party and, in 1895, Olaf Magnus.

Magnus rented the water to the Golden Beach Company and sold the water right to J. P. Lane when he took over the company in 1905.

Finally, in 1919 the Alexandra Borough Council acquired the water rights, race and dams by forfeiture. The race was sold to the Government in 1925 and sections of it are still used in the Last

Chance Irrigation Scheme.

Mountain Race: In the spring of 1863 James Coleman and partners began to construct a water race from the South Branch of Conroys Creek. Commencing at an altitude of 600 metres, it became known as the 'mountain race' and was almost certainly the first of the large water races constructed in the district. In a somewhat modified form it is still in existence.

From Conroys Creek, the race passed through a saddle into the valley of Butchers Creek. It continued down the Butchers Creek side of the dividing ridge and finally discharged into Chapmans Creek. From the lower course of this creek the water was picked up by the **Junction Race**, which ran along the steep rocky bank of the Clutha River to Frenchmans Point where every drop of water was immediately sold at high prices.

In 1869 the race was extended from the head of Chapmans Creek to a high point overlooking Frenchmans Point thus supplying claims above the level of the Junction Race. But in 1874 Craven Paget snr, William Noble snr, and Robert Ballantyne, who had bought the race, abandoned this high-level branch race and allowed the water to again flow down Chapmans Creek from where it was led to their new mine at the mouth of Chapmans Gully.

Olaf Magnus bought the race in 1896 and to save maintenance, diverted the water near the source of the race, into the nearby and nearly parallel, Caledonian race. This left the greater part of the Mountain race abandoned until 1908, when about four kilometres of the lower end of the race were restored and enlarged to serve as part of the Alexandra Borough water supply. In 1937 the whole of the Mountain Race was taken over by the Public Works Department and incorporated into the Last Chance irrigation scheme, but the lower part continued to be used for the borough supply until the 1970s.

Blackmans Race: In August, 1864 it was decided to bring water from Omeo Creek to Frenchmans Point. The race left Blackmans Gully, followed around the hill slopes at the southern end of Earnscleugh Flat, crossed Conroys Creek and continued skirting the hills until it joined the Junction Race. After the 1878 flood Conroys Creek water was fed into Blackmans Race and conveyed to workings along the river bank opposite Alexandra.

The race was taken over by the Golden Beach Company in 1896 who terminated it in a dam on Noble's property on the upriver side of Chapmans Gully, from where it was fed into the dredge pond.

Earnscleugh Races: The Earnscleugh or Fraser River carried at least 100 heads of water so it was early a prime source of water for nearby claims. During 1863 at least nine races, some carrying five or more heads of water, were cut from intakes just below the outlet of the gorge to mines on the West Bank[9] of the Clutha River. Mining companies such as the Albion, Sandy Point, All England Eleven etc. between Clyde and the mouth of the Fraser River were all supplied by these water races. Later more were constructed until at least 14 races furrowed Earnscleugh Flat. Many were used to supply dredge ponds and later still formed the basis of the Earnscleugh Irrigation Scheme.

Relics

A surprising number of the big water races are still recognisable. Many, such as the Manuherikia, Ovens, Caledonian, Mountain races and those from the Fraser River, have been adapted to become important components of Central Otago's irrigation system. Others such as the Rose, Thistle and Shamrock, the Tucker Hill race and the Golden Gate race are no longer used but can be easily traced by their more permanent features such as cuttings, tunnels and, particularly, the stone walls that supported the races. Even though these races have fallen into disuse, the remnants are reminders of structures that played a very important part in the progressive development of the Central Otago goldfields.

NOTES

1. Gabriel Read reporting to Vincent Pyke. *Otago Daily Times* 7 October 1862.
2. The first rules for apportioning water are in the 1862 Regulations to the 1858 Act drawn up by the Otago Provincial Government. They allowed one head (see Note 3) for two men, two heads for three men and so on. A later Act in 1866 introduced licensing of water races and the approved quantity of water was included.
3. This old mining term for measuring the flow of water was equivalent to one cusec, ie. one cubic foot per second (28 litres/sec).
4. When a water race came to a large gully the water was piped down one side and up the other where it discharged into a continuation of the race. Such a V-shaped pipeline was called an inverted siphon or simply, a siphon.
5. This stream was named by the pioneer runholders, Alex and Watson Shennan after a locality in their native Roxburghshire in Scotland, and the name was officially recorded by J. T. Thomson, the Provincial Surveyor.
6. It was necessary to keep the races at a higher than necessary level in order to cross the ridge which ends in the high and spectacular cliffs just above the bridge to Galloway.
7. Blacks No. 1 diggings were at Ophir township and Blacks No. 2 and No. 3 on the other side of the Raggedy Range on the slope overlooking the present settlement of Poolburn. Manor Burn water was never taken to Ophir.
8. *Dunstan Times* 21 March 1903.
9. 'West Bank of the Molyneux' was an address given by scores of miners. It referred to diggings along the western bank of the Clutha River ('Molyneux' was the name in vogue at the time for the river) from the Alexandra ferry to about Clyde.

6.

MANOR BURN VIADUCT

'The best mining engineering work yet constructed in Otago'; 'the most expensive water race.'; 'The greatest white elephant of all.' These were some of the epithets used to describe the great trestled structure that carried the water race of the Rose, Thistle and Shamrock Water Race and Sluicing Company across the Manor Burn.

Figure 6. 1. The lower end of the Manuherikia Gorge just above the old Chatto Creek railway bridge. The intake of the Rose, Thistle and Shamrock water race was just below the point where the river turns to the left in the distance. The track along the bank to the right almost certainly follows the line of the race.

A group of 10 'working men,' [1] including their manager John Cole Chapple, fresh from his success in organising major river diversions, was formed in December 1863 to take water from the Manuherikia River. The object was to tap the river in the gorge above Galloway Flat and cut a water race round the eastern side of the Flat. Water would be sold to claims along the southern bank of the Manor Burn. While money was thus being recouped, the race would be extended down the eastern side of the Manuherikia River to Tucker Hill where the company hoped to begin mining. Rich prospects had been reported here and the future looked bright if only water could be brought on to the ground. There was even talk that the race might be further extended down the river—perhaps to its junction with the Clutha River (where it would discharge at a height of 23 metres above river level) or even to Butchers Point about 6 kilometres down the Clutha River where water at a high elevation was at a premium.

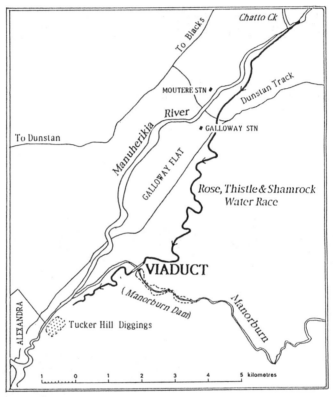

Figure 6. 2. The route of the Rose, Thistle and Shamrock water race and the Manor Burn viaduct.

The Race

Work started in early January 1864 and it was hoped that the race would be finished within three months, but this turned out to be optimistic. The first problem was to lead the race out of the rocky river gorge, and this involved making over 800 metres of cuttings, some up to 4.5 metres deep through solid rock. The whole party worked on these cuttings for seven weeks, using 200 kg of blasting powder. Then another two kilometres of the race had to be built up to a height of between 4 and 6 metres by stonework. The race wound its way for 11 or 12 kilometres in and out of the gullies and round the low spurs behind Galloway Flat with a steady fall of 50 cms to the kilometre.[2]

Figure 6. 3. For long distances the race ran through cuttings in solid rock, along built-up embankments and across slopes supported by long lengths of stone walling. Here, a remnant of the race, supported by a stone wall, makes its way round a large rock outcrop.

In early August[3] it was reported that the race was finished and that the men were busy on the greatest work of all—the giant set of trestles to support the flume which would carry the water across the Manor Burn. In all it was 250 metres long and 28 metres high at the centre where there was a clear span of 9 metres across the deep, rocky gorge. The whole structure was built of timber obtained from Lake Hawea, and the collection of this was a story in itself.

The Timber
Over a period of five weeks the whole party camped at the lake and cut 200 poles, each 7.5 metres long and 20 cms to 30 cms in diameter, from a block of bush near the shore that had suffered a bush fire shortly before. The trees, though dead, were still standing and the wood was dry. The poles were made up into three rafts and floated down the Clutha River to just above the rapids at Cromwell. Here the rafts were dismantled and the poles made up into bundles of four or six. These were refloated and allowed to find their way down to the Dunstan (Clyde) where they were reassembled into rafts. These continued down the river to the junction of the Manuherikia River where the poles were finally landed and carted to the building site.

Construction
Pairs of struts made up from poles, joined to make the necessary height and diagonally braced between the poles, supported the flume.

65

Figure 6. 4. The great wooden viaduct that carried the Rose, Thistle and Shamrock water race across the Manor Burn.

Figure 6. 5. A row of stone pylons supported the viaduct on the south bank of the Manor Burn.

These pairs of struts were placed 3.5 metres to 4.5 metres apart with more diagonal braces between the pairs. In the centre of the gorge it was necessary to fasten the feet of the struts to the solid rock. This was accomplished by attaching iron bars to the foot of each pole with 15 cm spikes. The bars were then set in molten lead in holes drilled 45 cms into the rock. At either end of the structure, where the height was less, stone towers were built between pairs of struts. These, apparently, had '. . . a considerable tendency to prevent oscillation.'

For some reason the viaduct was not straight but had a slight kink built into it at about two thirds of its length. This meant that the southern end of the structure ended up several metres further upstream than it would have done had the viaduct been straight.

The water was carried across this structure in a flume 60 cms wide and 30 cms deep, consisting of tongued and grooved Baltic pine set on 75 mm x 50 mm cross pieces 1.2 metres apart. These in turn rested on longitudinal, 100 mm x 500 mm rails, running the full length of the flume, which were attached and suitably braced to the tops of the struts. All of this timber used for the flume was brought from Dunedin.

Figure 6. 6. One of a number of iron pegs set in holes in the solid rock, to which the foot of the timber poles were bolted.

Water was turned into the race early in 1865 and the company began to supply water to miners, and do some sluicing itself, in shallow ground in a gully only a few hundred metres from the southern end of the flume. The company struck gold and in the first wash up in March it recovered 24 oz of metal. But the company had more ambitious plans and applied for an extension of the race to Tucker Hill diggings in May 1865. Construction recommenced but progress was not easy. Almost immediately another 250 metres of fluming was necessary to carry the race to the back of Heyward's store at the mouth of Edwards Gully. This structure was not nearly so high as that across the Manor Burn but the men had to go back to Lake Hawea for more timber. In all a total of 730 m of fluming was used in the length of the race.

Figure 6. 7. This is the point on the south bank of the Manor Burn where the viaduct joined a normal water race.

Long lengths of fluming were not the only difficulties. Many stone walls were required to support the race along steep hillsides as well as deep cuttings, and even a tunnel was needed to avoid a long loop round the end of a spur.

By February 1866 the race was within half a mile of Tucker Hill and a lease was taken out on a 10-acre (4 h) claim which the company hoped the race would reach in seven weeks. But costs were skyrocketing and the company attempted to raise more capital. This was not very successful and then everything began to go wrong.

Disaster
It was suddenly realised that the race, after all the effort, was too low to reach the claim that the company had acquired, and while discussion went on as to what to do, a tremendous storm blew down part of the high flume over the Manor Burn. This was the last straw: the shareholders agreed to sell the company by auction. The race and flume, which had cost £2,350, was eventually bought for £105 by the Manuherikia Water Race Company which had also recently taken over the big race from the upper Manor Burn built by the Ida Valley Water Race Company.

It is likely that the portion of the Rose, Thistle and Shamrock race from the intake in the Manuherikia River to Dip Creek was abandoned at this time and that water was supplied to the remainder of the race from the upper Manor Burn race via Dip Creek. The new owners did not operate a mine themselves but concentrated on supplying water to other miners.

Still in service as part of the Government irrigation scheme, the section of the original Rose, Thistle, and Shamrock Company's race from Dip Creek to the Manor Burn is now part of the 'Top Race' of the Galloway farmers.

Repaired after the wind damage of 1867, the big viaduct across the Manor Burn was eventually abandoned when the easily-recovered gold ran out on the Manorburn field. Although there is no record of its eventual fate, we can be certain that, once it fell into disuse, it would not survive very long in a land where timber and firewood were nearly as valuable as gold.

NOTES

1. Working partners as distinct from 'capitalists' who supplied money only.
2. The race and flume was described by a special reporter in the *Otago Daily Times* 21 November 1864.
3. *Otago Daily Times* 6 August 1864.

7.
RAIDING THE
JEWELLERS SHOP

Frenchmans Point

On the inside of the big bend where the Clutha River turns at right-angles to enter the gorge immediately below Alexandra, was an isolated remnant of a gravel terrace. Fronted by a sandy beach and lying against the rocky hillside behind, the crescent-shaped mass of gravel was about 400 metres long and perhaps 70 metres wide. Its surface was at the same level as that of the terrace across the river on which stands the township of Alexandra.

Figure 7. 1. This sketch of Manuherikia (Alexandra) from the track over the Knobby Range, was adapted from a work by Nairn and published in *The Illustrated London News* of 14 November, 1863. On the left is the feature that was later to be called Frenchmans Point. Miners are shown working on the Point even though the main discovery of gold was not made until June 1864.

The beach along the foot of the terrace, together with other beaches in the vicinity, had early on been tested for gold, but was publicly pronounced 'duffer ground.' It was not until June 1864,[1] when the river was once again as low as it had been at the time of the Dunstan Rush, that a party of miners was able to dig deeply into the bank at the back of the beach. The men struck a layer of wash from which they quickly obtained 84 oz of gold.

In no time 15 claims were pegged out along the river frontage and an almost equal number in a parallel row immediately behind, although it soon became obvious that these could not be worked satisfactorily until the front claims were worked out. And when the difficulties of working the ground became apparent, even many of the front claims, pegged out in the first rush of enthusiasm, were quietly abandoned.

There were two main problems. One was the thickness of the overburden that had to be removed to expose the wash. The 20 metres or so of only slightly compacted gravel, standing as an almost vertical cliff above the workings, was a constant source of danger. The second was that the gold-bearing wash was at, or below, normal river level so the workings were, at all times, subject to constant and rapid seepage from the river. And each time the river rose the workings were completely flooded. This meant that from the time the river began to rise with the spring thaw, until autumn frosts began lowering the river level, it was impossible to reach the gold-bearing wash. Work at the claims during summer and autumn was confined to stripping away the thick overburden and exposing a patch of wash in readiness for excavation during the relatively short period of winter low water.

Figure 7. 2. A photo taken by Joseph Perry in 1865 shows the Clutha River rounding Frenchmans Point and entering the gorge below Alexandra through the narrow 'Gates of the Gorge.' The Manuherikia River joins the Clutha River in the foreground.

Large Californian pumps, with water wheels to drive them, were essential to keep the excavations clear of the water which, even at times of low river levels, poured through the porous gravel. In this respect the miners at the terrace were fortunate in having the use of one of the earliest long water races in the district. Commenced in October 1863 by Coleman and party, it tapped the South Branch of Conroys Creek far up on the slopes of the Old Man Range and delivered the water to the West Bank of the Clutha River opposite Alexandra. Completed in the middle of 1864, Coleman said later that the race, which became known as the Mountain Race, had been built as a speculation. Its construction had no doubt been encouraged by good returns from earlier prospecting along the river banks. By fortunate coincidence it was completed at the same time as the discovery of the rich gold near its terminus.

The water was essential to the new workings but it was not cheap, as Coleman charged up to £6 per week for one head. So potential miners had to have sufficient money not only to buy water for the water wheels but also to purchase other elaborate equipment and to hire labour. This was no place for the enthusiastic miner and his mate—only groups pooling their capital could hope to succeed here. But for those who could command the resources the rewards were to be immense.

Perhaps the earliest front claim was the one financially backed by Jean Désire Feraud, described as 'a leading tradesman and investor' who had already established a successful 16 hectare fruit and vegetable farm near Clyde. This claim was to become famous throughout Otago for its fabulous returns—returns approaching, and perhaps exceeding, those obtained by the rich 'Gully' discoveries of 1862.

Three weeks after the initial discovery of this rich deposit, three front claims had been established, each employing machinery on a scale not hitherto seen in the district. Because of the height of the terrace it was necessary to strip away more than 25 to 30 metres of low-yielding gravel before the 1.5 metre-thick wash at the base was reached. But it was certainly worth the trouble. Each shovelful of wash yielded about 1.5 grams of gold. On each of the three claims, water from the Mountain Race was used to operate an overshot water wheel which was connected by an endless rope belt to a Californian pump on the beach below. After passing over the water wheel the water was conveyed down the hill in a canvas hose and used to loosen the terrace gravels and wash them through the sluice boxes.

All of the material from the whole height of the terrace was passed through the sluice boxes, but the gold came mainly from the wash at the base. The return was some 20 to 24 oz of gold each day and Feraud received a dividend of £100 on his investment in the first three weeks.[2] The claim soon became known as "The Frenchman's"[3] (Feraud had been born in France) and the area became 'Frenchmans Point.' The success of this field attracted others to try their luck on nearby beaches, and Butlers Point, just up the Manuherikia River, and Prospectors Point, directly across the Clutha River, became as busy as

Figure 7. 3. Jean Désire Feraud was the Frenchman after whom Frenchmans Point was named. Feraud, a Clyde businessman and farmer, certainly financed the famous 'Frenchmans Claim' but it is unlikely that he actually worked in the claim.

they were in the earliest days of the Dunstan Rush. Even the holders of the almost unworkable claims behind the outer ones on Frenchmans Point began to sink shafts in a desperate attempt to cash in on the bonanza.

Adjoining the Frenchman's claim was the United Bendigo claim, owned by James Coleman and John Tunnell and party, and further along was the Harp of Erin which was giving comparable returns to those of the Frenchman's claim.

In early August came the first of the floods that were to plague the claims. This one did damage throughout the goldfields but the low-lying claims at the Point suffered particularly. The Frenchman's claim was damaged to the tune of £170 and the Harp of Erin suffered even more severely when the race supplying the water wheel burst and washed out the claim. Although the damage was repaired within a month there were to be only a few more short periods of low river before the spring rise made the gold-bearing wash inaccessible.

Ironically, one of the answers to high river levels was to bring in more race water so that more pumping could be carried out and the overburden removed at a faster rate. Edmund Jones, a local entrepreneur, began to construct races to bring in water from Omeo Creek in Blackmans Gully. and from the Fraser River. Altogether an extra seven heads of water were delivered to Frenchmans Point by the end of 1864.

To lessen damage from river floods and to save the labour of removing 18 metres of overburden, the Harp of Erin decided to try tunnelling into the wash rather than excavating vertically. For a time it turned out to be very profitable. More than 12 oz of gold were recovered for each metre the tunnel was advanced, but all too soon they were forced to revert to 'paddocking' as they could not overcome

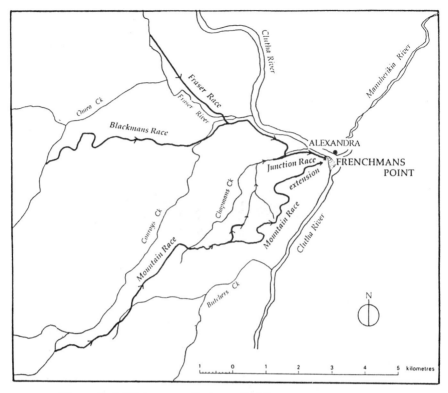

Figure 7. 4. Water races that supplied Frenchmans Point claims.

the water which seeped into the tunnel.

After another flood, which capsized the Harp of Erin's water wheel, James Coleman sold his claim and moved down the river to Butchers Point.

Frenchmans Point made a spectacular sight as work continued through the night under the light of kerosene lights backed by reflectors. The array of bright lights, and their reflections from the river, accompanied by characteristic sounds—the whirring of the water wheels and the flop-flop of the Californian pumps—gave the whole scene an air of bustling activity. The Frenchmans claim, managed by Michael Kett, was now employing 18 men at £5 a week each and typical gold production was 80 oz from a 'paddock' 45 ft x 15 ft (17.6 m x 4.5 m).[4] Little wonder business was booming in the village of Alexandra.

The Hit or Miss claim, established in January 1865, was soon stripping its overburden, or 'opening up' as the miners put it. Over the 30 metres by 45 metres area of the claim, 2 metres of gold-bearing wash lay under 18 metres of gravel. This turned out to be a particularly well managed claim and became the example for others to follow. The party consisted of nine members who worked two shifts of 10 hours each. Seven men worked in the mine and the other two kept the machinery in repair. Their plan was to strip off overburden while the river was high and then to work the underlying wash when the river had fallen to a low level.

Three heads of water were bought for £12 to £18 a week and the gravel was loosened with a hydraulic hose and washed through the 60 metre-long sluice boxes. An innovation was to use iron ripple bars to catch the gold in the boxes instead of the more usual flat stones placed in a ditch. This was a big step forward in gold saving and was rapidly copied by other nearby claims. Now for the first time, gold could be recovered from the gravels overlying the wash, and whereas it was not a great amount, it was sufficient to cover the cost of stripping. Work went on continuously and resulted in a flood of gravel pouring into the river. This caused miners working across the river on the beach at Prospectors Point to protest that the river was being filled up and the rising water was interfering with their claims.

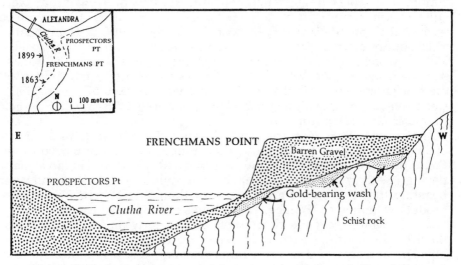

Figure 7. 5. A cross-section sketch (not to scale) through Frenchmans Point shows the wash containing the gold lying under a large thickness of relatively barren gravel.
Inset: River banks in 1863 (dotted lines) before the mining of Frenchmans and Prospectors Points, and in 1899 (solid lines) after mining.

Meanwhile John Miller, a shareholder in the new Hit or Miss Company, had built a water wheel over 4 metres in diameter, and this was opened with due ceremony on 16 June 1865.[5] It was connected to a Californian pump more than 14 metres long—so long in fact that its great length had to be supported by braces like a suspension bridge. Everything was made ready to handle the expected influx of seepage water when the river dropped sufficiently to allow excavation of the golden wash to begin.

New companies, such as Enterprise, United Bendigo, New Propriety and the Perseverance took up claims, flourished for a while but soon tired of the floods and moved out. At one time all of the 15 front claims were occupied, and over 100 men were employed during the winter when the river was low and the wash accessible. But it was the Frenchman's and the Hit or Miss claims that persisted and reaped the golden harvest.

As the miners worked their way deeper into the terrace, so the height of the face of gravel above the excavations became greater and slips and falls became commonplace. One, in the Hit or Miss claim, took several days to clear away but a more serious fall in the United Bendigo mine resulted in the burial of three men. Two were dug out uninjured but the third suffered a broken leg. This was followed in early July by a fall at the Harp of Erin claim that closed the mouth of the tunnel in which four men were working. Luckily one was outside and was able to extricate his companions.

The supply of gold pouring out of these claims seemed inexhaustible, especially when the miners suddenly broke through a false bottom to discover fresh riches beneath. Returns of 40 oz a day were quite common and it was known for 80 oz and even 100 oz to be recovered in one day. The Frenchman's claim took 400 oz from a patch of 12 square metres, over six days. Their first wash up for 1867 yielded 900 oz which, after deducting £1,000 for expenses (mainly wages), gave each shareholder £600. At the end of the winter wash up in 1868 the shareholders pocketed £1,000 each after expenses of about £300 a week were paid. The Enterprise claim recovered £7,575 worth of gold in one season of eight months.

That year, 1868, was the peak. During the following year several claims were put up for sale and the number of men employed at the Point dropped to 30. This did not prevent the Frenchman's claim paying its shareholders £300 each after nine days work in July and boasting that this was a greater return than that offered by the most productive mines at Thames. Then things started to go wrong.

A mild winter saw the river begin to rise early and the mines were flooded two months earlier than expected. Then Michael Kett, the very efficient manager of the Frenchman's claim, left to operate his own claim at nearby Halfmile Beach.

By early August 1870 all the claims except the Frenchman's and the Hit or Miss had been worked out and abandoned. A month later the Hit or Miss Company became the sole survivor when it took over the Frenchman's claim. It struggled on for another year but by 1872 Frenchmans Point was finished—finished not only as a gold field, but as a landform.

In seven years, half a million cubic metres of gravel had been sluiced into the river. The whole terrace had been washed away, right down to bedrock. In its place was a large water-filled hole in the midst of a gravel shoal. Today the bare rock is clothed with sparse vegetation and the hole has filled with gravel.

Because the 'companies' were groups of private individuals, there was no obligation to disclose their recoveries of gold, so figures quoted in newspapers were often the results of information 'leaks,' exaggeration and sheer speculation. For these reasons it is impossible to know now how much gold was recovered from Frenchmans Point diggings or from individual claims.

Figure 7. 6. The site of Frenchmans Point today. The gravel terrace has been completely removed and all that is left is a shoal in the river.

A clue, however, was given by Michael Kett, the manager of the Frenchman's claim, when he admitted that for the first 12 months he had recovered £3,000 worth of gold but another £2,000 worth had escaped through poor gold-saving techniques. From these values, and other information, it seems probable that the output of the Frenchmans claim was about 2,000 oz per year or 12,000 oz, worth £46,500, over the six years of its life. On today's price of gold ($NZ600 oz) this would be worth about $NZ5 million. Not a bad investment for the £555 (or $NZ86,000) that J. D. Feraud and three others paid for it in 1865!.

NOTES

1. *Otago Daily Times* 6 June 1864.
2. *Otago Daily Times* 13 June 1864.
3. It is commonly believed that it was Feraud who discovered gold at Frenchmans Point but there is little evidence for this. It is more likely that it was Feraud's friend Bladier and his brother who were the discoverers. But there is no doubt that Feraud financed the claim.
4. *Otago Daily Times* 21 December 1864.
5. *Otago Daily Times,* 23 June 1865.

8.

DISASTER IN THE GORGE

It didn't take the early miners very long to discover small amounts of gold in the patches of gravels lying high above the river in the gorge below Alexandra. A few lone fossickers prospected and stayed, but most miners were after greater wealth and quickly moved on. It was only when more persistent men dug deeply into the gravel cliff opposite Alexandra, later to be called Frenchmans Point, and extracted 84 oz of gold in a few days, that the potential of these terrace remnants was realised.

James Coleman was one of those who was early on the scene at Frenchmans Point, but finding it too crowded for his liking, decided to try what he saw as a similar formation about six kilometres further down the gorge. He was right. At Butchers Point, in March 1865, he struck thick washdirt,[1] with abundant coarse gold.

At Butchers Point the eastern wall of the great gorge is broken by the steep, rocky defile of Colmans[2] Gully. At the mouth of this gully a narrow terrace stands about 25 metres above the river level and stretches several hundreds of metres in both directions along the river bank. A thick veneer of large boulders, washed out of Colmans Gully during past intensive rainstorms or fallen from the steep slopes above, covers the river gravels that make up the terrace. The terrace remnant is at the same level as, and was probably once continuous with, the extensive terraces on which the towns of Alexandra, Clyde, Cromwell and Roxburgh are built. The gravel was deposited when the Clutha River flowed at a higher level.

As Coleman excavated down to the wash which was lying on a 'bottom' of solid schist rock sloping towards the river, he began to have difficulties with water seeping through the porous gravels into his workings. Normally he would have lifted the water out with a Californian pump[3] driven by a water wheel. But there was too little water in the small stream that splashed down Colmans Gully to turn a water wheel, so his pumps had to be turned by hand. It was estimated[4] that pumping cost £64 a week in labour, as it required four

Figure 8. 1. Looking down the Clutha River gorge below Alexandra. Butchers Point protrudes into the river in the centre with Colmans Gully behind. Butchers Creek joins the river lower right.

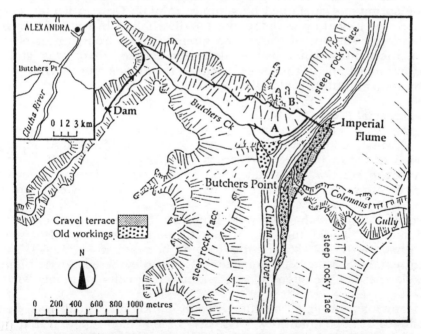

Figure 8. 2. Map of Butchers Point. In 1866 a water race, marked 'A,' conveyed water from Butchers Creek across the Clutha River by way of the Imperial Flume to gold workings at Butchers Point. In the 1890s John Magnus used a flume on the same site to convey water, brought from a dam in Butchers Creek by way of a high-level race, marked 'B,' to his hydraulic elevator at Butchers Point.

men on each of two pumps night and day to keep the seepage under control. But the rewards were worth the effort as a return of 80 oz of gold from one 'paddock' [5] was reported.

No doubt an invention[6] of Coleman's was welcomed with gratitude by the men working these pumps. He constructed a propeller, with four blades set at $45°$ in a frame attached to poles, which projected a considerable distance over the water. The propeller was turned by the current and was connected to the Californian pumps by a long belt. So successful was the machine that it was able to keep two claims clear of water.

The small stream in Colmans Gully was, of course, hopelessly inadequate to supply water for sluicing and, in fact, it dried up completely in the summer and autumn. So the gold-bearing sand had to be carried down to the river for washing in cradles, but in spite of this miners were making £3 to £4 a week each. How much more, they asked, could they make if they had sufficient water to wash the sand through a ground-sluice? No wonder frustrated miners were offering up to £30 a week to anyone who would supply a head (= water flowing at the rate of 1 cubic foot [28.4 litres] per second) of water. Much thought was given to ways and means of satisfying the demand.

Immediately opposite Butchers Point a large stream, Butchers Creek, joins the Clutha River by way of a narrow, deep rocky cleft. The stream itself rises far back on the Old Man Range and is fed by melting snow in the spring and sustained by summer rainfall. Only in winter when the water is locked up by frosts does its flow falter. In spite of the fact that a large amount of water was already taken from the creek by water races at various points along its course, there was still a substantial volume in the lower reaches. But it was on the wrong side of the wide and turbulent Clutha River.

The Imperial Flume
So great was the attraction of an abundant water supply, however, that Cornish and party (calling themselves the Imperial Company) decided to try to bring water across the river by means of a flume. They began erection in August 1865 amid a rising clamour for water from the crowd of miners that had been attracted to Butchers Point by the steady gold returns.

Cornish thought that he could bring up to seven heads across and estimated it would take six weeks to build the flume. But seven months later he was still saying it would be ready in six weeks. Three months later it was to be finished '. . . in a few weeks.' [7] He blamed the slowness of the shareholders in answering calls for money for the delays.

Meanwhile, in spite of the difficult conditions, gold was being produced in large quantities. One party of four men reported that they were recovering 12 oz of gold each week and another said that, when they finally reached bottom, they were getting close to 2 oz per shovelful and some of the pieces weighed two pennyweights (1/10 oz).[8]

The flume was finally finished in early November 1866 and was opened with the christening ceremony traditional for such events.

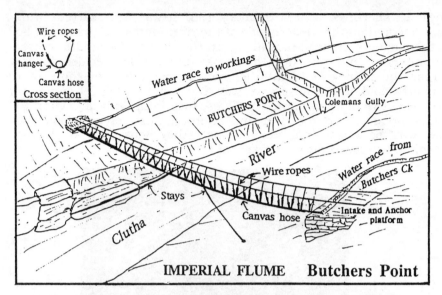

Figure 8 . 3. A sketch, based on descriptions, of the Imperial Flume.

People made their way across the Manuherikia River by the ferry at Alexandra and then down the rough track along the left bank of the Clutha River. The flume made a gay sight festooned with bunting and flags. After speeches, a Miss Henderson broke a bottle of champagne on the structure and named it "The Imperial Flume."[9] The water was turned on, toasts drunk, Mr Robinson (Warden of the Goldfield) made a speech, and everyone retired to the refreshment table.

The flume was certainly an impressive affair. Two parallel wire ropes stretched for 150 metres across the turbulent river and were securely anchored on either side. Between the two ropes, closely spaced canvas straps formed a long hammock in which lay a large-diameter canvas hose. Various rope stays were used to keep the main ropes taut and to prevent, as far as possible, excessive sway caused by the wind howling down the gorge.

A small dam had been built across Butchers Creek about 400 metres from its mouth and water was led in a race along the northern bank of the creek to a point about 30 metres above the river. Here the water was fed into the canvas hose and eventually gurgled from the other end into a race, which led it along the hillside to the claims. The Imperial Company took most of the water for its own use but rented some to the neighbouring claim-owner, Parker and party, who were then able to sluice off the overburden on their claim rather than strip it off by hand.

Coleman wasn't interested in the flume water even if it had been offered. He began to use his propeller-driven pump to lift water eight or nine metres from the river to his claim.

Disaster
The joy of achievement of the proud owners of the Imperial Flume was,

however, shortlived. On 31 January 1867 it was necessary to bring a boat, moored on the western side of the river, across to the claim. Four of the partners, instead of walking up the river to Alexandra, crossing on the punt and returning down the other side, decided to crawl across the flume. At about the midway point one or more of the supports holding the hose gave way and the men fell 20 metres into the river. Two of them miraculously escaped injury but one, Oran Bell, was swept away by the river and another, Goss, struck some rocks and was seriously injured. Although they took him to Dunstan Hospital, he died shortly after arrival.[10]

Figure 8. 4. Looking across the Clutha River, along the line of the Imperial Flume, from the intake platform on the West Bank. On the opposite (eastern) bank traces of a water race lead away from the point where the flume ended. The large rock in the foreground has marks that may indicate it served as an anchor for Magnus's flume.

At the inquest into the two deaths held soon afterwards, the manager of the Imperial Company, John Miller, admitted that he knew of the faults in the supports but then so did the partners. It was ruled that the victims were the authors of their own misfortune.

This accident was the final blow that broke up the Cornish partnership. The flume had taken much longer to erect, had cost much more than expected, and then had not delivered the promised amount of water because of the need for constant repairs. It was taken over by the manager, John Miller, and his brother, along with a Mr Scott. They decided to rebuild the flume but dispense with the canvas hose and replace it with the new galvanised iron 'tubes' that had recently become available. Although expensive, it was thought that the pipes would pay for themselves because of the need for fewer repairs.

The Flume Rebuilt

These 18.5 cm diameter pipes, or 'tubes' as they were referred to, were in 6 metre lengths and were joined with bands of rubber cemented in place with a special composition supplied by the maker. Again the pipes were laid in a canvas hammock between the two wire ropes.[11] The system had been used successfully by the Golden Gate Company in building their flume across the Manuherikia River at Blacks. It was calculated that the pipes could carry four heads of water but apparently they never delivered more than two heads.

Figure 8. 5. Looking up the gorge of Butchers Creek towards the site of the intake of Magnus's high-level race. The remains of the race can be traced along the middle of the steep slope on the right.

Eventually Nicholas Anderson became the owner of the flume and of the water right to four heads from Butchers Creek, but in 1878 the great flood swept down the gorge and destroyed the structure.[12] We do not know whether the wire ropes themselves were washed away but the flume was not reinstated.

James Coleman had never taken water from the flume, possibly because of its cost, but struggled on with the small quantity delivered by his pump. At last, however, he was forced to start cutting a race[13] from Speargrass Creek, a tributary of the Manor Burn, and with this water he carried on for 10 years. After passing through several hands, Coleman's claim was acquired in 1894 by John Magnus and John Everitt who called themselves the Butchers Point Company.[14]

Another Flume

Magnus, like others before him, planned to flume water from Butchers Creek across the Clutha River, but unlike previous miners, Magnus intended to work his claim by hydraulic elevating.[15] This system required a fairly large quantity of water at high pressure so Magnus applied for eight heads from Butchers Creek. When he found that the water right was still held by Anderson, Magnus immediately applied to have the right forfeited on the grounds that Anderson had not used the water since 1878. Magnus won and was granted four heads.

Figure **8. 6.** An extension of **Figure 8.5** towards the right. On the left, Magnus's high-level race from the dam in Butchers Creek skirts a very steep face then crosses a scrub-filled tributary gully and, on the right, comes towards the Clutha River.

A race was constructed, by contract, from a dam in Butchers Creek gorge, along the almost vertical western wall of the gorge and then, as the creek turned at right angles towards the river, along the northern side until it terminated about 80 metres above the Clutha River. From here the water was conveyed down the steep hillside in a pipeline which was taken nearly 200 metres across the river, suspended from either the original wire ropes put in place for the Imperial Flume or, more likely, from a new, heavier rope. The pipeline climbed the eastern side of the gorge and discharged into a high-level race that carried the water along the back of the Butchers Point diggings. From this race the water was piped down to the elevator in Magnus's claim, providing sufficient pressure for gravel to be lifted 10 metres. Magnus's claim was busy, with nine men employed, but high river levels frequently brought the work to a standstill and in May 1896 a decision was made to pull out and move all of the equipment to a new claim at Poverty Beach on the Clutha River, about, one kilometre above the Alexandra Bridge.[16] And that effectively was the end of mining at Butchers Point.

Relics

The old low-level race which fed the Imperial Flume is still visible, although badly overgrown with briar, as is the platform on the western bank of the river which provided the anchor site for the ropes. A few centimetres of 15 mm-diameter galvanised wire rope protruding from this platform may well be the remains of one of the ropes that supported the flume. Remnants of a race can also be traced for some distance from the outlet of the flume on the eastern bank of the river.

Figure 8. 7. Rock platform at the western side of the Imperial Flume. It was here that race water entered the canvas hose of the flume and the supporting wire ropes were anchored at the back of this platform.

John Magnus's high-level race is much better preserved and can be easily traced from the dam site in Butchers Creek to the point where the water entered the pipeline. Coils of 3 cms-diameter wire rope, partly buried in the ground near the low-level race, may be the remains of the ropes that carried Magnus's pipeline across the river, but they could equally be part of a mooring line from one of the dredges that later worked in the river. It is possible that a large prominent rock, now not far above lake level, was used for anchoring the rope of Magnus's flume.

Figure 8. 8. Magnus's water race (right foreground) from Butchers Creek terminated at the edge of a very steep slope. Here water entered the pipeline the intake of that lay between the two rocks. The pipeline dropped steeply into a gully (partly hidden by a briar bush) ran down the slope to the right towards the river and across the flume.

It is known for certain that by 1930 no ropes crossed the river[17] and it is likely that they were removed during the dredging boom of the early 1900s, either to provide mooring lines for a dredge or perhaps to avoid dredges fouling them during periods of high river level.

NOTES

1. The 'washdirt' (abbreviated to "wash') was the layer of sand and fine gravel that contained the bulk of the gold. It ranged from a few centimetres to more than a metre in thickness and generally lay on solid rock or other hard layer (the 'bottom'). It could be overlain by many metres of relatively barren gravels.
2. Modern maps give the name of this gully as 'Colmans' but it is undoubtedly named after James Coleman who, in Electoral Rolls and in a signed letter to the newspaper, spelt his name with an 'e.'
3. See Chapter 7 for a description of this pump.
4. *Otago Daily Times* 1 July 1865.
5. A claim was generally divided into blocks or 'paddocks' which were excavated in turn.

6. *Otago Daily Times* 3 August 1865.
7. *Otago Daily Times* 8 June 1866.
8. *Otago Daily Times* 21 August 1865.
9. *Otago Daily Times* 2 November 1866.
10. *Otago Daily Times* 11 February 1867.
11. *Dunstan Times* 7 June 1867.
12. *Otago Witness* 15 February 1894.
13. This race was noteworthy because it crossed under the saddle between Shanty Creek and Colmans Gully by way of a tunnel 150 metres long ⸴
14. *Dunstan Times* 9 February 1894.
15. See Chapter 5 for description of this device.
16. Magnus, with others, formed the Golden Beach Company to work this claim.
17. According to Mr E. V. King of Alexandra (personal communication) who mined in the gorge during the Depression of the 1930s.

9

LEVANTING TUNNELLERS

At the point where Conroys Creek leaves its lower gorge and begins its journey across Earnscleugh Flat, it has to make a U-bend round a hill. The miners said it was a 'made hill'—their term for a landform that was not composed of solid rock. They were right. The hill was, in fact, comprised of schist gravel brought down from the Old Man Range by Conroys Creek and dumped at the outlet of its gorge. Gold was, early on, detected in the gravels of the hill.

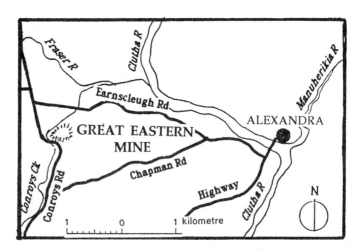

Figure 9. 1. Location map Great Eastern Mine

In late 1865 John Bennett, John Benny and others pegged out the hill as a claim. They intended to sluice it using water from Conroys Creek. But instead of building a race which followed a circuitous route round the hill, they decided to bring the water to their claim by way of a tunnel driven straight through the hill. Beginning on the upstream side of the hill—that is, on the side facing up Conroys Creek—Bennett and his mates were greatly encouraged by recovering payable amounts of gold from the material they excavated. Eventually, after 150 metres of tunnelling, they emerged on the other side of the hill in March 1866.

Then John Bennett had an idea. Instead of sluicing the hill from the outside, they would mine it from the inside. Wooden sluice boxes were laid in the floor of the tunnel along its length so that the creek water flowed through them. Then they began to enlarge their tunnel, throwing the spoil into the sluice boxes where the water washed away the stones and sand, leaving, hopefully, the gold behind.[1] Eventually the main tunnel was nearly 5 metres in width and over 4 metres in height. They were not game to make it any larger in case the whole thing collapsed, so they began to excavate side tunnels and chambers. Eventually the hill was fairly honeycombed with over 400 metres of side tunnels. According to the *Dunstan Times,* some of the chambers were:

> . . . sufficiently large to entertain at luncheon, at least two dozen guests, without their being discommoded.[2]

It was suggested that townspeople should visit the mine because, the local paper claimed, probably no underground mining in the province was carried on so systematically and extensively. In fact, it was because there were so many subterranean corridors and 'rooms' in the mine that it was named "Great Eastern" after a fancied resemblance to the interior of the huge ship[3] of the same name which was in the news after its recent launching in Britain.

There was apparently a constant change of partners—Bennett dropped out and Luke and Martin came in. Then James Simmonds, later to be mayor of Alexandra and a prominent contractor, bought a third share in the enterprise which continued to prosper.[4] It is

Figure 9. 2. Air photograph taken in 1949 when the site of the Great Eastern mine was being used as a source of gravel (the light area to right of lower centre). Only a narrow rocky ridge (Figure 9. 3) remains between the mine site and the valley of Conroys Creek. The lower gorge of Conroys Creek is to the left and the orchards of Earnscleugh Flat to the right.

recorded that each partner was making £8 a week and several wages-men were employed. Then they made an error of judgement—they brought in three more partners. But the returns were not sufficient to support so many extra people. Simmonds saw the writing on the wall and sold his share back to the company for £30 and got out.

The downward slide continued and debts to local storekeepers began to accumulate. There was nothing unusual in this. It was a tradition of the goldfields that storekeepers would 'grubstake' miners—in other words extend credit—until they struck gold. Then the storekeeper expected to be paid in full, and most often he was.

One morning, towards the end of 1868 and about six months after Simmonds had left, word flashed round the district, "Men are trapped in the Great Eastern." Without a second's hesitation miners took up their tools and ran, or grabbed horses, or clambered into drays. Sure enough, a length of one of the branch tunnels had completely collapsed. The men were obviously trapped as their hut was open, their working clothes and tools gone and dishes were on the table just as they had left them as they set off for the day's work.

In no time sweating gangs were inside the tunnel shovelling frantically at the fallen debris while gulping tea provided by women also perspiring as they stoked fires under boiling billies. Hour after

Figure 9. 3. Today the view from the south gives the impression that the 'made' hill, in which the Great Eastern mine was located, is still intact. But the feature is actually a ridge, only a few metres wide, comprised of a veneer of gravel draped over a rock core, which not only protected the original terrace from stream erosion but also prevented both the miners and the quarrymen from removing the last remnants of gravel from the site. The entrance to the tunnel was under the right-hand clump of trees growing on the slope.

hour the work went on. Then the shout went up—the rescuers were through. But relief turned to puzzlement—where were the trapped miners? The mine was searched by men growing increasingly excited as they realised that it was empty. Then they remembered the rumours about unpaid debts. The truth quickly dawned on the rescuers—the tunnellers had absconded. "The beggars have levanted,"[5] was the expression of the time as the angry men gathered up their tools and made their way back to their interrupted work.

Some months later it was reported that the missing men had been seen working on the Thames goldfield in the North Island. It was reported, too, that a number of Alexandra storekeepers had had to write off some large debts about this time.[6]

James Lees and Party took over the abandoned claim in 1870 and, with water from Conroys Creek, began wholesale sluicing. Good results were reported. The already honeycombed hill did not last long under this onslaught and in mid-1871 what was left of the claim and the mining plant were offered for sale.

There is no sign of the Great Eastern tunnels now. Lees' sluicing destroyed them and, what little of the 'made hill' left was used for some years, as a County gravel quarry. Only a level patch of bare, firm gravel, devoid of topsoil, backed on the south side by a narrow ridge of rock thinly veneered with gravel, marks the site of one of the district's more interesting gold mines.

NOTES

1. *Otago Daily Times* 8 September 1866.
2 *Dunstan Times* 24 August 1866.
3 The *Great Eastern* was launched in 1858 and at 18,914 tons and with a length of 213 m was by far the largest ship in the world.
4. Simmonds, J. *Otago Daily Times* 27 November 1912.
5. 'Levant' was a legal term commonly used during the mining days and means to `abscond without paying debts—to 'shoot through' in modern parlance.
6. Verbal communication, the late Alex Taylor of Alexandra, 1952. Mr Taylor first heard the story from his father-in-law, Richard Dawson of Conroys Gully, who was one of the would-be rescuers.

10.

THREE CHRISTMASSES
- NO PRESENTS

The Golden Gate Water Race

The McNally boys, Patrick and John, had prospered at Blacks diggings some 32 kilometres up the Manuherikia Valley from Alexandra. They had seen how shortage of water was holding back the development of this otherwise rich area, so with a few mates they set out in mid-1864 to remedy the deficiency.

Calling themselves the Golden Gate Company[1] they began to construct a race from Thomsons Creek (or Spottis Creek as it was then called), a stream flowing across the broad Manuherikia Valley from the Dunstan Mountains and joining the Manuherikia River near Blacks (now Ophir). The water was carried across the Manuherikia River gorge in a flume supported by high wooden trestles. Although the flume was damaged by wind and then destroyed by a flood, it was rebuilt and continued to supply water not only to the claim of McNally brothers and their partners but also to several nearby mines. After six years rewarding work, however, the end of the easy ground came into sight and the lads began to look for another claim.

New Ground
During June 1872 the McNally brothers appeared, along with their mates, on a number of occasions in the Dunstan Warden's Court to apply for several claims at the Waikerikeri Valley diggings about 5 km north of Clyde. In an often-used device to acquire and hold a large area of ground, various combinations of partners applied for separate claims. First, Patrick McNally, along with three other partners, applied for an Extended Claim of four acres in Connews Gully; then his brother John, along with John Hastie, applied for another Extended Claim of two acres in neighbouring Deans Gully. Later other claims were applied for by other combinations of the partners. They finished up with a number of claims totalling more than 20 acres (8 h) that

they intended to mine as a group.

Having secured their ground, the partners now turned their attention to a water supply. Ideally they wanted the same arrangement as they had had at Blacks—sufficient water for their own use and a surplus to sell to other claims. They had their eyes on the east bank of the Clutha River below Clyde where mining was greatly hampered by lack of water. Whoever could supply reliable water to these claims stood to make a good profit.

The partners first applied for a race and water right from Waikerikeri Creek, which was the nearest source of reliable water. But they knew very well that James Holt held the first right from this stream and used the water to drive the pumps and hoists at his colliery near Clyde. To cover the possibility of their application being refused, they also applied to construct a race from the headwaters of Chatto Creek.

This was a bold scheme. The race would be difficult and expensive to construct. It was planned to take five heads of water from Leahys Creek (one of the tributaries of Chatto Creek near its head) and convey it along the foothills of the Dunstan Mountains by a race which would terminate on the banks of the Clutha River near the Dunstan Hospital. The race would be about 25 kilometres long and on its way would pick

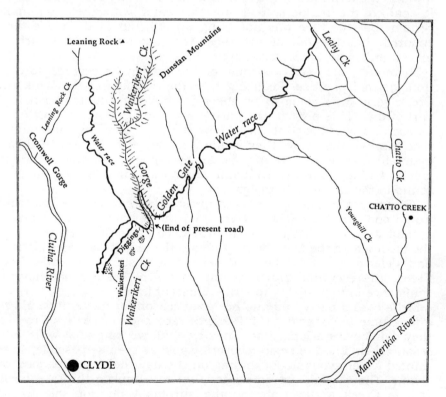

Figure 10. 1. The Golden Gate Water race was built from Leahy Creek to the Waikerikeri diggings over the years 1872 to 1874.

93

up water from a number of small streams flowing from the mountains and would finally deliver about 14 heads.

Sure enough, the group's application for water from Waikerikeri Creek was strongly opposed by Holt and his supporters, and was refused. So the partners turned their attention to the emergency scheme. But they met with opposition again.

The Manuherikia Ground Sluicing Company pointed out that it had held first priority rights for 14 heads out of Leahys Creek and Younghill Creek since 1864. This Company also pointed out that during many seasons it was fortunate if it got three heads in total out of the creeks.

Nevertheless the application was granted and the group, now consisting of eight miners[3] and calling itself the 'Golden Gate Company,'[4] began construction work soon afterwards. Newspapers were speculating that 10 heads of water would be available in two months and all 14 heads would be at the claims within six months. Little did they know!

Work started about half way along the route on relatively easy country north of Waikerikeri Creek. This was unusual. Normally race construction began at the source of the water and worked 'downhill' towards the terminus of the race, and there was a good reason for this. It enabled the builders to 'bring the water with them' so making certain that the race was not going up hill, but at the same time it ensured that the fall of the race was just sufficient to carry the maximum amount of water at optimum speed.

There were also good reasons for the Golden Gate group to depart from normal practice. Realising that the crossing of the Waikerikeri Creek gorge was going to be the most difficult and time-consuming part of the whole project, the partners wanted to make a start on this as soon as possible. But they knew very well that, as they built the race through the gorge, they would need water to 'take with them' to maintain their levels. So they began by tapping into one of the small creeks falling from the Dunstan Mountains and leading the water round to the entrance to the gorge.

Building a segment of a race in isolation carried the risk that it would end up at a different level from the remainder. If the separate section were too high the result would be disastrous. However, from the point where the team began to build the race it was possible to see, and determine levels, for a considerable distance towards Leahys Creek, the eventual source of the race. The team must have had confidence in their ability to strike the right levels.

McNally and party had another good reason for haste. It would take a long time to construct a full-length race back to Leahys Creek and they didn't have a long time. They were all working men with limited resources and had to begin recovering gold as soon as possible, so they wanted water available for mining on the day their race reached their claims. There would be time after that to complete the race back to Leahys Creek and so provide the surplus water for sale to other miners.

Progress along the gravel terraces was quite fast and before the end of 1872 the race had reached the Waikerikeri Gorge. But the newspapers were no longer so optimistic. Seven months after the work started the *Dunstan Times,* estimated that it would take another year to complete the race and by July 1873 the paper was only guessing when it estimated that the race would cross the Waikerikeri Creek by Christmas.

Gorge of Waikerikeri Creek

Waikerikeri Creek rises below Leaning Rock, a prominent landmark on the summit ridge of the Dunstan Mountains, and flows south down through a rugged valley that narrows to a gorge, with the stream flowing between steep rocky slopes only a few metres apart. After leaving the gorge the creek flows towards the Clutha River in a broad flat-floored valley cut across the terraces of the Manuherikia Valley.

Figure 10. 2. Waikerikeri Creek rises on the Dunstan Mountains below Leaning Rock (right, skyline) and passes through a rugged, narrow gorge before flowing across the terraces of the Manuherikia Valley to join the Clutha River. With great labour the Golden Gate water race was built along the left bank (right foreground), across the creek and down the right bank (left of photograph).

When the Golden Gate race reached the eastern edge of the gorge it was about 45 metres above the level of the stream. At this point, and at this level, the walls of the gorge are about 200 metres apart, so the simplest crossing would have been to pipe the water down one side of the gorge and up the other and then continue with the open race. Presumably the partners could not afford the cost of pipes so they faced the very laborious task of building the race along the side of the gorge. For more than a kilometre the race wound its way up the gorge until it finally reached the level of the creek. Then the Company had to turn round and build the race for a similar distance back down the opposite side.

Work commenced in the gorge just before Christmas 1872. So rugged was the country that it was necessary to support the race on stone walls for much of the distance until the steadily rising valley floor was reached. The creek itself was crossed on a short flume and then the stone walling began in earnest as the race was carried back down the gorge. On this western side the slopes were even steeper and more rocky so the stone walling was continuous for long distances and, in places, reached heights of 8 metres or more.

Figure 10. 3. The Golden Gate race running down the right bank of the Waikerikeri Gorge.

It is difficult to imagine the labour involved in this work. Any rocks of suitable size and shape lying within reasonable distance would be collected and carried to the construction site. This in itself was a difficult and dangerous job on the near-vertical slippery slopes. Large rocks would be slid down-slope with the help of crowbars and manoeuvred into position—no doubt at the expense of skinned knuckles and bruised fingers. With the supply of easily collected rocks exhausted, attention would then be turned to breaking up large slabs of schist into suitably-sized pieces by means of a heavy hammer and gads.[5] The space behind the growing wall had to be back-filled with well-rammed earth and the race itself, which was about a metre wide and half a metre deep, had to be lined with silt or clay to make it reasonably watertight.

The slopes of the gorge were furrowed with numerous shallow, steep gullies separated by rocky ridges. Provision had to be made for storm water to pass beneath the built-up race where it crossed these gullies. Cuttings had to be made through the rock ridges either by hammer and gad or, on rare occasions, by blasting.

The construction took so long that newspapers ran out of things to say about it. In July 1873 it was reported as being 'pushed ahead.' By March 1874 it was still 'pushing ahead' but the paper conceded that it was a long job and hoped that the party might be rewarded for its perseverance. And then on 18 September the *Dunstan Times* announced that McNally and party were through the gorge. "After three Christmases in one valley" as an old-timer expressed it[6] picturesquely even if not quite accurately.

By this time the party apparently had had enough of race building so tenders were called for the final 10 kilometre section between the outlet of the Waikerikeri Gorge and the claim in Connews Gully. This section of the race was finished in June 1875, and the party were able to start sluicing shortly afterwards. Long gone, apparently, were any ideas of extending the race out to the banks of the Clutha River.

The newspapers admitted that building the race through much broken country had proved a tough job and even the Warden commented that it had been too big a job for such a small party to

Figure 10. 4. Stone walls about six metres high were required to carry the Golden Gate race over a shallow steep gully in the Waikerikeri Gorge.

attempt. It was said that so far the race had cost £8,000 and had been financed by the six men themselves. They had taken turns at working on outside jobs to support those still working on the race.

Gold mining

Sluicing started on the Golden Gate claims at the end of July 1875 but very little information about returns was reported. This lack of information almost always meant that returns were disappointing.

The Waikerikeri diggings were frustrating for miners. Returns in the main were just sufficient to pay wages but every once in a while a rich patch would be struck. Lindsay and party for instance, who had a claim near the Golden Gate ground, struck such a rich patch shortly after starting work. They also had brought in a race,[7] with great labour and expense, from a creek high on the Dunstan Mountains but, it was said, were able to clear the debt on their race from this one lucky strike. It was the chance of making such a strike that kept miners plugging away year after year. Fortunately, what gold there was at Waikerikeri lay at shallow depths, but to recover payable quantities it was necessary to work large areas of ground, and to do this an adequate supply of water was necessary. In spite of all their work, the Golden Gate party did not have adequate water because their race had not been completed back to the main source of supply. Their only water was from one or two small creeks which may well have dried up in the summer and frozen in the winter.

Under these circumstances it is perhaps not surprising that the temptation to divert water from Waikerikeri Creek into their race at the crossing point became too strong for the partners to resist. On April 28 1876 James Holt, who had first priority from Waikerikeri Creek, accused McNally of diverting his water. McNally was fined one shilling by the Warden, who obviously was sympathetic to the group and the work they had done. But things did not improve and two years later the Golden Gate Co was again accused of pinching water, this time by J. D. Feraud who was farming in the lower Waikerikeri Valley. The case was dismissed.

The party had originally planned to sell water to other miners but this was not possible, not only because they did not have sufficient for themselves, but also because almost all the other miners had tired of waiting for the Golden Gate race to be completed, and had left the field. Only Lindsay and his party remained and they had their own ample supply of water from Leaning Rock Creek.

Disillusioned by the poor returns, members of the Golden Gate party began to sell their shares in the enterprise and seek better fortune elsewhere. B. R. Baird of Cromwell bought the shares as they became available.

Finally John McNally himself called it a day. Exhausted by hard work and financially crippled, he decided to leave the district and he put his assets up for sale in February 1878. These comprised a one-sixth share in the Golden Gate Company, which included the race itself and the claims at Waikerikeri, which consisted of 16 acres in three claims in Connews Gully; a two-acre claim in Deans Gully and a four-acre claim in Hanlons Gully. In addition he listed a one-sixth share in the flume across the Manuherikia River at Blacks. His shares were bought by Baird of Cromwell who now owned half the shares in the group.

Figure 10. 5. Photographs of Waikerikeri Diggings taken from about the same spot.
(a): In 1905
(b): In 1998

Public Company

Borthwick Robert Baird[8] had been the Clerk of the Court at Cromwell but was at the same time the principal shareholder in the very lucrative Cromwell Quartz Mining Company at Bendigo. Now he was a very wealthy man and his occupation was listed in the Electoral Roll of 1880 as 'Gentleman.' He decided to form a public company and the Golden Gate Mining Company with a capital of £6,000 was registered on 22 February 1878. B. R. Baird with 3,500 shares was the principal shareholder and five others held 500 shares each. Only two, David McFerron and John Shepherd, were members of the party which had constructed the water race.[9]

One of the first things the new company did was to call tenders and let a contract for the construction of the remaining 6 kilometres required to complete the race to Leahys Creek. Once the race was completed, 10 heads of water were available at the diggings and when miners realised this they began to drift back. Gradually claims were taken up again so that by October 1880 eight claims were working with water supplied from the Golden Gate race.

The results of this mining are unknown but the *Dunstan Times* was probably accurate when it said:

> As the whole of these parties have now been working on the commonage for a number of years, the inference is that they are making wages, or they would not with such limpet-like tenacity stick to it.[10]

As the pattern was set, so it continued year after year. In 1887 it was noted[11] about 20 men were employed on the diggings. Work was carried on night and day and it could be assumed 'that they were making fair wages.'

It is one thing to pay fair wages to workers but another to pay dividends to shareholders. Two of these shareholders, John Crawford, who had a substantial farm in the valley, and James Campbell, apparently managed the company in its later years. With the help of an occasional rich patch, such as the 100 oz washed up for a few months' work in 1894, the Company continued on its erratic financial way.

By 1895 the Company was no longer mining but was renting all of its water to other miners such as John Leamy's party in Scrubby Gully at Springvale, and Neil Nicholson, who had a claim near the 'Springs' in Waipuna Valley, a tributary of the Waikerikeri Valley. In fact by 1896 all of the Golden Gate water was in the hands of Neil Nicholson and Walter Anderson. But this did not give the return that Baird wanted from his investment and in July 1899 the Company was wound up.

The career of the Golden Gate Company and the effect of its eventual liquidation is perhaps best summarised by a pathetic death notice in the *Dunstan Times* of 16 January 1911 which stated that Jimmy Campbell, an old man living alone at Waikerkeri Valley, had died. Jimmy, the paper said, had been a miner all his life and had, through hard work and some luck, accumulated substantial savings but had lost everything in the Golden Gate Company. Jimmy Campbell had invested £500 (equivalent to about $40,000 today) in the Company.

Today

The remnants of the Golden Gate race can easily be traced as it wends its way across alluvial fans and in and out of the gullies of the foot-slopes of the Dunstan Mountains. But the most interesting part of its long course lies in the Waikerikeri Gorge where the impressive stone walls built with so much labour 125 years ago still stand in good order. A walk of a kilometre or so along a reasonably well formed track leading from the end of the Waikerikeri Valley road will give a good idea of the amount of effort men will expend when they have the glint of gold in their eyes. It is especially sad when so little return was achieved from the effort.

NOTES

1. Not be confused with Golden Gate claim at Frenchmans Point, near Alexandra nor with the Golden Gate Gold Dredging Company which operated below Island Block from 1895 until 1915.
2. Application to Wardens Court, Clyde 5 June 1872.
3. The original group consisted of Patrick and John McNally, John Hastie, John Shepherd, R. Block. Thos Kenney, David McFerron and another. The bulk of the race construction was apparently done by six of these.
4. The relationship between this new 'Golden Gate Company' and the former one which built the race to Blacks is not clear. The McNallys may well have kept the registration alive and brought in the others as shareholders. According to the *Otago Daily Times* (15 May 1872) the water right of the old company was to be used in the new race. This may refer to the water right from Thomsons Creek. As far as is known the old Golden Gate Company (1866) did not have a water right for Leahys Creek.
5. A gad is a steel spike, generally up to 60 cms in length , with a wedge-shaped end which, when inserted into a crack or seam and struck repeatedly with a heavy hammer, was quite effective in splitting the rock.
6. Late Mr Joe Davidson of Clyde—tape interview, New Zealand Broadcasting Company, 1948.
7. Lindsay's race started in the headwaters of Leaning Rock Creek at an elevation of 900 metres.
8. Parcell, 1951 pp. 133-139.
9. The others were James G. Campbell, a miner of Matakanui; Lindsay Davison, a miner, and John Crawford, a shepherd of Matakanui
10. *Dunstan Times* 23 September 1881
11. *DunstanTimes* 9 December 1887

11.

WATER FOR THE TOWN

A year after the new Alexandra Borough Council took office in 1867, 'Ratepayer,' who was to become a regular newspaper correspondent and critic of the Borough Council over the next 40 years, made a suggestion:

> There are two large water races running near the town, at a sufficient elevation that, were pipes laid from either there would be sufficient pressure in case of fire to throw water over the highest building in Alexandra.[1]

As there were, as yet, no buildings of more than a single storey in the township, 'Ratepayer' was probably correct in his prediction about available water pressure. The correspondent was referring to the two water races from Chatto Creek, the Manuherikia Ground Sluicing Company's race (also known as 'Drummey's' after the builder), and the Ovens Company's race which, only a few metres apart, ran along the edge of the Terrace on their way to the bank of the Clutha River. This is the first recorded request for a town water supply and may have been the stimulus that moved the council to begin a battle that was to last for nearly a hundred years.

When, as a first move, a Dunedin engineering firm was asked for an estimate for supplying one kilometre of piping, plus all the fittings suitable for a water scheme piped from one or other of the races, it was clear that the cost would be too great for the small borough to sustain. But the council was not allowed to let a matter of such importance rest. Three months later a committee of council began to collect information as to the best method of supplying the township with water and to find out what the two local race owners would charge for a supply guaranteed for 14 years.

The Manuherikia Company offered to supply '10 ins'[2] (a quarter of a head) of water 'without pressure' (that is, in an open race) for £2 a week. This was expensive water but not as expensive as that offered by the Ovens Company—it wanted £5 a week for the same quantity. This information, together with quotations from several Dunedin firms, was presented to a public meeting called by the mayor in November 1869, to discuss ways of raising funds to provide the town with a permanent water supply.

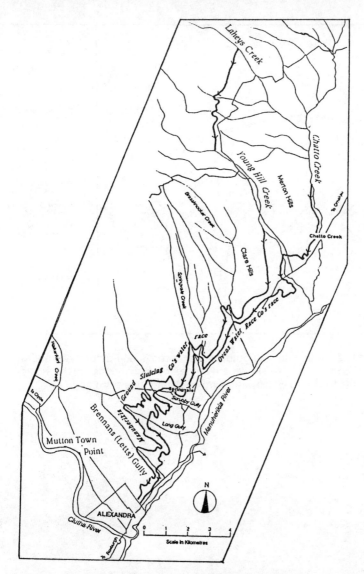

Figure 11. 1. Two large water races were constructed from Chatto Creek, or its tributaries, to Alexandra during 1863-65. The Ovens Water Race Company's race was bought by the Borough Council in 1873 and provided the water supply for the borough for the next 30 years.

The meeting felt that the race water was too expensive and that there were cheaper ways of attaining the objective. Why, for instance, couldn't the power of the river current be used to pump water up to the township? This had always seemed a particularly attractive method of obtaining cheap water for mining and had given rise to the invention of a number of devices. One designed[3] by J. T. Thomson, the Provincial Surveyor, was a simply-constructed, multi-bladed propeller

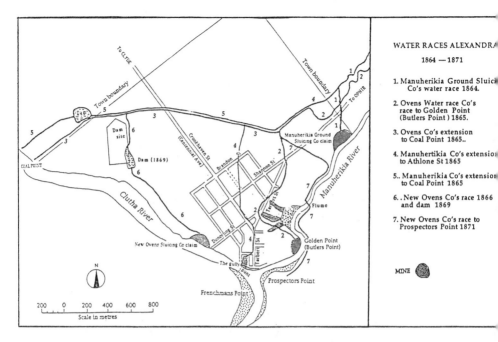

Figure 11. 2. Main and distributory water races in and around Alexandra 1864-1871. Also shown are some of the gold mines in the vicinity of the township which were worked during the period.

Figure 11. 3. Today's Royal Terrace is exceptionally wide because it follows a Water Race Reserve that once carried the two large, parallel water races—the Ovens Co's race and the Manuherikia Co's race.

104

(Thomson called it a screw or fan) which was suspended from a punt moored in the river. When revolved by the current it worked a reciprocating pump. The inventor calculated that a propeller one metre in diameter, set in a current flowing at 10 kilometres an hour, would lift 150 litres each minute 30 metres above the river. This quantity, he thought, would serve a population of 1,000 people and so would supply Alexandra adequately.

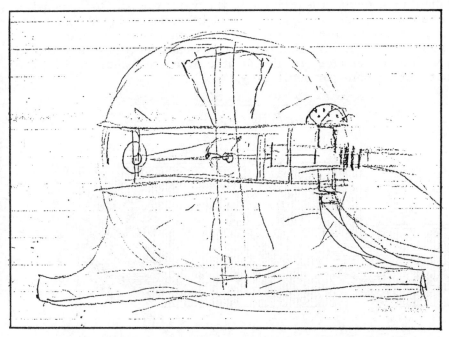

Figure 11. 4. This is believed to be J. T. Thomson's original sketch of his device for pumping water from a river by using the power of the current. It was discovered by Dr John Hall-Jones in a book which was part of Thomson's library. The device was designed to be submersed at right angles to the current which turned the propellor connected to a single-acting, reciprocating pump by a crank.

Undershot water wheels worked by the river current were already widely used to power the Californian pumps which kept beach claims clear of water, and others were used for lifting water on to the early spoon dredges for gold washing. The idea of current driven pumps for town supply kept surfacing over the next 30 years but none was ever built.[4] In spite of the various inventors' claims, it was quickly discovered that a machine to lift the required volume of water would be so large and costly as to be beyond consideration. The fact that such a contrivance had to be moored in mid-stream and adequately secured against floods also counted against its adoption.

First Water Supply
Apparently the committee did not come up with any practical ideas for a cheap water supply, so council was forced to go back, cap in hand,

to the owners of the water races. These latter were not really interested in supplying the town, as they could sell all of their water to miners, but they were rather enjoying the experience of having the town over a barrel. Perhaps, councillors thought, asking for a guaranteed supply for 14 years, as they had two years before, had frightened the water race companies and caused them to quote a high price. So now, at the end of 1871, council asked them for a price for 10 inches of water for six months. It made little difference—the water was still too expensive. What about a supply of 5 inches (one eighth head)? council asked. The Ovens Company wanted £2 a week. Negotiations went on and council was forced to settle with Manuherikia Company for a miserly two inch (50 mm) diameter pipe of water (a little over one twelfth of a head—about 1,875 gallons per hour).

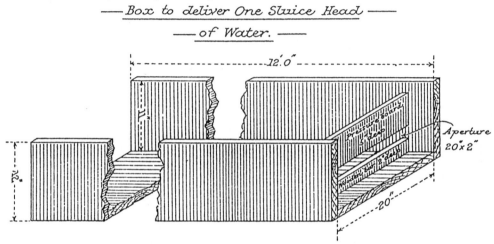

—— Box to deliver One Sluice Head ——
—— of Water. ——

Figure 11. 5. A standard gauge-box for measuring water. The slot at the end of the box was 20 inches (500mm) long and 2ins (50mm) wide. It allowed one sluice head to pass through when the box was placed level in a water race.

It is believed that this small flow of water was conveyed to the 'head of Tarbert Street' [5] by a branch race which had originally been constructed to deliver water to a sluicing claim on the banks of the Clutha River between Athlone and Ennis Streets. It had left the main Manuherikia Company's race on the Terrace at the point where Simmonds Street now crosses Royal Terrace, and ran straight across the uninhabited flat and down the main street to the claim. Such was Alexandra's first water supply—apart from the water cart.

The routes followed by the two big water races from Chatto Creek to the town boundary and along the Terrace are well documented (the races themselves, in modified form, still exist over part of the route). But their branches to the various gold mines within the town are now difficult to trace because of the scarcity of records, lack of physical remnants and even confusion between the two races. Both races played a part in supplying the town with water and, in fact, one was to become the principal town supply for more than 30 years.

In June 1872, however, the Borough Council, fed up with the unreliability of the supply from the Manuherikia Company, and still smarting over the price, decided to try again for an independent supply. It called for tenders[6] for pumping 200 gallons (900 litres) of water per hour from the Clutha River into a reservoir. Although this is somewhat less than the quantity supplied by a present-day household tap it was apparently regarded as sufficient. The Provincial Government was asked to allow its district engineer to report on the best site for the reservoir. We hear nothing further of this pumping scheme. Either there was no response to the call for tenders or the prices received were too high. But at least Mr Bews, the engineer, did inspect and report on a site for the proposed reservoir.

There was a pause while the council pondered its options. Suddenly a solution to the problem presented itself. On 3 January 1873 the Ovens Company's assets, which included its water rights, water races and all its mining gear, were advertised for sale by an auction to be held three weeks later.

The Borough Race.

James Rivers, a member of the Borough Council and a prominent storekeeper in the town, boldly suggested to the council at its meeting on 10 January 1873 that it should buy the race and the water rights. The council moved with uncharacteristic but commendable speed. By the next day the Mayor and Cr Rivers had arranged an overdraft of £900 with the Bank of New Zealand, and with this the race was

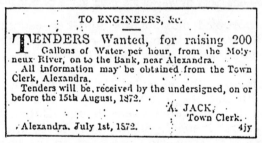

TO ENGINEERS, &c.

TENDERS Wanted, for raising 200 Gallons of Water per hour, from the Molyneux River, on to the Bank, near Alexandra.
All information may be obtained from the Town Clerk, Alexandra.
Tenders will be received by the undersigned, on or before the 15th August, 1872.

A. JACK,
Town Clerk.

Alexandra, July 1st, 1872.   4jy

Figure 11. 6. There was either no response to this advertisement for tenders or the quotes were too dear. Nothing further was heard of this proposed scheme for pumping water from the river.

purchased. This was a large sum for about 60 ratepayers to repay, but the newly acquired race was to provide the main water supply for the town for the next 30 years and, as part of the Manuherikia Irrigation Scheme, much of it is still in use today. Just what did the Borough Council get for its money?

It got a first priority water right from Chatto Creek[7] for five heads. In addition it also got the Chatto Creek water race, in future to be known as the 'Borough race,' and its branches. One of these, which had been the main race originally, came across what are now the Convent grounds and then followed generally the eastern side of the track that was to become upper Tarbert Street. It cut through the garden of J. C.

Figure 11. 7. Now part of the Manuherikia Irrigation Scheme, the Borough race is still much the same as when it was constructed in 1864-65 by the Ovens Water Race Company. Here it is about to descend into Letts Gully by way of the 'drop' in the trees in the background.

Chapple, who occupied most of the land between the present Skird and Walton Streets, and then swung round the site of the present Centennial Swimming Pool before sidling round the hillside to Golden Point.

The arrangement with Butler of Golden Point apparently did not work out, as although the race was completed to the claim, very little water was actually delivered even though Butler took the Ovens Company to court. Instead, during late 1865, the race had been continued along the Terrace to Coal Point on the bank of the Clutha River where water was sold to a number of parties who were sluicing the low terraces along the river. But now, as the Borough took over, the water was being diverted, just before it reached the Coal Point, into a branch race that ran southwards along the river bank into a small dam. From here water was led to a claim further down the river.

In a last desperate attempt to find payable gold, the Ovens Company had opened a mine near Prospectors Point at the confluence of he rivers. Making use of a much earlier race, water from the old Golden Point race had been led through the rocky gorge of the Manuherikia River below the present 'railway' bridge. It crossed the river in a flume just upstream from the Shaky Bridge, and then continued in a race along to the claim.

Problems of Race Ownership
More than money was required to become the owner of a water race.

The purchaser had to have a Miner's Right before a licence for a water race could be applied for, but this Right could only be held by individuals—not by a Borough Council. So the agent of the Bank of New Zealand held the Right in his name. But later, when the debt had been paid off, this arrangement was no longer feasible, and first the town clerk, and later William Theyers, a prominent citizen and borough councillor, acted as trustee for the Borough and held the Miner's Right.

The large flow, of several heads, in the newly acquired race was far more than the borough needed, so a week after purchase, tenders for leasing the water were invited from mining concerns. There were good reasons for this haste. Under the Mining Act of the time it was quite tricky to use water for other purposes than mining. Had a mining concern wanted the water, and felt so inclined, it may well have succeeded in obtaining a Decree of Forfeiture against the Borough Council. So it was much easier for the council to obtain the water 'for mining purposes' and, by leasing the water to mining concerns, fulfil its legal obligations. A second reason, and equally important, was that the water was a valuable asset and the council needed every penny it could raise from its use to repay the £900 overdraft.

A number of conditions had to be met by the tenderer—the lease was for 12 months; the race had to be cleaned out so it could carry 10 heads and, most important, half a head was to be constantly supplied to the Borough.

JOHN C. CHAPPLE

1871 — 1872

Figure 11. 8. John Cole Chapple (1828-99) was a pioneer miner associated with some of the first mining companies in the district. He was an early mayor of Alexandra. Later he farmed at Tiger Hill. One of his sons became a well-known medical practitioner and was a Member of Parliament both in New Zealand and the United Kingdom.

It was arranged that the Borough's allocation would be discharged from the main race on the terrace into the now abandoned branch of the Manuherikia Company's race.[9] Water in this branch race (now referred to as the 'Town race') was measured at a gauge-box inserted in the race as it came through what was to become Pioneer Park[10] at a point opposite the newly-built manse. From here water passed down the main street in one or both gutters and unused water fell, by way of a 'by-wash,' into the river at the lower end of the street

At last the town would have a reliable water supply of its own—or so it was thought.

A minor complication following the change of ownership led to the first of the innumerable court cases involving the Borough Council and its water supply. The old race to Golden Point still carried some water as it passed through ex-mayor J. C. Chapple's property[11] and he irrigated his garden from it. Shortly after the council took over the race, it reformed the upper part of Tarbert St and cut through the old

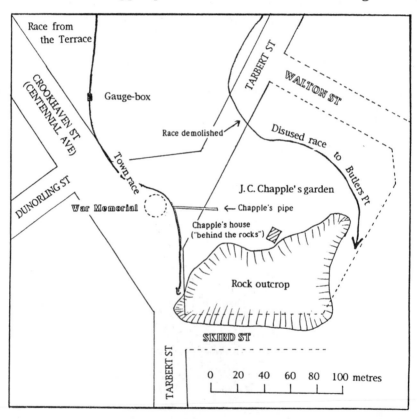

Figure 11. 9. J. C. Chapple lived 'behind the rocks' at the 'head of Tarbert Street.' His property occupied the block between the present Skird and Walton Streets. He was something of a 'stirrer' and he ran foul of the Borough Council when he laid a pipe across Tarbert Street to tap the Town race to replace the supply cut off by council road works.

110

race, effectively putting a stop to Mr Chapple's free irrigation water.

Chapple told his story at a public meeting called by the mayor to discuss the newly acquired water race. Chapple said he wrote to the council for permission to pipe the water across the street from the town race, but received no reply. Not one to be messed about, Chapple went ahead and laid a pipe across the newly formed road to recover his water supply. The council came down on him for interfering with the road.

Chapple, the recently retired mayor, decided that if he were going down he would take others with him. So at the meeting he pointed out that he knew that one councillor had dug up the footpath to take water into his section; that the town clerk himself had dug up a main street to take water into his garden, so had Mr Theyers (an ex-mayor), the Bank of New Zealand agent and numerous others. Why were none of these people being proceeded against? asked Chapple. He suggested that the meeting should not only pass a resolution condemning the mayor (William Beresford), but call on him to resign. But the meeting refused to do this. Several people pointed out that it was difficult enough already to get someone to stand for mayor 'in a one-horse municipality.'

In spite of this public linen washing, the council decided to go ahead with the case against Chapple but it fizzled out over a technicality. So Chapple, with studied innocence, wrote in next month agreeing to remove the pipe but asking if he could substitute a stone culvert. Council gave him permission to remove the pipe but refused permission to install a culvert!

Troubles with Lessees

Fawcett and Party, the first lessees, agreed to clean out the race for £130 and lease the water for 12 months for £180, so the Borough made £50 profit. Each year tenders were called for leasing the water and each year the price offered was lower. It was £130 for 1874, £86 for 1875 and by 1877 John Terry was simply offering to clean out the race in return for the water. Mining was in the doldrums and there was now little demand for water.

Fawcett and Party gained the lease again in 1878 but now began a struggle which lasted for 30 years—a struggle by the Borough Council to persuade or force the lessees to stick to the terms of the lease and allow the agreed allocation of water to flow down the town race. Letters threatening that, unless the agreed 20 inches of water was delivered at the gauge-box at the head of Tarbert Street, the council 'would take steps,' brought no results.

Things began to get serious when the council decided in January 1883 that Thomas Jackson, the lessee at the time, would be fined 10 shillings for each day that he fell short on the borough's water allocation. It was calculated that the fine was already £7 but this was reduced the following week to £2. Council's magnanimity was not rewarded, however, and by May it was threatening to cancel the lease. The situation was so bad that, come the end of the year, the council was prepared to pay Fawcett 5s. a week to supply the borough with its own water!

The Dam Site

W. A. Bews, District Engineer for the Provincial Government, who was based at Cromwell, recommended that if a borough reservoir should be required it should be sited near the small dam built by the Ovens Company. An old channel formed by the river in some past time had been made use of by the company for their dam, and it was a convenient place also for a Borough reservoir. Now that the Borough Council owned the Ovens water race and dam it decided to have the site properly surveyed. Accordingly, in November 1875 the council wrote to J. T. Thomson, Commissioner of Crown Lands, Dunedin, asking for the 15 acre site recommended by Bews to be set aside as a reserve for a town reservoir.

The survey was carried out in June 1876 (at a cost to the Borough Council of £4 - 5s.) and the famous Block 19 came into being. From that day until fairly recently this small block, marked 'Dam site,' was a prominent feature on cadastral maps of the town. Its prominence was made more so because of its shape, which resembled that of a church Gothic window and by its isolated position which was out in the wilderness about a kilometre north-west from the township.

No reservoir was ever built within the surveyed area but the Ovens Company's dam (later called Halpine's dam) did serve as the first town reservoir and it also served the various mining claims that leased the borough race. It was still holding water at the time of the coal mine fire in 1906.

The dam-site was the subject of a rather complicated land deal during 1913[12] when it was exchanged by the Borough Council for a block of Crown land already planted out in productive orchards, but threatened with dredging by the Karaunui Dredging Company. The dam-site was finally destroyed by the Clutha Gold Dredging Company's dredge, during the late 1940s.

Piped Water

James Rivers, as part of his platform for contesting the mayoralty in July 1874, promised that if he were elected mayor, there would be a piped water supply within the year. The present supply in open channels, he said, was a temporary expedient. But, as he was not elected mayor at that particular time, we hear nothing more about a piped water supply until 1878, when he did become mayor. Rivers then brought up the matter of a piped supply again and asked that the ground be measured out for pipes to give some idea of cost. Once more prices were obtained from Dunedin firms and the Bank of New Zealand was to be approached about money for a water scheme. But it was not the time. The country was sliding into depression, Alexandra's population was falling and business was stagnant. Not even Jimmy Rivers's energy and fertile imagination could beat the odds. Fifteen long years were to pass before a piped water supply would be discussed again.

NOTES:

1. *Dunstan Times*. 10 July 1868.
2. This was yet another way of measuring water. A wooden box was designed with one end closed apart from a slot 20 ins (500 mm) long by 2 ins (50 mm) wide so the aperture was of 40 square inches. So when the box was set level in a water race the slot passed '40 inches' of water or one head. So '20 inches' equalled half a head, '10 inches' one quarter head and so on.
3. Described in a paper read by J. T. Thomson to the Otago Institute in 1872.
4. In 1908 a current-driven pump was built on the pontoons of an old dredge, to pump water into the pond of the *Alexandra Lead* dredge. It cost many thousands of pounds and although it worked satisfactorily, it sank and was lost after only a short working life.
5. During the 1860s and early 1870s the name 'Tarbert Street' (or 'Broad Street' as it was unofficially called) was still applied only to the lower part of the street — the part regarded as the 'main street' today. The upper part of the street leading to Manuherikia Road was simply a track through an uninhabited wilderness. So the 'head of Tarbert Street' was the top of the main street—where the War Memorial is today. People who lived thereabouts were regarded as living on the outskirts of the town.
6. Minutes Alexandra Borough Council meeting 28 June 1872 . Advertisement *Otago Daily Times* 4 July 1872.
7. This stream was named by the pioneer runholders, Alex and Watson Shennan after a locality in their native Roxburghshire in Scotland and the name was officially recorded by J. T. Thomson, the Provincial Surveyor.
8. The Borough Council gained extra water from Younghill Creek, a tributary of Chatto Creek.
9. The Manuherikia Ground Sluicing Company renamed the 'Manuherikia Water Race Company', had abandoned its mining operation in the Borough and moved further afield to Muttontown Point and the terraces of the Manuherikia River.
10. A large block of about 10 acres (4h) had been set aside as a reserve for recreation during the late 1860s but for many years it was a rough wilderness used by wagoners as an overnight camp for their animals. It was developed during the 1880s and became known as the 'Recreation Ground' or 'Rec' in popular parlance. It was named 'Pioneer Park' after the 1912 Jubilee of the Gold Rush of 1862.
11. *Dunstan Times* 11 November 1873. The report says that Chapple 'lived out of sight of the main street, round the rocks'. He lived in upper Tarbert Street between the intersection of Crookhaven Street (Centennial Avenue) and the future Walton Street. His small house, constructed of stone with mud mortar, was still in existence in the early 1960s.
12. *Alexandra Herald* 11 June 1913 and 13 May 1914.

12.
GULLIES ON THE HILL

Once it was called Bugle Hill, because the coach, as it came down the hill, sounded a bugle to alert the puntman to have the punt ready.[1] Then it was just 'the Hill' where people, who did not wish to pay town rates but still wanted to enjoy some of the town amenities, lived in little cottages scattered among the huge outcrops of schist rock. Nowadays part of it is 'Bridge Hill,' the upmarket suburb of Alexandra across the Clutha River bridge, which is dotted with elegant homes enjoying expansive views out over the older part of the town and across the Manuherikia Valley to the Dunstan Mountains beyond.

Figure 12. 1. A 1949 air photo of part of Bridge Hill shows the trellis pattern of shallow gullies. Many were floored with rich gold-bearing wash overlain by Clutha River gravel which partly filled the gullies. The large sluicing claims in Ketts Gully and Gilberts Gully are prominent.

A prominent feature of the hill is a deep, straight gully that drains into the Clutha River at the now submerged Halfmile Beach—so named because it was half a mile down the river from Alexandra. Not unnaturally, the gully itself was called 'Halfmile Gully' and the steep pinch by which the main road from Alexandra to Roxburgh climbed out of this gully was 'Halfmile Hill.'

On air photographs of Bridge Hill we can see that Halfmile Gully is only one of a number of shallow, mostly dry, parallel gullies spaced a few hundred metres apart. Furthermore, other sets of similar, parallel gullies cross the first set, so forming a distinctive, trellis pattern. A few, such as Halfmile Gully, carry small streams of water, probably mainly seepage from nearby irrigation races. The gully floors lie high above the present level of the Clutha River and any water from the gullies falls into the river by way of very steep water-courses or even waterfalls.[2]

It is likely that the gullies follow along zones of weakness in the underlying rock, such as lines of major jointing. Intense weathering of the schist rock in ancient times penetrated more deeply into these weakened zones than into the intervening firmer rock, and when the softened rock was subsequently removed by erosion, the pattern of gullies was revealed. Most are 10 to 30 metres deep and have flat floors about 50 metres wide. Not all the gullies are straight—some are offset as they cross other gullies.

When early miners began to sink shafts into the flat floors of these gullies they were surprised to find they were underlain by river gravels identical with those known to have been deposited by the Clutha River. Invariably the sinking of the shafts was stopped by striking schist rock at shallow depths, and much effort was expended for little return. It was only when the miners began sluicing in the gullies that it was realised that the infilling of river gravel was of considerable depth and scattered through it were numerous very large boulders of schist rock—some several metres across. It was these that had impeded the shaft sinkers.

The excavations also revealed that the sides of the gullies, hidden by the infill of gravel, are vertical and often marked by vertical, semicircular flutings, some a metre or so across. These are the half-sections of 'potholes' formed in the bed of a former stream by stones swirled round by the force of the current. The evidence of former potholes, together with the presence of Clutha River gravels, indicates that at some past time substantial quantities of river water flowed through these gullies when the river was at a higher level—probably when it was at the level of the terrace on which the aerodrome is located.

Michael Kett was the first to demonstrate that payable gold lay on the rock floor of these long abandoned river channels. Regarded as one of the foremost miners of his time, Kett was manager of the famous Frenchman's claim at Frenchmans Point. But he eventually fell out with his employer, J. D. Feraud, and went his own way. In November 1869, he bought the very productive Caledonian claim at Halfmile Beach for the unheard of sum of £2,800.[3] He used water from the

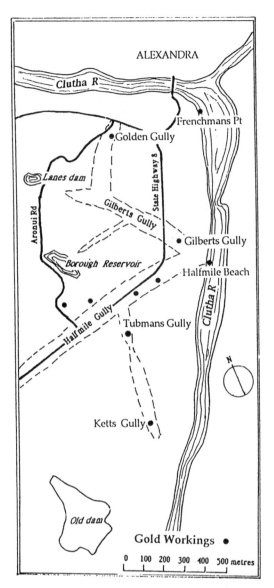

Figure 12. 2. Notable gold workings on Bridge Hill and other features.

Caledonian race, which he acquired along with the claim, to turn water wheels to drive Californian pumps which kept the mine clear of water. In spite of all his skill and experience, and the expenditure of £3,500,[3] Kett could find little gold in the mine—perhaps the previous owners had taken the lot. After a couple of year's fruitless work he cut his losses and abandoned the claim.

Ketts Gully

Michael Kett tired of battling with the vagaries of the river, so for his

116

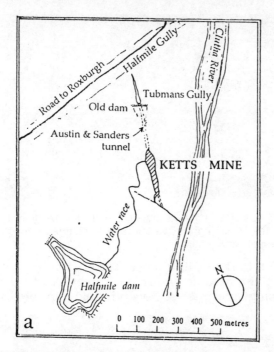

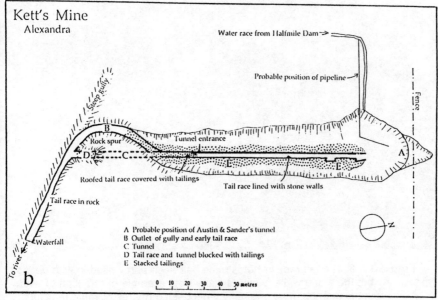

Figure 12. 3. (a): Location of Kett's mine, its water supply and other features.

(b): Sketch plan of Kett's mine (measured but not surveyed).

next mining venture he applied for a three acre Extended Claim in a gully that lay 60 metres above the river. The gully is the southern end of a clearly defined depression that runs in a northerly direction right

Figure 12. 4. Kett's mine is situated in a shallow gully high above the Clutha River (right). The tail race discharged through a tunnel into the gully at the right.

across Bridge Hill to the Clutha River. The part of the gully where Kett pegged out his claim became known as 'Ketts Gully.' [4] Here Kett began the largest sluicing enterprise so far undertaken in the district.

Figure 12. 5. The tail race in Kett's mine has been partly filled in with debris but the stone walls, which are the best example of this kind of work in the district, must originally have been 6 metres or more in height.

Opening up the mine was not easy. Before any sluicing could be done a tail race had to be constructed to allow the debris from the sluicing to be washed into the river, and for this to happen the tail race had to be fairly straight and have considerable slope or fall. To achieve these conditions Kett began excavating a channel on New Years Day 1874. Commencing above a 6 metre-high waterfall in a steep gully below his proposed mine, he lowered the solid rock floor of the watercourse by three metres for a distance of 70 metres. Then, employing up to six men and working day and night shifts, he drove a tunnel, 50 metres long and two metres high, from the side of the gully through a high rocky ridge which separated his tail race from the proposed mine. Once through the ridge he continued cutting an open channel through rock for another 70 metres before he could begin opening out a working face in the gravel infill of the valley.

Figure 12. 6. Kett's mine today looking south along the tail race towards the outlet.

Using Caledonian race water stored in a dam he had constructed at the top of Halfmile Gully between the main road and the river, Kett was able to bring six heads into his mine. Of these, two and a half heads were led through a large canvas hose to a nozzle which directed a jet against the gravel face which was reputed to be 35 metres high. The remaining water washed the loosened gravel through 35 metres of sluice boxes where the gold was trapped. The debris, or tailings, from these boxes clattered down through the tail race and out through the tunnel into the river.

Very large schist boulders, fallen from the rocky slopes bounding the gully, were scattered through the river gravel and were a great danger to the men working below in the mine. The breaking up of these boulders once they dropped on to the floor of the claim and stacking the pieces neatly on both sides of the tail race, greatly slowed the pace of mining. But it has resulted in the largest and most impressive example of a stone-walled tail race in the district. In fact such a huge quantity of rocks were produced from the sluicing that Kett was forced to roof over much of the open tail race with slabs of rock so that large quantities of stones could be stacked above the tail race.

It was reported that the claim was very rich and that Kett quickly recovered the £1,000 he had spent in opening it up. In less than a year a great chasm some 220 metres long, up to 50 metres wide and averaging more than 20 metres deep had been torn out and all the gravel it contained sent on its way down the tail race.

In the light of the reports of Kett's rich returns, Alexandra was surprised when, in September 1875, after only nine months work, the mine and gear, including Kett's house and the Caledonian race, were all put up for sale. The reason given was that Kett's health had broken down. But the mine was also becoming increasingly difficult to work as the thickness of gravel lying over the gold bearing wash steadily increased up the gully. The race and mine was sold to Garty of St Bathans for £800 and Michael Kett faded from the scene.[6]

Figure 12. 7. An indentation on the hillside filled with thick briar marks the outlet of the tail race tunnel. The deep tail race cut in solid rock leading away from the tunnel (between the rocks in the foreground) has been filled in with tailings.

So far as is known, Garty did not operate the mine and kept the Caledonian race for less than a year before selling it to George McNeill who, with changing partners, was the owner of the race for the next 20 years.

The Tunnellers
Meanwhile Kett's mine lay abandoned until late 1889. Then Thomas Sanders and James Austin, calling themselves the Nil Desperandum Company, were granted a claim over the remaining, unworked floor of 'Ketts Gully.' Their four-acre claim stretched from the end of Kett's mine over a low divide into Tubmans Gully which was part of the same

120

long depression but drained northwards into Halfmile Gully. Instead of attempting to sluice the dangerously high gravel face of Kett's mine they decided to extract the gold-bearing wash by tunnelling along the rock bottom. Water from the Halfmile dam, now owned by Dawson and Foxwell, was rented to wash the material through the sluice boxes.

For two years Sanders and Austin tunnelled along the floor of the gully from the end of Kett's old workings. They were greatly helped by their pony which pulled the trolley of excavated wash along rails to the outlet of the tunnel. In the end the claustrophobic darkness became too much for the partners and the pair went off prospecting for coal around Gorge Creek for a couple of years. But by September 1893 they were back, this time pegging out a claim of two acres in Tubmans Gully presumably with the intention of continuing their tunnelling but this time from the opposite direction. The scheme was not very successful, however, and within a year they had shifted their operations to nearby Gilberts Gully.[7]

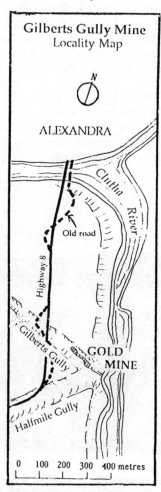

Figure 12. 8. Location map of the mine in Gilberts Gully.

Kett's mine remains much as he left it more than 120 years ago. Certainly debris has fallen from the sides but, although the tailrace is partly filled in, the high stone walls on either side are still well preserved. The outlet of the tailrace tunnel is blocked and a thick growth of briar makes exploration difficult but the mine is undoubtedly the most complete and impressive example of a sluicing claim in the district.

Gilberts Gully

Gilberts Gully is another of the dry gullies of Bridge Hill and was formed in the same way as the others but it lies almost at right angles to Ketts Gully. Gilberts Gully is better known to the people of Alexandra because, shortly after crossing the Clutha River, the State highway cuts across it. But what is not so well-known is that only 60 metres from the busy road lies a spectacular gold mine, much smaller, but similar in many ways, to that of Kett's.

As with other neighbouring dry gullies, early miners prospected Gilberts Gully and, as in the other gullies, were frustrated by striking huge boulders at shallow depths when they tried sinking shafts.

Peter Campbell was a master stonemason who had been responsible for much of the stone work on the piers of the big, new suspension bridge across the Clutha River at Alexandra. It was shortly after the bridge was completed in 1882 that Campbell, with two mates, James Austin and Jack Allen,[8] decided to try some serious mining in Gilberts Gully. Their first task, begun in March 1883, was to construct a tail race and it was necessary to commence this well down the bank towards the river to obtain the necessary fall. As they neared the

Figure 12. 9. Access shaft to the tailings tunnel at Gilberts Gully mine. A number of vertical shafts were constructed along the length of the tunnel to allow men access to clear any obstructions.

122

mouth of the gully their work was made doubly difficult by the narrow width between the schist walls of the gully—there was no room to stack the stones and rock from broken-up boulders. So the miners adopted the same system as Kett had done some years before—they covered over the tail race with slabs of schist rock and then stacked the tailings on top. However, they left narrow access holes at intervals along the length of the tunnel so that a man could let himself down into the tail race to clear away any boulders that might get jammed in the race.

Figure 12. 10. The long semi-circular grooves in this vertical schist wall of the Gilberts Gully mine are the remnants of 'potholes.' These structures were formed by abrasive action of stones swirled round by a strong current of water. Their presence indicates that the chasm, in which the gold-bearing wash lies, was cut by a substantial stream—perhaps by a part of the Clutha River.

A wire rope ran the length of the claim and suspended from this was a block and tackle that was used to lift heavy boulders. It took the partners two years to construct their elaborate tail race and only when it was finished could they begin mining. Water, rented from the owners of the Caledonian Race was stored in a shallow dam in the part of the gully that lay above the main road. It took six hours to fill the dam but

Figure 12. 11. The face of the mine in Gilberts Gully as it is today. At extreme right foreground is the vertical schist wall of the chasm. It was filled in with Clutha River gravels and large schist boulders (centre foreground).

only two hours to empty it—'six hours dry and two hours wet' as the miners put it—so only two hours sluicing could be done in every eight. From the dam water was led in an open race to the edge of the mine. Here it cascaded over the lip of the growing excavation eroding the gravels and washing the material, loosened by the water and by the picks of the miners, through the sluice boxes.[9, 10]

It was a dangerous mine. As the gravels were removed, the vertical rock walls of the old stream course, only about 5 metres apart, were exposed. Above the rock walls hung huge blocks of schist rock precariously encased in gravel. At the head of the claim the vertical working face of gravel and giant boulders towered some 12 metres above the miners' heads. The falling of these boulders into the mine, as the surrounding gravels were washed away, must have been a regular and frightening occurrence. Little wonder that after the long and expensive job of constructing the tailrace there was disappointment that the gold was so difficult to reach. It became a race as to whether they would reach payable gold before their funds became exhausted. After only a few months of real mining they had to give up and ask the Warden's Court in September 1885, for 90 days 'Protection.' A Certificate of Protection prevented their claim being declared 'Abandoned' and therefore open to anyone to peg it out.[11]

Campbell and Austin were unsuccessful when they sought a further extension to their Certificate of Protection in December 1885. Campbell went off to work at Roxburgh and Austin, after a few years prospecting, teamed up with Tom Sanders and started tunnelling in Kett's old claim in 1889.

Eight years later, in August 1894,[12] James Austin came back to Gilberts Gully with Thomas Sanders. They cleaned out and repaired the 275 metre-long tailrace, and rebuilt the two metre-deep dam in the upper part of the Gully. This time, with more experience, and probably more capital, they made better progress and had much more success. Although the work was no less hazardous than before, the pair continued mining for several years and were mainly responsible for the spectacular gulch that today, although hidden by pine trees, is only a few steps off the State Highway.

The Disappearance of Jack Allen[13]

Although Peter Campbell, James Austin and Jack Allen were partners in opening up the Gilberts Gully claim in 1883, Allen left after a year and another partner named Brown was taken in. Allen apparently was not a man for partnerships—he liked to work alone, and for years he fossicked in the gullies of Bridge Hill, particularly around Halfmile Gully. He lived alone in his little hut at the Gully and callers could tell where he was by noting which of his clothes were hanging on the nail at the end of his bunk and by whether or not his mining tools were leaning against the outside wall near the door. If his suit was on the hook and his tools and working clothes gone, then Jack was out on the job, but if his working clothes were on the hook and his tools at the door then Jack was wearing his suit, which meant he had gone to town.

It was as well that people took some interest in his movements because Allen's work was hazardous. He was constantly digging new tunnels or working in old ones and had met with a number of accidents over the years. In 1886, for example, he had been seriously injured when he fell from a height after the rope he was using to climb down into some old workings, gave way.

One day in 1899 it was reported that Jack Allen had not been seen for several days and the party which set out to visit his hut found his tools and working togs missing and his suit hanging on the nail. They carried out a search but found no trace of the missing man. It was surmised that he was working in one of the tunnels that were common on Bridge Hill when a boulder fell on him. No one was enthusiastic about searching scores of dangerous tunnels for a body, so Jack Allen still lies undisturbed in his last workplace.

NOTES

1. According to the late Mr S. R. Stevens (Personal communication).
2. Park (1906 p.12) refers to one of these gullies, Gilberts Gully, as a 'hanging valley', a term now more commonly used in describing glaciated landscapes. It is not clear whether Park was implying that Gilberts Gully was excavated by ice. If he were, then modern Earth Scientists would not support this view.
3. Equivalent to 732 oz and 915 oz of gold, respectively, valued at £3. 17s. 6d per

ounce. With the present price of gold at $NZ600 oz it seems that these sums were equivalent to about $440,000 and $550,000 respectively.

4. Miners gave their own names to almost every locality where there were gold diggings. The gully where Kett had his claim became known as 'Ketts Gully.' Diggings further north along the same depression, where it drains into Halfmile Gully, were said to be in 'Tubmans Gully.' The same depression can be traced northwards right through to the Earnscleugh Road and here the diggings were described as being in 'Golden Gully.' But the area at the mouth of Chapmans Gully was also variously referred to as 'Golden Gully,' 'Golden Flat' and finally 'Golden Beach.'

5. These measurements are taken from air photographs and differ from those given in *Dunstan Times* 18 September 1874 and 5 March 1875—which differ from each other.

6. *Dunstan Times* 1 October 1875.

7. Records of Warden's Court, Alexandra held in Regional Office of National Archives, Dunedin. Also Personal Communication. Mr Ivan Sanders, Alexandra.

8. Not to be confused with John Allan, a well-known miner from Springvale.

9. *Dunstan Times* 21 July 1882.

10. Peter Campbell Jnr, son of the stone mason, taped interview in 1963 by Les Thomson of Alexandra.

11. Records of Alexandra Warden's Court. Regional Office, National Archives, Dunedin

12. *ibid.*

13. Peter Campbell, tape 1963 (Note 10).

13.

THE MOLYNEAUX HYDRAULIC

Alexandra's fortunes fluctuated widely after it was founded during the heady days of the Dunstan Gold Rush. Always, however, when the future looked particularly bleak, another development in gold mining would come along to boost confidence and business. First, there had been the fantastic gold returns from the 'Gullies ' on the Old Man Range and as these died away, there was the rise of the big water race companies and sluicing concerns. Then came the boom in primitive dredging appliances, but by the middle 1870s, these had been put out of action by the increasing quantities of gravel coming down the river from sluicing operations. There were brief flurries of excitement as gold-bearing quartz reefs were investigated at Conroys Gully and Butchers Gully but they petered out. The great expectations aroused when the first steam dredge set to work on the river above Alexandra in 1881, were dashed when, after a few years, it moved down to Coal Creek in search of richer harvests.

New Zealand was in depression during the 1880s and Alexandra was particularly hard hit. In fact, with the dredging boom still in the future, there seemed little future for the tiny town. Apart from some activity on the quartz reefs on the Old Man Range, the outlook for mining was bleak. As people drifted away, and the population fell to fewer than 400, houses remained empty and business was in the doldrums. There was a real chance that the place would become another mining ghost town.

Robert Finlay, the mayor, called a public meeting in 1889 to discuss the situation, and from this a committee of prominent citizens was elected and charged with finding some suitable undertaking that would benefit the town.

Opening a gold mine on the outskirts of the town was the committee's proposal. As a number of the committee members were also members of the Borough Council, it was easy to gain a promise of full cooperation from that body—including a promise to lease the Borough water race to the new enterprise.

There was a great deal of excitement amongst the townspeople when it became known that a company had been formed to work a claim that was right in the town. The fact that Louis Gards, a respected citizen, who was the local blacksmith and owner of a successful dredge, was the principal shareholder gave standing to the venture. Understandably, it was seen as bringing employment and prosperity to a town that was in decline. In fact, the directors claimed that the company had been set up deliberately to bolster the economy. This may well have been so, but the spirit of community service did not last very long, judging by the later disagreements between the company and the town. The company was strongly supported by local citizens of Alexandra and, indeed, it boasted that most were shareholders, though it was disappointed that it did not attract much support from outside the town.[1]

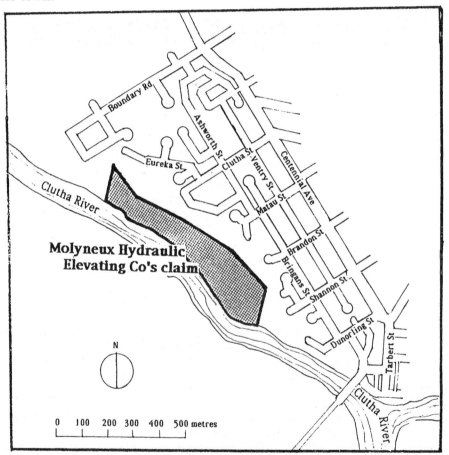

Figure 13. 1. A map of the streets of the western part of modern Alexandra with the 33 acre (13 h) claim of the Molyneux Hydraulic Elevating and Mining Co. Ltd taken up in 1890.

Although the new company was officially and ponderously called "The Molyneux Hydraulic Elevating and Mining Company (Limited),"[2] it was

Figure 13. 2. At Brennans (Letts) Gully the Ovens race was led from the top of the high terrace to the floor of the Gully. In this 'drop' it lost about 40 metres of altitude. Today the drop still exists and is marked by the line of willow trees in the centre of the photo that looks across the width of Letts Gully. The arrow marks the short race cut by the Molyneux Hydraulic Company in 1892 to lead the race water into their pipeline.

always known locally as the 'Molyneux Hydraulic' or simply, the 'Hydraulic.'

The new company proposed to sluice the upper gravels from a narrow strip of the terrace that formed the eastern bank of the Clutha River, and then to work the underlying gold-bearing wash by the relatively new method of hydraulic elevating. To do this successfully required a large quantity of water under high pressure, and arranging for this became the company's first consideration.

Directors of the new company approached the Borough Council about the use of the Chatto Creek race. Some would say later that this took little effort, as they were mainly the same people! The truth was that by 1890 the Borough race had become an embarrassment to the council. Through lack of maintenance it had fallen into disrepair and now could barely carry two of the ten heads it was registered for. Council simply did not have the money to keep the race fully operational but nevertheless was worried that someone would seek Forfeiture of the other eight heads. So it was only too ready to lease the race to someone who would renovate it. The outcome was that the council agreed on 15 December 1890:

> 1. To grant the Alexandra Gold Mining Co (sic) a lease of the water race for 21 years on condition that the Company will at all times allow one Government sluice-head of water to flow into the town under the

control of the Council. The water to be supplied from the pressure pipe.

2. That the company be granted the lease at a peppercorn rental on condition that the company pay all expenses of preparing lease transfers or other legal documents connected with same.[3]

The rental was, in fact, one shilling a year but the council was to receive, in addition, a one-off payment of £100 in consideration of the work carried out in widening and improving the race.

Later there were to be accusations that the race had been given away and, what was worse, that the directors of the company 'had

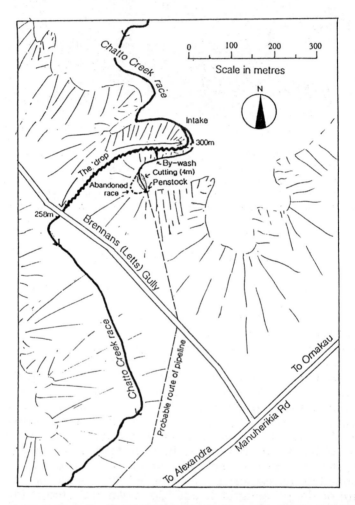

Figure 13. 3. From the top of the 'drop' in the borough's Chatto Creek race at Brennans (Letts) Gully the Molyneux Hydraulic Co constructed a short race to a penstock at the end of a spur where the water was fed into a pipeline. Later a cutting through the spur shortened this race. The area in the rectangle is covered by the air photograph, Figure 13. 4.

given the race to themselves'—a reference to the fact that a large number of borough councillors were directors of the company.[4] One newspaper correspondent even sarcastically referred to 'The Molyneux Borough Hydraulic Council.'[5]

There is little doubt, however, that even those councillors who were not directors of the new company agreed to the arrangement willingly. To be relieved of the considerable expense involved in the upkeep of the race and at the same time have a water supply guaranteed by a large company must have seemed to be a good deal. The fact that fellow councillors, who were seen as honourable men, largely controlled the company, was regarded as an advantage.

The Pipeline

It was a stroke of luck that the company was able to buy all of the assets, including thousands of metres of pipe, from the liquidated Commissioners Flat Gold-mining Company of Roxburgh East. By reselling everything except the pipes the Molyneux Hydraulic gained almost sufficient material for its proposed pipeline at a cost of only a few hundred pounds.

On the northern side of Brennans (Letts) Gully, at a point just before the Chatto Creek race plunged down the 'drop,' a short branch race was constructed out on to a spur overlooking Manuherikia Road. Here the water entered a pipeline that conveyed it some 3.4 kilometres to the claim. The pipeline followed roughly along the now disused part of the race to the Alexandra town boundary and then took a direct route down Shannon Street to the mine.

For the first 900 metres the pipes were 22 inches (56 cms) in diameter but for the greater part of the pipeline they were 16 inches (40 cms). Wooden trestles supported the line along most of its length except at road crossings where it was partly buried, with its presence marked by annoying humps. The 260 feet (80 m) difference in level between the intake and the mine at river level would ensure adequate pressure, it was hoped, for sluicing and working the hydraulic elevators. The Prospectus quoted £6,293 as the estimated cost of the scheme.

The job was completed and the line tested under pressure by the middle of January 1893 and sluicing started soon afterwards with John Magnus as manager. But from the day that sluicing began there were problems. Even though the race from Chatto Creek was full to the brim, the manager still complained about shortage of water. It showed in the first washup—only 13 oz for seven days' work. The newspaper was trying to be optimistic when it said that the claim was just paying expenses but returns would undoubtedly improve when excavations reached 'bottom.'

Under these circumstances it is not surprising that the company found certain difficulties in supplying the borough with the promised one head and it was not long before citizens were complaining about lack of water in the Borough race.

Water for the Borough

Even before the Molyneux Hydraulic Company's pipeline was

completed the *Dunstan Times* was commenting:

> Alexandra has one of the best water rights of the country towns but suffers from an intermittent supply. Now water is being brought to the very door by the pipes of the Hydraulic Co. It is hoped Councillors will wake up.

Figure 13. 4. An air photo taken early in 1949 covers part of the area shown on the diagram in **Figure 13. 3.**

The council, of course, already had the agreement with the company to supply one head of water, under pressure, to the town. Until the pipeline was completed this water had been delivered by open race but now it was being discharged from the new pipeline, through a valve at Finlay's corner,[10] into the race which ran along the Terrace. But the valve was to be the source of much criticism because it was liable to become so choked with debris that no water could flow into the town race. And there were other complaints about the water. In March, for instance, one of the driest months, the water in the race was diverted into the river so that the race could be cleaned. Residents were without water for nine days, '. . . a nice state of affairs at this time of the year' as the newspaper commented.

Borough's First Pipeline

In February 1893 the council came to a new arrangement with the company whereby only a portion of the borough's allocation of water

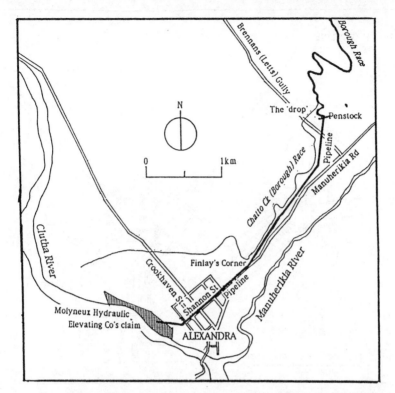

Figure 13. 5. The Molyneux Hydraulic Co's pipeline more or less followed the line of the Borough race to Finlay's corner (Ngapara St-Manuherikia Rd intersection) where the borough's allocation of water was discharged back into the Borough race. The pipeline then followed down Shannon St to the Molyneux claim on the bank of the Clutha River.

was to be discharged from the company's pipeline into the Town race. The remainder was to be discharged into a council pipeline that was to be connected to the company's pipeline where the latter crossed Crookhaven Street (Centennial Avenue). The council's pipeline was to be laid down the main street, with a branch along Limerick Street—a total length of 714 metres. It was intended to give the citizens their first piped water supply.

Council thought it had struck it lucky. The mayor and Cr Rivers attended a sale of mining pipes at Bannockburn and bought the required amount of 7 in (175 mm) pipe for £149 11s. 3d. Even with £18 extra for cartage they thought they had a bargain.

As the laying of the pipes through the main street in their 15 in (350 mm)-deep trench progressed, it was announced that it was intended to have a number of standpipes at intervals which would allow hosing of the street to lay dust and also to provide water for fire fighting. The local newspaper's suggestion that a dynamo should be incorporated to light up the town was not taken up. The pipe laying was completed by the end of November 1893 and trials commenced.

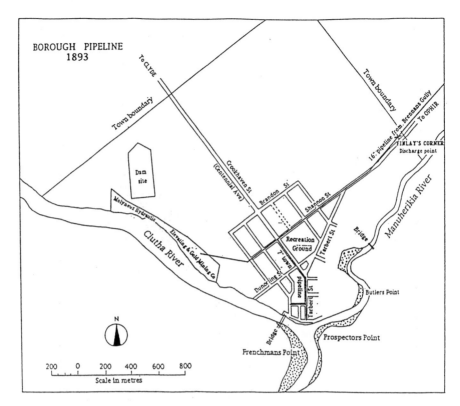

Figure 13. 6. The Borough Council laid a pipeline through the main street and connected it with the Molyneux Hydraulic Co's pipeline at the Shannon-Crookhaven Streets intersection. Unfortunately the Council's pipes failed under test and were ripped up and disposed off before any homes were able to enjoy the luxury of piped water under pressure.

Fiasco

There seemed to be some delay in turning the water into the new main. Was something wrong? There was no problem, assured the council, just some slight difficulties with the pipe joints:

> . . . but Mr James Simmonds, the worthy Mayor, came to the rescue and devised a plan of placing a thin layer of cement round the joints. The result is that they are thoroughly watertight. In a short time water will be at last in the houses.[7]

Unfortunately, the mayoral brainwave was not good enough. It was that regular critic of council, 'Ratepayer,' who blew the whistle in a letter to the *Dunstan Times*:[8]

> The Alexandra Borough Council find that after laying the pipes for a water supply they are of no use, being too weak to stand the pressure. They are to be lifted and sold and the ratepayers are to look on, grin and bear it until the Council sees some way of getting a water supply.

And, sure enough, in the same issue the council called for tenders to raise, clean and stack the town pipes. What had gone wrong?

The facts were that the metal of the secondhand pipes was too thin and a bit rusty here and there, so, in spite of the mayor's concrete bandages, the joints could not be made to withstand even the modest pressure they were subjected to. And there was also a suggestion (denied by council) that the pipes had been laid in trenches so shallow that the pipes could be crushed by the weight of wagon wheels.

The upshot was that before any houses could be connected, the pipes were ripped up, cleaned and stored at the recreation ground for sale. It was probably of little consolation to the Borough Council that the cost of lifting the pipes (£11 12s. 6d) was much less than that for laying them in the first place (£20) and when it sold them it received 3d. per foot more than it had paid for them.

So ended the Borough Council's first attempt to provide the citizens with a piped water supply. It was back to the open town water race.

Company in Strife

From the beginning, the directors of the Molyneux Hydraulic, few of whom were practical miners, had argued amongst themselves as to where the best gold was to be found in their claim. Those who thought they knew more than the manager, interfered in the working of the mine. As the *Dunstan Times* remarked:

> If it were not that the fighting and squabbling between the shareholders in the Alexandra (sic) Hydraulic Co is mischievous in its results it would be amusing.[9]

One section of the directorate wanted activities moved to the upper end of the claim where there was supposed to be a proven lead of gold, but this would have meant an expensive extension to the pipeline. Other directors wanted work to continue at the downstream end of the claim and were calling on the manager to excavate ever deeper until he reached 'bottom.' But this he found very difficult to do. It was easy enough to sluice away the overlying gravels but these contained only small amounts of gold. To reach the underlying, gold-bearing wash the manager had to use the hydraulic elevator to lift material out of the excavation so that the tailings could be dumped into the river, and he really never had enough water at sufficiently high pressure to achieve this.

It was at this time that the great flaw in the company's plan was exposed—a flaw that was to prove nearly fatal to the enterprise. Surprisingly for people who had spent their lives in Central Otago, the directors had overlooked the fact that the larger rivers and streams carried most water during the spring when snow on the ranges began to melt. In the winter when the country was held in an icy grip the streams shrank in volume. It was only for a short time in the spring that there was sufficient water in Chatto Creek race to work the hydraulic elevator. But this was also the time when the Clutha River was rising and water flooded the mine. The elevator spent most of its energy lifting water rather than gold bearing wash, hence the poor returns. When the river level fell with the approach of winter, and the wash was exposed, so also did the water in the race shrink so that elevating became impossible. No one had any doubt that the claim

135

contained rich gold—this had been proved on the rare occasions when the 'bottom' had been approached. The problem was getting it out.

The directors blamed a succession of managers for their troubles. John Magnus lasted only until July 1893. He was replaced by Scott who complained, at a testy shareholders' meeting in November, that the directors were constantly interfering with him. It would be better to get rid of him, he said bluntly, if the directors felt they could not trust him. They took his advice and sacked him there and then. Then the directors themselves resigned and John Pattison, the Chairman of Directors, and a miner, took over as manager until April, 1894 when John Stewart of Millers Flat was appointed.

Although the company owed the bank £600, with insufficient capital to meet the debt, there were still insistent calls from the floor to shift operations to the upper end of the claim even though this would cost £200 in new pipes. The alternative was liquidation. A newspaper correspondent writing about the history of the company had predicted:[10] "It is now elevation, soon will come depression, then prostration, followed by liquidation". It seemed that he was going to be proved correct.

Robert Gilkison, the Company solicitor, saved the company from immediate liquidation by raising a loan, with the existing pipeline as security, so that the bank overdraft could be repaid. This gave new life to the company, and to the meeting, which immediately resolved to order the necessary pipes to enable operations to move up to the top end of the claim.

Everyone realised, though, that this move was only delaying the inevitable. It would not solve the lack of race water or the high river levels but it gave the directors time to think about the future of the claim. It was admitted in the end that the gold, which was undoubtedly present in the claim, could not be recovered by sluicing or elevating. The only possible method was by dredging.

Where was the £4,000, or more, for a modern dredge to come from? Various schemes were suggested until it was remembered that of the £12,000 capital originally called for when the company was formed, only a little more than half had been allocated. So another issue of 4,310 £1 shares was authorised and those in the room promptly took up 650 shares. But that was about the sum total of takers— shareholders already had more than enough Molyneux Hydraulic shares, thank you. Then someone had a brainwave—make the second allocation of shares 'Preference Shares' returning dividends three times greater than those of the original ordinary shares. This did the trick and the new shares were disposed of quickly.

Having made the decision to change to a dredging enterprise, the company decided in September 1895, in the face of a rising river, to suspend operations and so cut its losses. And losses there certainly had been. The whole of the available capital of over £4,000 had been spent on gear and on operating expenses. And in addition there was the mortgage of £600 on the pipeline. Set against this expenditure was the 448 oz of gold, worth £1,726[11] recovered since the company began sluicing in January 1893.

The race and claim would be let out on tribute,[12] for at least a year to J. McLean the manager, who was now out of a job, and W. A. Theyers.[13] This arrangement gave the company time to organise the finance for the construction of the dredge and to enlarge the claim to

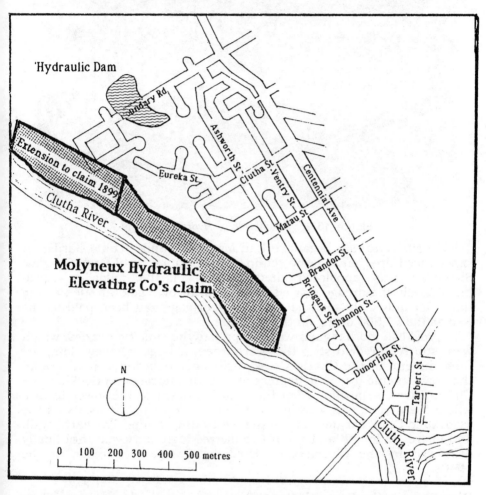

Figure 13. 7. After the arrival of the dredge a large shallow dam was built to store water from the Borough race for sluicing overburden. In 1899 the company extended its claim to 66 acres (26 h).

63 acres (27h) so that it now embraced the whole river bank from Brandon St to beyond the Town Belt.

The Dredge

The *Molyneux Hydraulic* was constructed beside the river about 400 metres above Dunorling Street. It was the largest, the most modern, and powerful dredge of the time. Its 40 large buckets lifted wash from a depth of 10 metres below water level and it could stack tailings to a height of 12 metres above the water line.

137

Figure 13. 8 . The *Molyneux Hydraulic* dredge.

Molyneux Hydraulic began work in May 1897 under Louis Gards, an experienced dredgeman, who retained the position until Carl (Charles) Simonsen was appointed dredgemaster in the following April. Immediately the dredge started it began to recover gold at such a rate that after only eight months the £600 mortgage had been paid off, as well as the £1,500 owing on the dredge.

To provide a more regular water supply to the sluicing nozzles, which were still required to strip the overburden, a large, shallow dam, fed from the end of the Chatto Creek race, was constructed just beyond the town boundary in a depression on the terrace overlooking the Clutha River. A pipeline from the dam led down to the lower terrace where the dredge was working. This dam, known to the locals as the 'Hydraulic Dam' became a favourite ice skating venue. The earth wall, 140 metres in length and about two metres high, survived until finally destroyed by the Clutha Gold Dredging Company's dredge in the 1940s.

Dispute with the Borough Council
The initial, somewhat idealistic, concept of working in a spirit of co-operation with the Borough Council for the good of the town, faded as the Molyneux Hydraulic Company, under pressure from share-holders demanding dividends, rapidly became a hard-nosed business. Relationships between the company and the council became difficult.

Almost from the beginning, council had had trouble in obtaining from the company the regular and full supply of water that had been clearly allocated to the borough in the agreement. It was obvious that the company had misjudged the capability of the Chatto Creek race to supply sufficient water for its own needs, let alone those of the borough as well. This led, not unnaturally, to a certain lack of enthusiasm on the part of the company for releasing the water—

matched only by a growing measure of impatience on the part of the council who had to explain the lack of water to the citizens. Many letters had gone out from the Town Clerk to the company complaining about shortage of water in the town where conditions were now vastly different from those in 1890 when the council had signed the agreement. For one thing, as a result of the rapidly increasing number of gold dredges in the district, the population had nearly trebled and every drop of water was needed. Nothing that threatened to diminish the meagre town supply could be tolerated and now new moves by the company had brought matters to a head.

Under the dredging system adopted by the company, water was needed only for sluicing off the relatively barren overburden and this did not require the water under the high pressure that had been necessary to work hydraulic elevators. The water could be supplied by open race again. So the company announced the pipeline from Brennans Gully was no longer needed and it would shortly be selling off the pipes. Furthermore, sufficient overburden had been stripped off during the years of sluicing to make further removal unnecessary for some time. So the company called tenders for leasing its water and gold miners at Springvale gratefully snapped it up. But this meant that the race from Springvale to Brennans Gully, a distance of some eight kilometres, now carried only the one head of water allocated to the borough.

The Borough Council became alarmed on several counts. First, there was nothing in the agreement with the company that allowed sub-leasing of the water. More important, the situation left the eight kilometres of race vulnerable to 'jumping.' It would be easy for someone to prove in the Warden's Court that, over that particular stretch, the race and water were no longer being used for mining, and this could bring about forfeiture. But the greatest cause of concern was that the agreement also said the company must have the permission of the Borough Council before any alterations could be made to the pipeline, and this it did not have. And here was the company talking about lifting its pipeline. How could it provide the borough water *under pressure* as it was bound to do if there were no pipeline?

Long and acrimonious argument followed. Perhaps this is not surprising when it is recalled that four of the seven councillors were shareholders and three of these were directors of the company. Mayor James Simmonds, who was not a shareholder in the company, was keen on taking the company to court to force it to carry out the terms of its agreement with the Borough Council. He listed other points of conflict. These ranged from a long-running dispute over who was to pay for bridges for sheep across the race, to a more recent failure of the company to supply efficient valves to release the borough's water from the pipeline. Cooler heads prevailed and it was finally agreed that the company could lift and sell its pipeline provided the lease was cancelled and the race handed back to the borough in good order and condition.[14]

The Borough Council, for its part, would supply the company with four heads of water at 10s. a head per week for four months of each year, for a term of 14 years. The borough was to receive at all times, as a priority, a minimum of one head of water. Some directors of the company thought they were silly to swap a race, for which they paid one shilling a year, for a water supply that would cost £24 a year. But as others pointed out, it cost the company about £200 a year to maintain the race and now they really only needed the water for a few months each year.[15] A new Deed of Agreement was signed on 27 January 1898 and the Borough, for better or worse, regained the Chatto Creek race.

Perhaps the sentiments expressed by 'Onlooker,' a supporter of the company who had carried out a spirited and prolific correspondence with 'Ratepayer' in the columns of the *Dunstan Times,* were appropriate:

'Now that the Borough is getting the race back again, we can afford to close this correspondence, and wishing the Borough all success from the new arrangement, and a Merry Christmas to 'Ratepayer' and all other ratepayers — I am etc.[16]

Onlooker

The company could hardly wait to sell the main pipeline (which it hoped might bring £1,000) but agreed to continue to supply water from it for two or three weeks to give the council time to clean out and enlarge the Chatto Creek race from Brennans Gully to Finlay's corner—which, over the last four years, had been maintained to carry only one head.

The renovation of the race proved to be a bigger job than the council expected and a month later, when the company asked for its promised four heads of water and, at the same time, said that it wanted the pipes emptied of water forthwith, the work was not completed. The mayor was forced to ask the manager of the Scandanavian Gold Mining Company of St Bathans if he would delay, for a fortnight, dismantling the section of the pipeline that he had bought, to allow the work to be completed. By the beginning of March the company was pulling up and stacking the unsold sections of the pipeline with the intention of selling the pipes in lots to suit customers. The prices ranged from 2s. 10d. per foot for the large pipes to 2s. 6d. for the 16 inch pipes.

New Company

In June 1900 the Molyneux Hydraulic Elevating and Gold Mining Company (Ltd) sold all of its assets to a new company, the Molyneux Hydraulic Dredging Company Limited. The original company was then voluntarily wound up.[17] This kind of restructuring was common amongst mining companies and for this particular company there were two reasons. First, the company had been formed to carry out mining by sluicing and hydraulic elevating but now it had changed to dredging, and secondly it was desirable to reduce the capital so that gold recovered represented a higher return on capital invested. The capital of the new company was fixed at £6,000 and shares were distributed amongst shareholders.

Dredging continued for many years with good returns. For example, for the year 1902-03, 1,608 oz of gold worth £6,190 were recovered allowing a dividend of 7s. 6d. a share to be distributed after setting aside £500 for reserves. Conditions were hard on the dredge. The engine room had to be lined in 1902 to protect the engine from drifting sand; a collapse of the 10 metre high gravel face buried the bucket ladder and twisted it so it had to be rebuilt and breakages of gear wheels and tumblers were fairly frequent. But these problems were common to dredges working into the terraces that formed the river banks.

Charles Simonsen left the dredge in October 1904 and was replaced by Sam Cameron who remained master of the dredge for the remainder of its life.

Year after year the dredge worked on, its steam whistle a familiar time-marker for the people of Alexandra. Working on average about 45 weeks a year, in that time it dredged its way through about half a hectare of gravel terrace bringing up wash from a depth of 10 metres and producing from 12 to 30 oz of gold a week.

Gradually, as the dredge worked its way further into the terraces the thickness of barren overburden became greater and gold production fell off in relation to the amount of gravel that had to be processed. By 1912 the dredge was 15 years old and nearly worn out. It came to a standstill in May and did not start again. It was sold in June 1912 for £235 to E. J. Isles who wanted the machinery for a quartz mine he was operating on the Carrick Range.

What did the Molyneux Hydraulic Company achieve?[18] It certainly provided a boost to the local economy. Over the lifetime of the company it produced 13,264 oz gold worth £51,126. Almost all of the operating expenditure, some £41,030, and the greater part of the dividends of £13,264 were spent in the district. The dredge employed 7 or 8 men regularly as crew and no doubt other support people ashore. But by the time the dredge began work, the dredging boom was beginning to develop and the individual benefit of the *Molyneux Hydraulic* to the town's economy was submerged in the general uprise of business. There is little doubt, however, that the founding of the company gave new heart to a town that was sinking into oblivion. It enabled the town to survive until, a few years later, it became the centre of the new gold dredging industry.

NOTES

1. Of 67 shareholders only 17 were from outside the Alexandra-Clyde district.
2. *Dunstan Times* 6 June, 1890. For some unexplained reason the word 'Gold' was omitted from the title but was used every time the company was named thereafter.
3. Alexandra Borough Council Minutes of Meeting 15 October 1889. The formal agreement was not signed until over a year later.
4. Four Borough Councillors —R Finlay (Mayor), J. Rivers. J. Kelman and W Theyers (out of seven) were also Directors of the Company when the decision was made to allow the company the use of the Borough race. Three councillors—Theyers (Mayor), Kelman and Rivers (out of six) were also Directors when the agreement was signed in December 1890.
5. *Dunstan Times* 24 December 1897.
6. Finlay's property was on the corner of Ngapara Street and Manuherikia Road.

7. *Dunstan Times* 9 February 1894.
8. *Dunstan Times* 27 April 1894.
9. *Dunstan Times* 8 June 1894..
10. *Dunstan Times* 21 April 1893
11. *Dunstan Times* 20 September 1895.
12. This means that the mine was worked by an outside party who paid a percentage of any gold obtained to the owners.
13. Not to be confused with his father, the venerable W. (Billy) Theyers.
14. *Dunstan Times* 22 October 1897.
15. *Dunstan Times* 24 December, 1897.
16. *Dunstan Times* 31 December 1897.
17. *Dunstan Times* 9 March; 6 April; 15 June 1900.
18. The original Molyneux Hydraulic Elevating and Gold mining Co Ltd (1890-1900) recovered 3,238 oz of gold worth £12,524 and returned dividends of £3,096. It should be noted that of these returns, 2,790 oz of gold worth £10,798, and all of the dividends, were provided by the first three year's work of the new dredge. The Molyneux Hydraulic Dredging Company Ltd (1900-1912) recovered 10,026 oz of gold worth £38,602, and returned dividends of £7,000. The total of 13,264 oz recovered by the company would be worth about $NZ 8 million today.

14.

RIVERS(S')WATER

The people of Alexandra were frustrated. They had watched pipes being laid in the street and had been looking forward with keen expectation to the luxury of piped water. Many had anticipated the supply by installing pipes and taps in their homes. But as they saw, with dismay, the pipes being ripped up again, their hopes of a permanent water supply faded. Renewed pressure went onto the mayor and councillors to provide a proper supply as quickly as possible.

Roberts' Scheme
James Rivers, elected Mayor for a second time in November 1894, was still dedicated to providing piped water. He had lost faith in the Borough water race as a source of domestic water because it was polluted and unreliable. He looked to the great river flowing at their front door. Almost immediately on gaining office, Rivers took the opportunity to buttonhole Edward Roberts, a Dunedin consulting engineer, while he was in Alexandra on other business. Rivers put to him some of his ideas about supplying water to the town. As a result Roberts, in January 1895, sent the mayor a report on one of the schemes that they had discussed. It was, simply, that the borough pump its water from the Clutha River using the current of the river to turn large paddle wheels, mounted on a barge, to provide the power. It was an obvious adaptation of the current-wheel dredges, some of which were still on the river at that time. The barge, said Roberts, would need to be 40 ft (12 m) long by 10 ft (3 m) wide and could be moored under the bridge. The two paddle wheels would work a slow-speed, three-throw pump which would pump water to a reservoir built some 60 metres above the river level on the rocky hill lying between the main street and the Manuherikia River.

The engineer calculated that such a set-up would supply 400 people with 80 gallons (243 litres) of water every 24 hours. He went on to detail the layout of the pipelines: a 4 inch (100 mm) pipeline up Tarbert and Crookhaven Streets to the Dunorling Street intersection and a 3 in (75 mm) branch main along Limerick Street, would serve most of the population. There would be ten fireplugs and all necessary sluices, valves, etc as shown on the plan that accompanied the report.[1] The whole scheme would cost £970.[2]

Roberts' report was discussed at the February meeting of council and given a mixed reception. One councillor suggested that the river water was polluted but the mayor vigorously denied this. Councillor Olaf Magnus thought it would be better to buy a water right from one of the races coming off the Old Man Range, which he thought could be obtained for £1,000.[3] The mayor again responded vigorously, pointing out that if they were looking for polluted water that was the way to get it—water travelling a long distance in an open race was subject to all sorts of pollution, including rabbit poison. In spite of the mayor's strong support for the Clutha River scheme, or perhaps because of it, most councillors expressed reservations, mainly about the initial cost and the maintenance of the pumping machine.

So Roberts was asked for more information on this aspect and to calculate how much saving would be made by pumping only half the amount of water suggested in the first proposal. He was also asked to compare the cost of the proposed reservoir with putting one up on Bridge Hill or using water tanks on high poles situated near the bridge.

At the same time Rivers took the opportunity to put forward another scheme. Why not, he asked Roberts, re-lay the pipeline from the Molyneux Hydraulic pressure line, using proper pipes this time, and use the water to drive a water wheel that would, in turn, operate the pumps or perhaps a hydraulic ram to lift river water. The place for this mechanism, Rivers proposed, was down on the river bank at the lower end of Tarbert Street.

Roberts was not impressed with this barrage of ideas. He pointed out that the great failing of the Chatto Creek race (which supplied the Molyneux Hydraulic pipeline) was its unreliability—it tended to run dry in summer and freeze up in winter and at all times was subject to washouts. He calculated that pumping half the water would save only £25 and he dismissed the other suggestions as being more costly than the original proposal.

Although, to the public, nothing much seemed to be happening in the matter of water supply over the winter, Mayor Rivers had not been idle. He had met up with another visiting expert. This time it was R. H. Postlethwaite, an electrical engineer of Dunedin, who was now subjected to a dose of Rivers' fertile imagination. Rivers asked Postlethwaite whether it would be possible to drive a dynamo for supplying electricity to the town from the same paddle wheels that were going to operate the water pumps.

Postlethwaite's Scheme
Ethics demanded that Postlethwaite consult Roberts but, having done so, he reported to the October council meeting in person.[4] He suggested drastic modifications to the original Robert's proposal. Instead of the paddle wheels driving pumps directly, they would drive an electric dynamo and the power would be taken ashore where an electric motor would operate pumps drawing water from a perforated cylinder sunk into the beach on the Alexandra side of the river. A pipeline would convey the water up to a reservoir above the town as in

the original proposal.

Postlethwaite pointed out the advantages of this modified scheme. First, an electric cable running ashore from the barge was far more flexible than a pipeline so could accommodate fluctuations in the river level much more readily; secondly, a much larger quantity of water would be raised; thirdly, river water would be filtered through gravels before reaching the pumps and cleared of fine silt and lastly, electricity would be available not only for lighting the streets and public buildings but for selling to the public. In this way most of the running and standing costs of the scheme would be recouped. If the council decided to go ahead, Postlethwaite would, with Mr Roberts, draw up working plans and specifications. This was agreed to, as was the placing of the required advertisements of the council's intention to apply for a loan of £2,500 to finance the scheme.

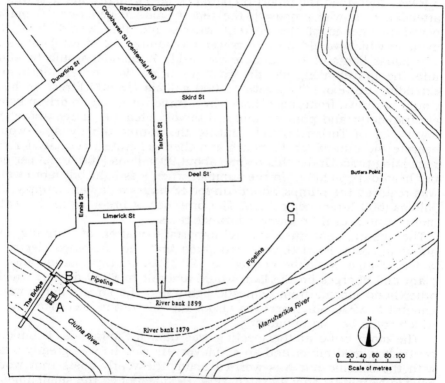

Figure 14. 1. The barge scheme. In the first scheme, designed by engineer Roberts, paddle wheels mounted on a barge moored near the bridge (A) worked pumps that lifted river water into a reservoir on the hillside east of the main street (C). From here water was piped through the town.

In a modified scheme, designed by engineer Postlethwaite, the paddle wheels drove a dynamo (A) which powered pumps on the river bank (B). Surplus power was to be sold to pay for the scheme.

145

There were over 100 people present at the public meeting called by the mayor, James Rivers, to explain the proposals. He outlined the history of the council's attempts to provide a decent water supply, pointing out that the Chatto Creek race was now heavily polluted by sheep, rabbits and vegetable matter and no longer suitable for a domestic supply. It had proved to be an unreliable source of water, practically drying up in the summer and freezing in the winter. Nor could the town count on the continued presence of the Molyneux Hydraulic's pipeline as the company was shaky and could well go into liquidation. The mayor pointed out that the combined electric lighting-water scheme would cost more than the original scheme and this was why it was necessary to increase the loan to £2,500. This would cost £250 a year to service and would require an extra rate on the citizens of 1s. 3d. in the £.

Rivers then read the report prepared by Mr Postlethwaite who was in attendance. It was proposed, the report said, to generate 10 horse-power by means of the current wheels and this would drive the dynamo which would provide power for pumps, 12 street lights and 100 house lights of 16 candle power each. A cylinder would be sunk into the gravel alongside the river to below low water mark and extending up above flood level. 3,000 gallons (13,600 litres) an hour would be drawn from this cylinder by a three-throw pump driven by an electric motor and pumped into a reservoir sited 14 metres above the lower end of Tarbert Street. During the winter the dynamo would operate the pumps for 12 hours and then generate electricity for the remaining time. Under this regime about 90 gallons (400 litres) per day per head of population. In the summer when less light but more water was required the pumps would run for 18 hours a day and supply 130 gallons (600 litres) per person. The presence of fireplugs in the water mains would result in lower insurance rates.

The report went into the all-important matter of running and standing costs. Postlethwaite estimated that the combined electrical-water scheme could be erected for £2,350 and the maintenance of plant and charges on the loan would amount to £250 a year. On the other hand income from domestic lights and the streets lights would amount to £220 but there was also 6 h.p. of surplus electrical energy which could be sold to industry.

The main critic at the meeting was James Simmonds, a building contractor, gold miner and an ex-mayor. He said he was greatly taken with the scheme but was worried about the yearly costs that would have to be met by only 90 ratepayers. He questioned the small amount of £75 per year allowed for maintenance and attendance at the plant. It would take rather more attention than the borough dayman squirting a little oil into bearings now and then. The whole scheme would need a full-time man and £400 a year would be a more realistic figure for total costs. This would require annual rates of £5 2s. per ratepayer as against £1 14s. at present, so it was vital that the scheme produce as much income as possible.

Others were concerned that ratepayers on the outskirts of the town, who would receive no direct benefit from the scheme, would still be required to pay half the new rate. But when the mayor asked for a show of hands of those approving the scheme, no-one was against it.[5]

At its next meeting the council considered ways and means of raising money. The mayor outlined the procedures necessary, including the holding of public meetings and a poll, before money could be borrowed from the Government. Backed by the mandate given by the public meeting, the council set the procedures in motion.

Saga of the Loans

At the official poll, the proposal to borrow the money for the scheme was carried almost without dissent. So the citizens were surprised to see another public notice appear in the newspaper less than two months later, and proceed to run for the required four issues, advising that the council intended to borrow £2,500 for waterworks and electric lighting. All was revealed at a public meeting called in March. Mayor Rivers had the embarrassing task of informing the 30 people present that:

> . . . unfortunately a slight hitch occurred—apparently a very slight matter, a few words in the Act having been over-looked by the town clerk.[6]

'Slight matter' it may have been, but it was enough to make the poll invalid. The Town Clerk had even written to the Premier (Richard Seddon) about it, but he had replied that nothing could be done and advised Rivers, as did the borough solicitor, to start the whole procedure again.

At this public meeting the mayor again had to face criticism of the scheme and this time he did not have Mr Postlethwaite present to help him out. Louis Gards, a man with much experience of mining machinery, was the outspoken one. He asked questions about maintenance, the expected life of the equipment, the small quantity of water to be pumped, permanency of the scheme and whether there was any guarantee that the estimate was anywhere near the final cost. Both Gards and the mayor became short tempered, with Gards reminding Rivers that, as mayor, he had refused to accept Councillor Gards' motion that the purchase of the Caledonian race from Butchers Creek be investigated as an alternative to the present proposals. Rivers came back at him and asked Gards if he had any better ideas about a water supply and finished by saying '. . . it rests with the meeting to decide who is the cleverest man, Mr Postlethwaite or Mr Gards.' At the conclusion of the meeting the inevitable show of hands showed only Gards and blacksmith William Fraser were against the proposal.

In the official poll held a week after the meeting, 51 voted in favour of the loan and only 4 against. But poor Rivers was forced to report to the council meeting held on 13 April that this poll, too, was invalid. He said that he had followed the borough solicitor's advice step by step and still the council had gone wrong. It had been pointed out by a Dunedin firm of solicitors, whose opinion was sought, that the Municipal Corporations Act made no provision for borrowing money for electric lighting. It would be necessary to hold yet another poll and this time ratepayers would have to vote separately for two loans—for

£2,150 under the Municipal Corporations Act, 1886, for the water works and for £350 under the The Local Bodies Loans Act, 1886, for the electric lighting.

Because the council had sought an opinion from the Dunedin solicitors, Bathgate and Woodhouse, the borough solicitor, Mr McDonald, took professional umbrage and resigned his position. To make matters worse, James Simmonds started an opposition campaign in earnest with a series of letters to the *Dunstan Times*. In his opening sally he reminded ratepayers of the cost of servicing the loan, pointing out the obvious that money is easy to borrow but difficult to repay. If the population fell because of a decline of the mining industry, he warned, or even if the town's revenue should be reduced by loss of one publican's licence fees or, heaven forbid, if the introduction of prohibition wiped the fees entirely, then the town's finances would really be in trouble. He went on to mention the physical risk to the generating equipment moored in the middle of a big, unpredictable river. What if a dredge broke loose upstream and swept the barge away? What would the town have? No power, no water, no equipment, nothing but the hefty interest and principal bill still to be met. Simmonds then went on to outline his own scheme for supplying water to the borough.[7]

Simmonds' First Proposal
Simmonds suggested a scheme that would make use of the one head of water the borough drew from the Molyneux Hydraulic Company's

Figure 14. 2. James Simmonds was a contractor who, with J. Drummey, had built the Alexandra Bridge. He built a number of buildings in the town including the Post Office. He strongly opposed the Postlethwaite water scheme and suggested instead a hydroelectric scheme in Brennans Gully. When he became mayor he put forward two other schemes.

Chatto Creek race. He suggested a dam be built in Brennans Gully large enough to hold about one month's supply of water and an hydro-electric station be established lower down the gully. The power would be taken into town for street lights and domestic lighting and the revenue from this would pay for the power to pump water as proposed under Postlethwaite's scheme. Simmonds thought his whole scheme could be installed for about £750. A bonus was the fact that the water, having passed through the generating station, would not be wasted but would flow into the lower section of the Chatto Creek race and thereby conveyed into town to serve those people not on the piped water supply.

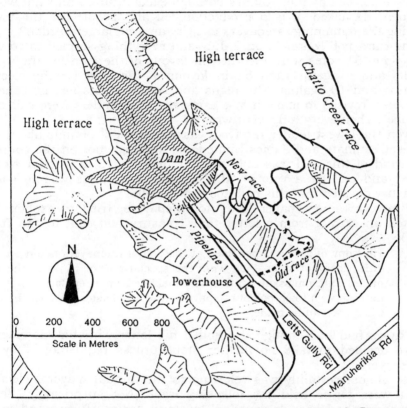

Figure 14. 3. Simmonds' scheme for a hydroelectric scheme in Brennans Gully using the 'drop' in the Chatto Creek race to provide hydraulic head. Power was to be used for pumping from the Clutha River.

James Kelman answered Simmonds' criticism, and reiterated the unreliability of the Chatto Creek race, pointing out that quite often there had been no water for a month at a time. He rubbished the idea of dredges breaking away in the river and thought it ridiculous that a thriving town such as Alexandra depended on the revenue of three publicans' licences. For several weeks Simmonds and Kelman slogged it out in the correspondence columns of the paper.[8]

Once more the loan proposals were advertised, following carefully the format set out by the Dunedin solicitors and once more Rivers called a public meeting. The townspeople were obviously getting tired of the whole performance as only 13 turned up.

This time it was Simmonds who had most to say. He went over again ("I'll be as brief as possible, Mr Chairman") his objections to the proposed scheme. There was no doubt about it, he had done his homework. His estimates for cost of maintenance and servicing seemed much more realistic than Postlethwaite's. His pessimistic prediction was that a total rate as high as 3s. 3d. in the £ on the valuation of property would be necessary to cover the shortfall on the scheme, as well as the ordinary borough expenditure. And what would happen, he asked, if gold production fell and people left the town, leaving the remaining ratepayers to carry an even larger burden?

The third poll was held on 2 July and everything seemed to go well this time. 51 votes were recorded in favour of the loan for the water works and 9 against and 51 in favour of the loan for the electric lighting and 10 against. The plans and specifications for the scheme had been revised to make it less expensive and tenders were called in October. Then everything went wrong.

Even the lowest tender received was hundreds of pounds above the highest estimate and James Simmonds, although not on the council, got wind of this and was able to crow over Rivers in a letter to the paper and call for a veto on the scheme. But worse was to come. Treasury decided that this poll, too, was invalid!

Rivers, in a newspaper letter to ratepayers, tried to explain. He quoted an extract from a letter that Treasury had sent to the Town Clerk:

> The copy of voting paper used at the poll of ratepayers taken on 2nd July, does not state upon what the special rate of 1s 3d in the £ is made. This omission cannot be considered an irregularity, but will necessitate a fresh poll of ratepayers, and all the steps, before the loan of £2,150 can be made.

Rivers had had enough. He ended his letter with the statement 'I have decided to take no further steps unless requisitioned by the ratepayers.' [9]

He almost certainly was referring to the annual mayoral elections that were to be held the following week. Not surprisingly, James Simmonds had been 'persuaded' to stand against Rivers and in the poll, held in late November 1896, he won by 37 to 30 votes.

At the first meeting of the council under the new mayor, it was decided, not unexpectedly, that Rivers's water scheme was too expensive and that was the end of it. Well, not quite—there was the matter of a bill for £70 from Postlethwaite for preparing working drawings.

As a stop-gap measure, the council asked the Molyneux Hydraulic Company if it could use the water that was normally running to waste down the overflow near the intake to the company's pipeline in Brennans Gully. This could be picked up by the abandoned part of the Chatto Creek race and brought into town to supplement the one head delivered from the company's pipeline at Finlay's corner.

Not forgetting that this was the race and water that the council had leased ('given away' according to some correspondents) to the company for the sum of one shilling a year, the coldly formal tone of the reply to the council's request to use what was virtually waste water gives an indication of the state of the relationship that had developed between

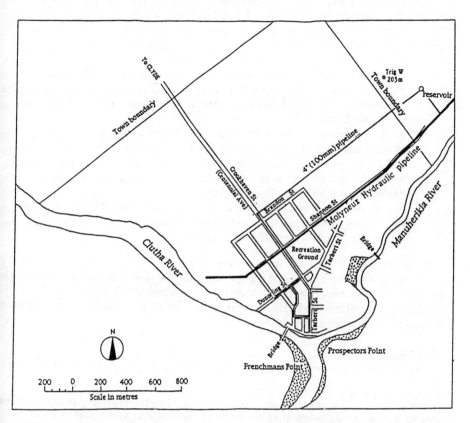

Figure 14. 4. When Simmonds became mayor he proposed to again use the Molyneux Hydraulic's pressure pipeline to supply the borough reticulation either directly or by way of a high level reservoir. The diagram is of the second option.

the two bodies. The Secretary of the company wrote:

> '. . . I beg to inform you that your application was considered at a meeting of the directors held this evening, and it was decided to grant the application for the term applied for, viz—five years . . . on the understanding that you do not allow anyone to interfere with the bye-wash, and further the Directors reserve the right to terminate this agreement at any time if they find it injurious to the working of the claim caused by people interfering with the bye-wash.[10]

Tenders were immediately called for cleaning and enlarging that part of the Chatto Creek race that had been abandoned when the Molyneux Hydraulic Company's pipeline was installed.

Simmonds' Second Proposals

Simmonds had had a lot to say against the various proposals of Rivers. Now, as mayor, it was his turn to put up proposals. But it wasn't until August that he produced his ideas on how to supply Alexandra with water. He explained that after consulting a number of firms, he had come to the conclusion that trying to lift water from the Clutha River was impractical and this meant he had also abandoned the idea of generating electricity from the Chatto Creek race at Brennans Gully. Nevertheless he was still determined that Alexandra should have a water supply under pressure. He produced three options:-

1. That a line of 4 inch (100 mm) cast-iron pipes be laid down Crookhaven and Tarbert Streets with branches into side streets. This pipeline to be fed from the Molyneux Hydraulic pipe line at the corner of Crookhaven and Shannon Street. The total cost of this scheme would be £746.

2. A reservoir to be built, complete with filter beds, high on the terrace north of the town and fed with a pipeline from the Molyneux Hydraulic pipeline. Street pipelines, laid out as in the first proposal, would be fed by a pipeline running from the reservoir to Crookhaven Street. Cost would be about £1,700

3. A water race be constructed along Crookhaven Street, from where the town race crossed Crookhaven Street, to serve people in the western part of the borough. Cost £28

Council agreed to call immediate tenders for the small amount of work required for the third proposal but further consideration of the other two was overtaken by events. The dismantling of the Molyneux Hydraulic pipeline and the return of the Borough race to the Borough Council made them obsolete.

NOTES

1. The reports and accompanying plans of this and subsequent schemes cannot now be located.
2. *Dunstan Times*, 13 September 1895.
3. The Caledonian water race, with a water right of 3 heads from upper Butchers Creek was for sale at this time. Olaf Magnus bought it himself later in the year for £650 and, as the managing director of the Golden Beach Co, used the water for sluicing at Poverty Beach.
4. *Dunstan Times* , 7 November 1895.
5. *Dunstan Times*, 29 November 1895.
6. *Dunstan Times*, 10 April 1896.
7. *Dunstan Times,* 22 May 1896.
8. *Dunstan Times* June to September 1896.
9. *Dunstan Times*, 20 November 1896.
10. *Dunstan Times*, 15 January 1897.

15.

WATER FROM ANYWHERE

but NOWHERE

During the late 1890s Alexandra's population increased rapidly because of the dredging boom, and the continuing and insistent demand for an adequate, high-pressure, piped water supply became a clamour. Many schemes had been discussed and sheets of plans drawn but there was still no sign of a water supply. Citizens were still making do with river water, supplied by carriers, for cooking and drinking purposes and with water from the Chatto Creek race (or the 'Town race,' as they called the branch that flowed through the town) for other purposes, including irrigation. But at least the race, and its full flow of water, were back under Borough Council control.

The Town Race

As settlement spread northwards across the flat, the races distributing water to various parts of the town from the main race on the Terrace, had to be realigned, extended and new branches constructed to meet growing needs. The Town race followed the old mining race from the Terrace across the flat to the 'head of Tarbert Street' (near the present War Memorial) and from there water flowed down the gutters on both sides of the main street.

In June 1873 a branch race was taken westwards from the Town race, under Crookhaven Street in a culvert which gave rise to a difficult hump in the roadway, and on into the western 'suburbs.'

When the four hectare block of land which had been set aside as a recreation reserve, was developed as a park in the early 1880s, the section of the Town race which cut through the reserve, was abandoned. In its place a new race was cut along the side of Crookhaven Street, from the point where the western branch race crossed that street, to the head of Tarbert Street.

The old race now stopped at the boundary of the Recreation Ground but it was extended east along Shannon Street and then south along Bantry Street in order to provide irrigation water for the poplar trees that had been established round the perimeter of the park.

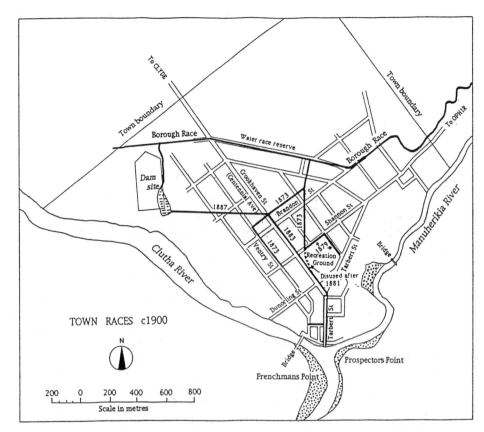

Figure 15. 1. As the population grew the town water race was extended and branches formed to supply water to as many properties as possible. At the end of the race the water was used for flushing the water tables of the main street. This map shows a possible reconstruction of the races, using all available evidence, as they were at the turn of the century.

For fourteen years the lessees of the Borough race had had the full use of the unused Borough reservoir, lying north-west of the township, for their mining operations, but in 1887 during a particularly dry spell, the Borough Council decided that the reservoir would be used to supplement the town supply. Fawcett, the lessee, was engaged to cut a race from the dam to link with the Town race in Crookhaven Street. He, not unnaturally, demanded payment but the council pointed out that, as it was already paying him to supply water to the borough and none was being received, it did not intend to pay him for work that he was obliged to do under the agreement.

Many tales about the water supply from the Town race have come down from those who had to make use of it. The race water was already polluted when it reached the boundary of the settlement and became much more so as it flowed through the town. It was quite unsuitable for drinking water and, indeed, some cases of typhoid fever

154

Figure 15. 2. Alexandra in the early 1890s. The main business street, Tarbert Street runs diagonally from the river bank at lower centre. The prominent intersection marks the former 'head of Tarbert Street' with upper Tarbert Street continuing to the right and the broad Crookhaven Street to the left.
Legend
1. The Terrace and the Borough race from Chatto Creek.
2. Town race leaves Borough race.
3. Town race cuts across the Flat.
4. Former Town race now used only to irrigate Park.
5. Recreation Ground (now Pioneer Park).
6. Race from first Borough reservoir (Halpine's Dam).

were traced to the water of the race. The main purpose of running water down the street water tables was to flush away domestic drainage and to provide water for fire fighting. Nevertheless, there is no doubt that many people, especially those living some distance out on the Flat where water carried from the river was very expensive, used the Town race as their only domestic supply.

Reynolds' Proposal
As soon as the Molyneux Hydraulic affair was settled Mayor Kelman asked Simmonds, who was still on the council and seemed to be regarded as the specialist on water schemes, to draw up plans for a piped water supply. But Simmonds, enthusiastic and capable as he was, knew that an engineer's oversight of a scheme would be required if money were to be borrowed from Government. The field of fresh engineers was getting limited now but finally Leslie H. Reynolds of Dunedin was asked to draw up plans based on utilising the Chatto Creek race.

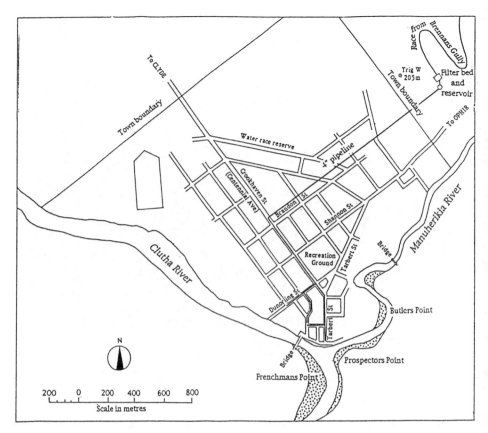

Figure 15. 3. The scheme proposed by Dunedin engineer, Reynolds, at James Simmonds' instigation, continued the Borough race at a high level from Brennans Gully to feed a reservoir on the high terrace overlooking the town cemetery. From here water was fed into the town reticulation.

Reynolds' plan was basically similar to one of Simmonds' schemes of a year or so before, but with modifications required by the absence of the Molyneux Hydraulic Company's pipeline. The Chatto Creek race, instead of being allowed to drop down the 40 metres at Brennans Gully, would be continued at the higher level and the water would flow though a system of gravel filter beds. Then it would be stored in a reservoir of some 30,000 gallons (143 cubic metres) sited well up on the scarp of the high terrace on Alexandra's north-eastern boundary. From the reservoir, water would be fed down into a reticulation of water mains laid in the streets of the town. The Borough Council adopted Reynolds' plans in October 1898 and the familiar procedures started for raising a loan, this time of £4,500. But the Chatto Creek race was giving trouble.

A major breakaway near Chatto Creek occurred early in 1899 and the resources of the council were fully extended in the repair work.

This was followed by other breaks and these, coupled with the annual cleaning, meant that water was not available from the race for nearly a year. It was not an auspicious time to discuss a scheme which, as a first requirement needed a reliable source of water, so for most of the year little was heard about the proposed water supply.

In fact, council was having doubts about using the race at all, and in mid-year a deputation visited Lye Bow, an orchardist at Butchers Gully, to enquire whether there was any chance of his water right of two heads from Butchers Creek becoming available. Lye Bow was not supposed to understand English but the deputation judged from his demeanour and his famous grin, that he might be receptive to a firm proposal.

Figure 15. 4. Looking across the the Clutha River in the foreground to the high terrace which is the background to the town. Reynold's proposed reservoir was to be sited on this high terrace at about the middle of the photograph.

Once the race was in working order again, Reynolds' scheme was resurrected and final details of the reservoir were discussed on site with the engineer in December. A public meeting, held early in 1900, heartily endorsed the proposal and a formal poll held in April approved the borrowing of the money. The council began preparations to call tenders for the work.

James Rivers makes a Proposal

Ex-mayor James Rivers, however, had different ideas. He was convinced that he could supply the borough from his race which brought water to his sluicing claim at Tucker Hill, just across the Manuherikia River from Alexandra. He lobbied councillors during the latter part of 1899 and then in early 1900 he 'went public' with a letter[1] to the *Dunstan Times* in which he pointed out that the feasibility of his scheme had been checked out and strongly recommended by

157

Dunedin civil engineers. He was of the opinion that if the citizens wanted a pure water supply they would be much better off spending the £4,500 on his scheme and leave the pollution-prone water of the Chatto Creek race for irrigation and street cleansing.

However, the mayor, Henry Symes, and some councillors, were still wedded to the idea of using the Chatto Creek race, and by the middle of the year the mayor was even telling townspeople that there would be money left over from the £4,500 loan. This, he told a sports gathering, could be used to plant trees in the streets and even build a pavilion on the Recreation Ground.

Other councillors, however, had misgivings about the scheme. The Chatto Creek race had cost a great deal of money to restore after being returned by the mining company and it was still costing a lot to keep it in order. It was certainly polluted and vegetation grew in the race quickly and luxuriantly so that a great deal of cleaning was required. And then there were those continuing, expensive breaks.

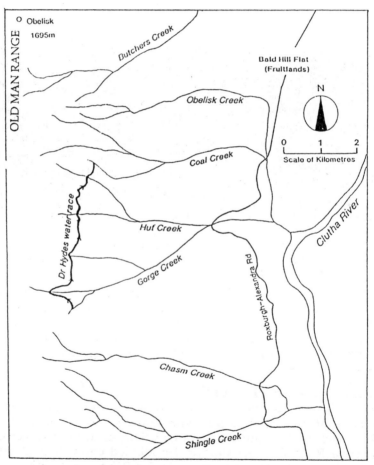

Figure 15. 5. Dr Hyde offered his race, which was high on the flanks of the Old Man Range, together with two heads of water, for £1000.

Dr Hyde's Offer

By early 1901 Mayor Symes, at least, had had a change of heart. Like most previous mayors he felt that he had to come up with his own project for supplying the town with water. At yet another public meeting,[2] called to discuss his proposal, he said that the council was not prepared to spend another pound on the Chatto Creek race. It had spent £1,000 over the last two years on maintenance and this was a substantial part of the council's revenue. It was keeping the place poor and preventing money being spent on other worthwhile developments in the town, he said.

Symes then told the meeting about an offer the council had had from Dr Hyde.[3] For £1,000 the borough could have a race and a water right for two heads from Coal Creek which drained the slopes of the Old Man Range at the back of Bald Hill Flat (Fruitlands). The mayor pointed out that it was the unanimous feeling of the council that it should secure this right.

Perhaps because the people were past caring where the water came from as long as they got a supply, or perhaps because the meeting had been loaded with supporters, a motion that this scheme be proceeded with was passed with only one dissenter. At the same meeting the council was informally given authority to borrow £7,000 to carry out the necessary work. An official poll of ratepayers to approve the greatly increased loan was to be held in a few days time.

Dr Hyde's race was high up on the slopes of the Old Man Range at an altitude of nearly 1,360 metres. It brought water from the head of Gorge Creek and discharged it into the headwaters of Coal Creek down which it flowed to be used by one or other of the mining concerns working on Bald Hill Flat. This was the race that Dr Hyde now offered, together with the water right for two heads, as a town supply.

At this distance in time the scheme seems particularly ill advised because of the difficulties associated with it. For one thing, at the altitude of the race, the ground, and any moisture in it, was frozen solid for a long period during the winter and for about six months each year the race would be under snow. Certainly, there would be ample water during the spring thaw but as the summer wore on and the snow disappeared, the supply would dwindle again just when water was in great demand in the town. Maintenance of a race so high up the range would also be extremely difficult and costly.

These were not the only problems, however. The race itself, connecting as it did the headwaters of two parallel streams, was relatively short and it stopped at Coal Creek. Presumably the water would flow down Coal Creek and be fed into a race at a lower level which would then take it the 15 kilometres or so to the town. Perhaps there was an existing race that could be used for part of the distance but there was no mention of this. It seemed that many kilometres of race would have to be cut between Coal Creek and the town. And then a storage reservoir would have to be built. Really all the borough was being offered for its £1,000 was the right to use the water.

Fortunately, the editor of the *Dunstan Times* was not as easily persuaded as those people of Alexandra who had attended the public meeting (perhaps because he lived in Clyde and could take a more distant view of the proposal[4]). The paper commented a few days after the scheme had been presented by the mayor:

> Mayor Syme's water scheme seems to have fallen flat and will find few supporters on polling day. A scheme that commends itself is lifting water from the river with two large wheels or floats. This is no doubt the best water and will eventually be the scheme by which the people of Alexandra will obtain their water.[5]

Nevertheless the official poll showed that 75 desperate citizens were for the scheme but 37 were against it which was in contrast to the almost unanimous approval that previous proposals had received.

It was pointed out by the newspaper that although people seemed to be under the impression that they had voted for Dr Hyde's scheme, this was not really so. No specific scheme had been mentioned in the poll. The only thing that they had done was given the council power to borrow money. 'It still remains,' the paper went on, 'with the ratepayers to see that a proper supply of water is procured for the Borough.'

Figure 15. 6. Dr James G. Hyde, (1856-1920) the greatly respected medical practitioner of Clyde and Superintendent of the Hospital from 1886 to 1914, was a strong investor in mining. He founded the successful Clyde Gold Dredging Company which brought a failed steam dredge from Wakatipu in 1892 and re-erected it on the Clutha River thus helping to establish the dredging industry.

After a long trudge up the mountain the following week to inspect the race for themselves, it was perhaps not surprising some councillors found that they no longer favoured the scheme. It was decided to hold a special meeting of council to discuss the matter thoroughly. This was done, but it was decided, nevertheless, by five votes to two, to take over Dr Hyde's water right under certain conditions. It was agreed, now the matter was settled, that the scheme would be pushed ahead with all speed.

Perhaps the doubts raised by the newspaper were registering with the townspeople, or perhaps Rivers's campaign was having its effect, because what was described as 'an indignation meeting' was held the following week. The hall was crowded with ratepayers and '. . . outsiders who looked forward to seeing some fun.' They were not to be disappointed. It was clear that the trend of the discussion was that the council had been too hasty in taking up Dr Hyde's offer and eventually it was resolved that a poll of ratepayers be held. If the majority were against it then the council would drop the matter.

It was then that the Mayor Symes dropped a bombshell by revealing the deed and documents had already been signed and the borough was now liable to Dr Hyde for £1,000. As the newspaper reporter said 'Tis a pretty kettle of fish anyhow, and it strikes me, we have not seen the end of it.' How right he was!

At the next council meeting:

> The proceedings were a wee bit warm at times and various compliments were passed about each other and on no account were they a happy family on that evening.[6]

The motion accepting Dr Hyde's offer was rescinded but we are not told whether the council paid out the £1,000 or, what is more likely,

Figure 15. 7. Henry Symes was the Town Clerk from 1893 until 1899. He served as Mayor 1900-1901 during the fiasco of the Dr Hyde water race affair.

Dr Hyde let the citizens off the hook.

This was the last meeting before the annual election for mayor and council and, of course, the water supply was the main issue. A 'Progressive Party' announced that it intended to contest the mayoralty with the object of supporting the Rivers scheme. Its candidate would be, guess who?—James Rivers. Furthermore the party let it be known that it intended to make sure that all nine councillors elected were in favour of Mr Rivers's water scheme and that they would get on and bring it into existence within the twelve month term of their office.

Rivers and the incumbent, Symes, tied in the mayoral contest and, following an old custom, the returning officer gave his casting vote to the sitting member. So Rivers missed out. Four new councillors were elected most of whom were supporters of the Rivers scheme.

Not surprisingly the new council was not a happy bunch and there were fights and squabbles which reached a climax at the July meeting when, at the close of business, the mayor, Henry Symes, announced his resignation. Councillors asked him to stay, as protocol demanded, but he 'could not see his way clear to fall in with their wishes' and at an extraordinary meeting held shortly afterwards, James Kelman, the former mayor, was elected.

Hay's Report

Council called in the services of Robert Hay, a prominent civil engineer of Dunedin, to assess all the proposed water schemes. In his preliminary report delivered at the August meeting he condemned, for various reasons, all of the proposals brought forward except the Rivers scheme.

It turned out that Rivers had firmed up his offer. He would supply the borough with half a head of water from his race for £1,250 with a further supply of another half head if necessary for another £100. Councillors gasped when they heard the price, especially when they realised it was unlikely that the supply would be constant over the winter months. They left the meeting with the distinct feeling the quantity of water would have to be increased and the price decreased if they were going to do business with Mr Rivers.

Rivers came back with a different deal. This time he offered one head of water for £1,200. And if council would come up with an extra £800 he would rebuild a large dam in Speargrass Creek that had been destroyed by a flood. He would make it much larger than before and the extra storage would make doubly sure that the borough would receive its head of water all the year round. The councillors were hesitant, but then, when they considered the money spent each year on the Chatto Creek race and the fact that under this arrangement Rivers was going to maintain the race and dams at no cost whatever to the borough, the deal began to look better.

Negotiations led to agreements that the £800 for the dam would be paid in instalments and the whole deal would be dependent on a successful application by council for loan money. In the end, all councillors, except one, gave their approval.

Once again the mayor called a public meeting and explained to a packed Town Hall the various proposals that had been considered and he read the engineer's report. All of the councillors spoke and all but two were in favour of Rivers's scheme.

A by-election in early January 1902 brought about by a councillor resigning, became, not so much a vote for the candidates standing, as a vote for or against the Rivers water scheme. Lewis Anderson, a supporter, was elected.

At the official poll of ratepayers held on 11 March to authorise the borrowing of £7,000, 106 voted for and only 10 against the proposal. Council now had a mandate to push ahead with the Rivers scheme with all speed.

NOTES

1. 23 March 1900 .
2. *Dunstan Times* 26 February 1901.
3. Dr James G. Hyde, the greatly respected medical practitioner of Clyde and Superintendent of the Hospital from 1886 to 1914, was a strong investor in mining. Amongst other ventures was the Dunstan Gold Dredging Company which brought a failed steam dredge from Wakatipu in 1892 and re-erected it on the Clutha River thus helping to establish the dredging industry. He was the principal shareholder in the Clyde Gold Dredging Company whose *Moa* dredges were very successful.
4. Nor, as far as is known, did he have mining interests on the slopes of the Old Man Range as did Mayor Henry Symes and his brother, Robert.
5. *Dunstan Times* 26 February 1901.
6. *Dunstan Times* 9 April 1901.

16.
RIVERS'S
"WRETCHED" SCHEME

The view from Observation Point, high on the ridge overlooking
Alexandra from the east, is one of the finest in New Zealand. It
embraces the whole of the Manuherikia Valley from the Old Man
Range in the south-west through the Dunstan Mountains in the north
to the Hawkdun Mountains in the far north-east, with glimpses of the
Remarkables and the Pisa Range in between. Immediately below,

Figure 16. 1. The front ridge of the Knobby Range forms a backdrop to
Alexandra which is just out of the photograph to the right. Along the
foot of the ridge lie the Tucker Hill diggings and the steep road to
Little Valley is prominent on the right. In the middle ground the
Manuherikia River is hidden by willows.

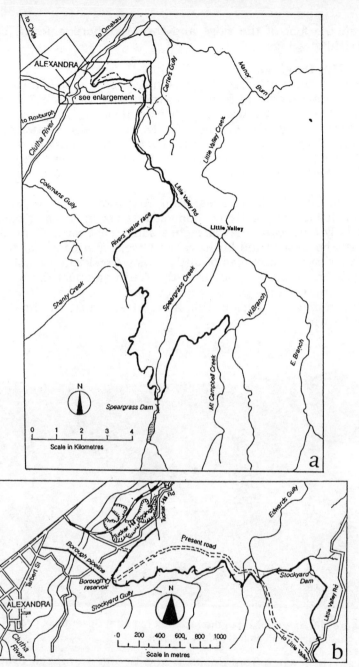

Figure 16. 2. (a): The water race from Speargrass Creek to Tucker Hill diggings was built with prodigious effort by Thos Jackson and George Campbell during three years 1891-1894. It was taken over by James Rivers in 1896. He built the dam in Speargrass Creek in 1902-1903.

   (b): The final stretch of race with Stockyard Dam, the Borough Reservoir and Tucker Hill diggings.

between the foot of the ridge and the Manuherikia River, lie the old Tucker Hill diggings.[1]

Tucker Hill Diggings

In the early days of these diggings no water was available and some keen miners carried sackfuls of particularly rich 'dirt' down to the Manuherikia River for washing. It was obvious, however, that, if the ground were to be worked successfully, an adequate water supply had to be provided on the site. But where was a stream which could provide water at a sufficient height to allow efficient sluicing of the gravels? The miners' answer lay in the hills to the south, beyond Little Valley.

Little Valley, 12 kilometres from Alexandra, is now an oasis of irrigated fields and scattered homesteads set in a small basin in the rocky, hilly landscape that stretches south-eastwards from Alexandra. Through the basin runs Little Valley Creek, a substantial tributary of the Manor Burn. Branches of Little Valley Creek such as Mt Campbell and Speargrass Creeks rise far to the south amongst the rolling ridges and swampy uplands of the Knobby Range. It was to these streams that the miners of Tucker Hill had early turned in their desperate search for water.

Figure 16. 3. A remnant of the race that ran from Speargrass Creek Dam to Tucker Hill as it is today.

It was 1891 when Tom Jackson and George Campbell first began to repair an old race that Coleman had used to take water from Speargrass Creek to Butchers Point. It took them three years to extend it, through some of the most difficult country imaginable, to the crest of the ridge overlooking their claim at Tucker Hill. In spite of all this effort Jackson and party were disappointed to find that they had only enough to water allow them to sluice for seven months of the year. Nevertheless, they were sufficiently encouraged by the amount of gold they won in that time to use the off-season to build an eight metre-high dam in Speargrass Creek. Another small storage dam, Stockyard Dam, was built in a narrow part of a dry, rocky gully, known to the miners as 'Edwards Gully,' some three kilometres east of Alexandra.

Tucker Hill Sluicing Company

However, the fact that they were working on borrowed money finally compelled Jackson and Campbell to give up and the claim, race, dams and water rights were sold in 1896 to James Rivers, the mortgagee.

In view of the controversy that arose later, it is interesting to note the information in the advertisement for the sale.[2] With the race went a prior water right of two heads from Speargrass Creek together with another water right of eight heads from Mt Campbell Creek. This latter water right was a second right and had not been utilised by Jackson and Campbell.

Rivers took into partnership John Gartley and, calling themselves the 'Tucker Hill Sluicing Company,' they started sluicing with George

Figure 16. 4. Jackson and Campbell built the small Stockyard Dam in Edwards Gully near the Little Valley road. It later provided storage for the Alexandra water supply.

Campbell as mine manager. But they, too, soon found that shortage of water was the great constraint in developing the mine. So early in the New Year of 1898 Rivers and Gartley began to construct a 10-kilometre race to bring the unused water from Mt Campbell Creek into the Tucker Hill race. When this was completed, and a pipeline constructed to the top of the ridge overlooking the diggings, they were able to sluice

167

IMPORTANT AUCTION SALE

OF

**VALUABLE MINING PRO-
PERTIES**

MANORBURN AND TUCKER HILL,
ALEXANDRA.

Under powers of Sale conferred by
Mortgage; Further Charges; and
by Consent.

At Ryan's Hotel, Alexandra,
on
TUESDAY, MAY 19TH, 1896.
At 2 p.m.

The under-mentioned Valuable
Properties will be offered by Public
Auction, in one lot—

(1) Head Water Race, 19 miles
in length (including extension), commencing at Swamp
near right hand branch of
Manorburn (also called Speargrass Creek), and terminating
at Butcher's Point, with extension to Tucker Hill. Lic-
ense, last renewal, No. 7584,
dated 17th December, 1895 ;
Two heads.—This is the first
right from Speargrass Creek.

(2) Right from Mt. Campbell (or
Gibraltar) Creek, 8 heads ; a
Second Right.

(3) Special Claim No. 153/94A,
dated 19th March, 1894, of
section 1, block VI, Cairnhill
District, containing 11ac, 2r
5pls.

(4) Dam of 20 acres, Speargrass
Flat, certificate 35383, 11th
March, 1892. The area of
Reservoir is nearly three-
quarters of a mile long, and
embankment is 2¼ chains long,
25ft high, and 70ft at base.

(5) 600ft of iron piping, and all
plant on said claim—well-con-
structed tail-race and all other
rights and easements occupied
or enjoyed along with said
properties.

Intending purchasers are invited
to inspect the claim and properties,
and may apply to

JACKSON & CAMPBELL,
On the Claim.
Or to
MR R. GILKISON,
Solicitor, Clyde.

Figure 16. 5. The advertisement in the *Dunstan Times* of 15 May 1896 for
the auction sale of Jackson and Campbell mining property, sets out
clearly the status of the water rights.

successfully at Tucker Hill with the enhanced water supply. However, operations came to a standstill early in 1902 when a flood carried away the dam in Speargrass Creek.

Speargrass Dam
Rivers had apparently never been very happy about the condition of the dam which he had acquired in Speargrass Creek. Within three weeks of his purchase he was talking about building a new dam just downstream from the existing one. He even went as far as preparing plans for a dam, with a reservoir covering 100 acres of Speargrass Flat, but they were not approved by the County Engineer. It wasn't until the old dam was destroyed in 1902, and he got £800 from the

Figure 16. 6. The Speargrass Creek Dam at Speargrass Flat, built by James Rivers in 1902-3, was a large engineering undertaking. Here, construction is in progress.

Alexandra Borough Council towards the cost of a new one, that there was action.

Leslie Reynolds, an engineer from Dunedin, designed the new dam which was completed in March 1903. It was quite a massive undertaking. The wall, built of local schist rock, towered 17 metres above the foundations and the reservoir stretched upstream for nearly two kilometres.

The Agreement
Alexandra Borough Council, desperate for a reliable source of water for the town, had in August 1902, finally entered into a legal agreement with James Rivers. He demanded a high price for his water but the

Figure 16. 7. The Speargrass Creek dam and a small portion of the reservoir as it is today. It is now used for water storage for irrigation in Little Valley.

council drove a hard bargain too. Rivers had to agree that, in return for £1,200, the council would have a tenth share in his enterprise—including his races, dams and, most important, his 10 heads of water. To make certain, the agreement stipulated one head of water, suitable for domestic use, had to be supplied at all times.

It was agreed to pay Rivers, in instalments, the additional £800 to enable him to build the new dam in Speargrass Creek. He also had to maintain the dams and races at his expense. But the whole agreement was to be dependent on the council's success in obtaining a £7,000 loan from Government.

The fact that the four fifths of Rivers's water was from an inferior right seems to have been overlooked by the council in these negotiations. Did the borough solicitor not check the records before the agreement was signed? Or did the sense of relief that the borough was at last to get a water supply over-ride this simple precaution?

The council, secure in the knowledge it now had a reliable supply of water, proceeded to raise the waterworks loan to carry out the comprehensive scheme designed by their consultant engineer, Robert Hay of Dunedin. The loan was to cover not only the cost of buying into the Rivers water holdings but also the reticulation of the town with water mains, and the construction of a reservoir.

The Tank on the Hill

A contract was let to a Mr O'Rourke and he arrived in town in mid-January 1903 with a large staff of workmen to build the reservoir high on the ridge overlooking the town. It would be only a few metres away from Rivers's water race at the point where it crossed the ridge and entered the pipeline. A hole was blasted out of the solid rock and then

170

lined with concrete. It was 30 metres long, 10 metres wide and more than 3 metres deep, with a capacity of nearly 200,000 gallons (900 cubic metres). There was a metre-high partition across the width which divided the structure into two compartments. Water from the race entered the first compartment where any debris such as sand or gravel settled. The clear water passed over the partition into the second compartment and into the pipeline that led out of this compartment by way of a small valve-box. There was an overflow, a pipe for draining off sludge and various control valves.[3]

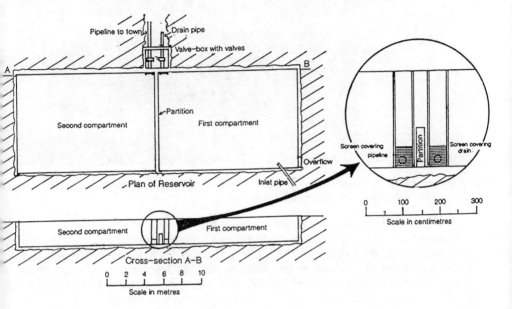

Figure 16. 8. Plan of the town reservoir.

Another contract was let to McKechnie and Fleming to lay pipes to connect the reservoir with the town mains. From the control box at the reservoir, a line of pipes led down the precipitous slope and crossed the Manuherikia River on a low level bridge which was supported by a wire rope[4] slung across the gorge. This crossing was about midway between the Shaky Bridge and the railway bridge which was by then under construction. The pipeline from the reservoir then found its way through private property until it joined the mains already being laid in Tarbert Street.

Pipe Laying in the Streets
Messrs A. & T. Burt of Dunedin won the contract for the supply of pipes for the reticulation of the town. The same firm also gained the contract for carting the pipes from Ida Valley, the railhead at the time, and for laying them in the streets.

Pipe laying began in June 1903 and by the time severe frosts caused suspension of the work in August, all of the 6 inch (150 mm) mains in Tarbert Street and the greater part of the 4 inch (100 mm) mains in

Figure 16. 9. The reservoir was blasted from solid rock and stands high on the ridge overlooking the town.

Crookhaven Street (Centennial Avenue) had been laid.

Meanwhile the big dam at Speargrass Creek was filling and Rivers had men busy cleaning out the race to Tucker Hill. Early in September he began sluicing at his claim with a full and satisfactory supply of water.[5] Unfortunately water could not yet be fed into the borough water mains as the reservoir still had to have its interior plastered. By early October 1903 the mains laying in the town was completed and the pipes ready for testing.

Council was being badgered to extend the mains system and eventually decided to call tenders for the supply of one mile of 1-1/2 inch (36 mm) pipe to be used to serve the outlying parts of the town. The Central Otago Foundry supplied the pipe.[6]

Water at Last

The great day arrived at last and the mayor decreed a half-holiday for Friday, 13 November 1903 to celebrate the opening of the waterworks. Council voted £15 for a picnic in the Recreation Reserve in the afternoon and a social in the town hall in the evening. Although the afternoon was uncharacteristically wet, it did not stop a crowd turning up to the ceremony, which consisted of the expected speech making and then the turning on of the water by the mayor's daughter, Miss Jessie Kelman.

At last Alexandra had a supply of piped, high-pressure water even though the scheme had, in the end, cost the very large sum of nearly £8,000 [7] After a lot of correspondence, the council managed to extract £600 subsidy from the Mines Department.

There was no doubt about the high pressure obtained in the town

172

from the nearly 120 metre hydraulic head of the new supply. The newly formed Volunteer Fire Brigade had the utmost difficulty controlling their fire hoses and tap washers were worn out in only a short time. But these were minor difficulties and did nothing to stop the town revelling in its new amenity. What a joy it was to have water on tap over the sink instead of having to carry in every drop from the barrel at the back door. Gone at last were the clattering water carts with their inconvenience and expense.

Trouble Ahead
However, even before the opening there were ominous signs of trouble ahead. O'Rourke, the contractor for the reservoir, required water on the site, presumably to mix concrete, and the Borough Council had undertaken to supply it as part of the agreement with Rivers. It was not long before O'Rourke was complaining he was not getting water when he wanted it and, in fact, he went so far as to demand the council pay his expenses for four days when he could not work through lack of water. The first of many, many letters went out from the council office to James Rivers, pointing out that under the terms of the agreement he had to supply water and if he didn't the council would be forced to take action.

Figure 16. 10. James Rivers (1837-1910). Pioneer storekeeper, mining investor, local body politician, racehorse owner, churchman, man of ideas. For years nothing happened in Alexandra without Jimmy Rivers having a hand in it. He was a Borough Councillor almost continuously from 1871 until 1896 and twice served as Mayor.

There is no doubt that the race was most difficult to maintain and there were many breaks and washouts, so that interruptions to the supply were not unexpected and some, perhaps, unavoidable, but others were deliberate.

Less than a month after the opening of waterworks, Rivers notified council that he was going to turn off the water so he could clean out the Stockyard Dam, and warned that his intention was to flush the silt and other debris from the dam down the race to seal any leaks. This was a fairly standard practice and was the cheapest and easiest way to seal leaks in a new race or after the winter frosts had opened up cracks. But it meant the race water would be unfit for use for some time.

Council replied[8] reminding Rivers the agreement stipulated he must supply one head of water, fit for domestic use, at *all* times so therefore he must not turn off or pollute the town supply.

In spite of this warning Rivers went ahead and turned the water off for most of two days. A great deal of slime and 'offensive matter' (probably mainly rabbit and sheep droppings) from the Stockyard Dam ended up in the borough reservoir and rendered the water unfit for consumption for three days.

Figure 16. 11. Stone walls of the old Speargrass Dam —Tucker Hill water race lie high above the road to Little Valley

Borough Council v Rivers

The council took Rivers to the Warden's Court for damages and for an injunction to prevent such things happening in the future. During a three-day hearing in March 1904 it was suggested that Rivers should have cut a short race to by-pass the Stockyard Dam while it was being cleaned out. This would have allowed an uninterrupted supply of clean water to the borough reservoir. The Court held that there had been a breach of contract, but as no actual damage had been proved, the damages asked for and awarded were purely nominal—£2. The request for an injunction failed.

Borough Council v Rivers again

By mid-June 1904, the parties were back in court. Council was again accusing Rivers of failing to continuously supply a head of water fit for domestic use. The 'Burgesses had suffered great loss and inconvenience' and damages of £200 were claimed and again an injunction to restrain Rivers from further failure to supply was asked for.

Much evidence was given by experienced people that they had inspected the races at various times. There were as many as 10 heads of water seen flowing in Mt Campbell Creek on one occasion, but none was going into the race. Much water was seen leaking from the long race between Speargrass Creek Dam and Stockyard Dam. Evidence was given of loss suffered in the town by the foundry, butcher's shop and livery stable through lack of water. Water had to be carted from the river and was charged for at as much as 2s. 6d. a barrel.

Then the Mining Registrar dropped a bombshell. He produced the titles (which, of course, were public documents and had been available for inspection all along) for the various water races and pointed out that Robert Campbell and Sons, owners of Galloway station, had a

Figure 16. 12. The race from Speargrass dam approaching the Borough reservoir. Towards the left the race has been buried by debris from road construction.

prior right to the water of Mt Campbell Creek. They could take four heads of water from 1 December to the following 31 May in each year for irrigation and wool washing.

Furthermore there was in existence an Order dating from 1881 that obliged Rivers to allow two heads of water to flow down Speargrass Creek 'for general use.' This virtually meant Campbell and Sons had a prior right to the water of this creek also. So during the driest part of the year Rivers (and the borough) could only have the water, if any, left over after Campbell and Sons had taken their share. There was insufficient water in the creeks to supply all of these demands, especially during the particularly dry season that was being experienced.

The warden pointed out that the agreement between the Borough Council and Rivers was for one tenth of the water that Rivers had, and when it was revealed that Rivers was entitled to much less than was thought, the council could only be entitled to a tenth of what he actually had. It was no use demanding the one head agreed to if it simply was not available.

Then there was an interesting argument as to whether the council could claim damages for losses sustained by individual citizens and the ruling was that, generally, it could not. Only loss suffered as a corporate body, such as lack of water for street cleaning, could be taken into account and the warden awarded damages of £10 for this.

The council also got an Order against Rivers restraining him, during the period when Campbell & Sons could not take water, from allowing any water to go past the intake in Mt Campbell Creek until at least four heads had been turned into the race. The whole episode cost Rivers £22 17s. 6d.[9]

Meanwhile Rivers was given permission to clean out the dam again but only if he agreed to run the sludge down Edwards Gully and not into the race feeding the town reservoir.

The Viewing
The warden made two attempts to visit Rivers's races and dams but was beaten by bad weather and lack of time. However, he finally managed the journey on 7 February 1905. It must have been quite an occasion. Rivers provided a four-horse conveyance, and the party, which consisted of the warden and solicitors, the mayor and councillors and Rivers and some of his employees, was transported to Little Valley. From there the warden, Rivers and some others rode on horseback to the intake of the race in Mt Campbell Creek and then followed the race round to Speargrass Dam where they met up with the remainder of the party.

Rivers, ever the politician, could not let the opportunity pass without making a speech. He addressed the party, no doubt from some vantage point, such as from the top of a rock or from the conveyance. As the council was apparently not satisfied with what he had done in the way of carrying out his part of the agreement, he said, he saw three options. First, he was prepared to refund the money it had paid him and so buy out council's interest in the property. A second option was for him to transfer to council his nine-tenths interest in the Mt Campbell race enabling it to connect this race into the Speargrass Creek Dam if they wished (this race joined the Tucker Hill race below the dam). One of the conditions of this deal would be that council completed the dam to a height of 63 ft (20 m)—the height granted under the original licence. A third option was to sell all his interest in the property to the council.

To complete the misery of the party they were caught in a sudden downpour on the ride home and completed the journey back to Alexandra in heavy rain.

The Borough Council was not satisfied. It had spent a vast sum of borrowed money, and reduced the borough to poverty, to provide water and still there was no reliable supply. So council adopted the view that a contract is a contract and, come what may, it was entitled to a head of water and if it didn't get it then it was entitled to damages. The question revolved around whether there were limitations to the contract.

Borough Council v Rivers yet again

It was decided to test the matter in the Supreme Court. To set the scene the council sued Rivers in the Warden's Court in March 1905 for the nice round sum of £1,000 damages for failure to supply water. It was agreed the points of law would be referred to the Supreme Court and, after they had been resolved, the warden would give his judgement.

Figure 16. 13. Justice Joshua S. Williams was the highly respected judge of the Supreme Court who heard the dispute between James Rivers and the Alexandra Borough Council over the non-supply of water.

177

The matter was argued before Mr Justice Williams in the Dunedin Supreme Court on 29 September 1905. A number of questions were put to the Court:

(1) Was the contract absolute or could Rivers be relieved from his undertaking by reason of drought or other causes?

(2) Could Rivers be forced to increase water storage by increasing the height of the Speargrass Creek Dam to ensure that the borough got its one head of water?

(3) What was the amount of damage sustained by the borough through Rivers's failure to honour his contract?

(4) What was the amount of damage sustained by individual citizens?

His Honour didn't take too long to sort things out. He was already familiar with the evidence, so was spared the dreary recital of waterless days, leaking races and empty reservoirs. He was mainly interested in points of law and these, it seemed, were quite clear to him. On the first question he said the contract was about supply of water and if there was no water the contract could not operate. If the water failed through natural causes such as drought then Rivers was not bound to supply it. The agreement also set out what Rivers had to do in the way of providing storage and he had done this, so he was under no obligation to raise Speargrass Creek dam. So far as damages were concerned His Honour repeated the decision already given by the warden. The Borough Council was not a trustee for individual citizens therefore could not claim damages on behalf of individuals. The contract was with the corporation not with individuals.

Chatto Creek race Scheme again

Meanwhile the supply of water had become so bad that the council was forced to feed water from the Chatto Creek race into the town's water mains. An automatic pressure valve was installed so water from the Chatto Creek race could only enter the mains when the pressure in the mains fell below a certain point—in other words when the water from Tucker Hill was off. Similarly when the high pressure water entered the mains again the valve closed and prevented mains water blowing out into the race. This arrangement was accepted by townspeople in the knowledge that the water was polluted and that it emerged from the taps with very little pressure. Still, it was better than buying barrels of water.

The final part of the legal saga was played out in the Warden's Court in July 1906 when the warden gave his judgement after taking into account the Supreme Court ruling. He found that, apart from the failure of the water supply through drought, Rivers could have done more to ensure whatever water was available did reach the borough tank, so the council was entitled to judgement. However, no damages could be awarded for losses suffered by individual citizens nor could the expense that the council had been put to in piping the Chatto Creek race into the borough pipes, be allowed. Of the £1,000 claimed for damages, only £2 were awarded as minimal damages. Costs of £11 5s. were awarded against Rivers. Always a trier, Rivers wrote to council asking that it refund his costs!

Whatever satisfaction the parties may have received from these repeated litigations, they did nothing to produce more water. It was abundantly clear that the water supply would never be really satisfactory. There simply wasn't sufficient water in the streams during a dry season to supply both the borough and Rivers's gold mine, although, according to Rivers, he engaged in sluicing only when Speargrass Creek Dam was full. Furthermore, the upkeep of the long and torturous race through steep and rocky terrain was going to be a constant problem. But the basic problem was the lack of water in the catchments, apart from the time of the spring thaw.

The summer and autumn of 1907 were particularly dry months and brought matters to a head. There was not sufficient water to flush the gutters in the main street. As a result there were complaints in the correspondence columns of the *Alexandra Herald* about the deplorable condition of the main street and the stench from household drains that discharged into the water tables. Many dredges were laid up because of low water levels and the newspapers were full of stories of crop failures.

It was obvious that the town's water supply was in a precarious position, so the council began to look around once more for yet another supply. When this search was brought to a successful conclusion, Rivers's water was finally turned off, without any regrets, in early June 1909.

Rivers's Motives

It is interesting to speculate as to why Rivers was so keen for the Borough Council to accept water from his race for the town supply. He lobbied councillors, wrote letters to the paper and finally stood again for the mayoralty in a clear attempt to clinch the matter.

Even though James Rivers was a public-spirited man—as evidenced by his many terms as mayor and long years as a borough councillor, it is most unlikely that he offered his water in a spirit of public benefaction. The high price he demanded of the council pointed to a straight business deal and the fact he accepted, in return, a tough agreement, which he must have known would be most difficult to keep, supports this view.

It is perhaps important to note that Rivers, at the time he made his offer to the Borough Council, had practically worked out the Tucker Hill diggings and was anxious to move to 'Richmond Hill,' a couple of kilometres further up the valley, where he believed there was rich gold. But his experience at Tucker Hill showed that he needed a more adequate and reliable supply of water if this new claim were to be successful. This could be provided by a large dam in Speargrass Creek which, he believed, would give him more than adequate water for his purposes. But such a dam would be expensive. The need for money to build the dam, enlarge the long race, build a second small dam in Edwards Gully and generally develop his new claim was perhaps the motivation behind his proposal to share his water with the borough.

Rivers's plans, almost certainly assisted by the desperate straits in which the borough found itself over water, came to fruition. But things began to go wrong almost immediately. There simply was not enough water to supply the borough and his own needs and he was stuck with an agreement that gave the borough priority. It is difficult to believe that Rivers was ignorant of the fact that he did not have prior rights to the water of Mt Campbell and Speargrass Creeks, and it is equally difficult to believe that the council did not check his water rights before joining in the scheme. But what really beat them was the old Central Otago problem of inadequate water. Only during the few short months of the spring thaw was there sufficient water for everyone.

There may well have been political and personality overtones to the whole matter that are not obvious at this distance in time. The lobbying, the forming of a party to push Rivers as a candidate for mayor, the resignation of Mayor Symes, are all indicative of activities behind the scenes. And then we have the forthright remarks of 'Citizen' in a letter to the *Alexandra Herald* in 1907:

> It is well known the ratepayers cannot afford to pay higher rates, and three shillings in the pound with high valuations is a higher rate of taxation than is to be found anywhere in New Zealand. Now how was this state of affairs brought about? Why, from the time that wretched water scheme of Rivers was entered into the serious trouble began. One cannot help wondering how a clever, shrewd man like the late James Kelman (peace to his ashes) allowed himself to be talked into that water scheme by a lot of toadies or sycophants boasting of a knowledge they never possessed.[10]

Few of us today would be happy about paying 15% of our property valuation in rates. There is little doubt that the large loan taken out to finance this waterworks scheme was a great imposition on the small number of ratepayers called upon to meet the charges. The heavy loan commitments retarded borough development for years to come.

Aftermath
The dismantling of the pipeline from the borough reservoir and the opening of a new water supply from Butcher's Creek was not the end of the Rivers scheme by any means. Rivers apparently thought it was, and immediately the pipes were lifted, he shut off the water to the borough reservoir at the Stockyard Dam. In spite of demands and threats from the council, he refused to turn it on again. Council took the view that it still owned its one tenth share of the water and, as one councillor expressed it, 'water is money.' Once more council prepared to take Rivers to court but then he fell ill and proceedings were delayed until he recovered, but it was not to be. James Rivers died in January 1910 and his interests in mining claims, the Tucker Hill races, dams and water rights passed to his family.

Borough Council v Rivers — the final round
The Rivers family apparently upheld the views of their late father so far as the borough's rights were concerned because in October 1910 the Borough Council began proceedings against Ada Mary Rivers, Mary Christina Rivers and Edith Ann Rivers. The women (a daughter and two daughters-in-law of James Rivers) were joint owners of the

'Middlesex' claim—a mine on the eastern side of the Manor Burn still worked by Rivers' manager, George Campbell. They had also inherited James Rivers's share of the Mt Campbell Creek water rights and the dams and races.

So in March 1911 we find the matter in the Supreme Court in Dunedin with the Corporation of Alexandra asking for a resolution of the position, damages and an injunction to prevent the Rivers family from continuing to deprive the borough of what it saw as its rightful share of the water. The family took the view that as the agreement concerned a supply of water for the borough, once the borough had taken away the connecting pipeline from the reservoir the contract was finished.

His Honour ruled, however, that James Rivers and the Corporation were a mining partnership and neither Rivers, nor his heirs, could deprive the borough of its share of the water no matter what it wanted to do with it.[11]

Later in the year the Secretary of the Middlesex Sluicing Co, George Rivers (a son of James) suggested selling Rivers's and the borough's water interests. Council's reaction, reinforced no doubt by the results of the recent court case, was, basically, 'you do as you wish with your interests but please remember that council owns one head of water and that must be available at all times.'

Then it was found that George Rivers had leased all of the water to miners at Doctors Point, about eight kilometres down the river from Alexandra. There were mutterings around the council table about the man having no authority to lease the council portion of the water to anyone without council's permission.

As a result of the Supreme Court judgement, Rivers's Estate owed council £90 in damages and costs, but George Rivers pointed out that the estate had no money at all. He suggested that the council take control of the whole Tucker Hill race and lease the water to recoup the money owing. In the end a new agreement was drawn up, with the Rivers group virtually handing the race and water rights over to the council. Almost immediately the council leased the water to a party who were mining at Doctors Point.

In mid-1914 the solicitor, W. A. Bodkin, approached council on behalf of one George Neill, offering to buy the borough's share in the Little Valley water for £500. Some councillors were reluctant to sell but when it was pointed out it would cost at least £1,500 to repair the race to bring water back to the old borough reservoir, minds were changed. And, even if they did bring the water back, what were they going to do with it? It was finally agreed to sell and when the deal was signed in November 1914 Council thought that that was the end of the Rivers scheme as far as the borough was concerned.[12]

It was not quite the end of the matter, however, as Council still had control of the remainder of Rivers's water which by now was leased to the Doctors Point Mining Company. Midway through 1916 this company ceased operations and the £40 still owing in damages and rent had to be written off.[13]

A year or so later Little Valley was opened up to settlement with irrigation water supplied by Mt Campbell Creek and Speargrass Dam. George Rivers took up a farm there and no doubt derived much more profit from the water than did his father.

For those who know where to look, the remains of the Stockyard Dam and fragments of the race that connected that dam to the borough reservoir can still be found. But the most obvious relic is the large concrete reservoir, its smooth walls now well splattered with graffiti which, lying only a few metres off the much-travelled road to Observation Point, is an object of curiosity to tourists and locals alike. Looking out over the town as it does, it serves as a memorial to the most expensive blunder the town ever made.

NOTES

1. A local story is that the name was derived from the fact that miners could always count on obtaining enough gold from these diggings to provide 'tucker.'
2. *Dunstan Times*, 15 May 1896.
3. See diagram. There was a small concrete valve box about 2 m by 1 m midway along the outside length of the reservoir. Two pipes led through the wall of the reservoir, one from each compartment, close to the partition near the floor. Their outlets were covered by a screen, probably of copper gauze, held in place by wooden guides. so that the screen could be pulled up for cleaning. The bolts which held these guides are still embedded in the concrete wall. When the valve opened, the accumulated debris in the first compartment would be sluiced down the hillside. The pipe from the second compartment would also have a valve in the valve box to control the water flow into the pipeline leading down the steep hill towards the town.
4. *Dunstan Times*, 15 May 1896. This bridge gave trouble. The wind, changes of pressure in the pipeline, and perhaps temperature, caused a great deal of movement which resulted in major leaks in the pipeline crossing the bridge. Attempts were made in 1905 to stabilise the bridge by guy wires. The wire rope, from which the bridge was suspended, remained long after the bridge had disappeared. It was a favourite swing for children during the 1930s and 40s and at least one fell from it but survived. It was finally removed in the mid 1950s during the clearing of the river banks before Lake Roxburgh was filled.
5. *Alexandra Herald*, 10 September 1903.
6. More than 50 years later the Alexandra Volunteer Fire brigade wasted valuable time during a fire at the Alexandra Primary School trying to get water from a fire hydrant in Bringans Street. Later investigation disclosed that the fire hydrant was fed by a 1-1/2 in pipe—no doubt a relic of the 1903 pipe laying.
7. According to the *Cyclopaedia of New Zealand* Vol 4 p. 710.
8. Published in *Alexandra Herald*, 21 January 1904.
9. *Alexandra Herald*, 28 July 1904.
10. *Alexandra Herald*, 10 April 1907.
11. *Alexandra Herald*, 15 March & 5 April 1911.
12. *Alexandra Herald*, 8 July; 22 July; 11 November 1914.
13. *Alexandra Herald*, 5 February 1919. Control of Rivers's share of the water had already been returned to the Rivers family.

17.

THE HAZARDOUS GORGE

It was the success of the primitive *Manuherikia* dredge that started it all. Cobbled together from bits and pieces by an enthusiastic band of local men,[1] it made use of a discarded bucket ladder from the first steam dredge, *Dunedin*, and the pontoon of the unsuccessful *Glen Rock* 'pneumatic' dredge. Powered by two paddle wheels, turned by the current of the river, this small craft ventured through the 'Gates'[2] into the fearsome gorge immediately below Alexandra.

The Gorge
At the township, the east-flowing Clutha River turns sharply towards the south and enters a narrow gorge.[3] Confined between steep, rocky walls more than 300 metres high, the river, before it was impounded by the Roxburgh Dam at the lower end, raced and swirled through the gorge at a rate of something over 16 kilometres an hour. There were several rapids, formed where large landslides had slid from the gorge walls, and there was even a spectacular waterfall, a couple of metres high, where huge slabs of rock had fallen from the cliffs above and obstructed the river. This obstacle effectively prevented any sort of vessel passing through the gorge unless in times of high flood, when the falls were overwhelmed and disappeared.

Miners had moved backwards and forwards through the gorge from the earliest times so that by the mid-1890s there were well defined, if rough, paths on both sides of the river. Although it had spectacular scenery, the gorge was an unpleasant place to live or work in. From swelteringly hot in summer, the bottom of the gorge quickly became an ice-box in winter when little sun penetrated its depths. It was a dangerous place too. Apart from the ever-present risk of falling from the narrow paths, which in places climbed high above the river, there were the floods. A moderate fresh in the river which might cause a rise of a couple of metres at Alexandra was converted into a rapid rise of eight metres in the gorge. This was the environment into which the *Manuherikia* party gingerly eased their small dredge early in 1893.

Early Dredges
Manuherikia was not the first dredge to risk the dangers of the gorge. Several primitive spoon dredges, active in the early days, apparently

had more success than the elaborate 'Pneumatic dredge' of the early 1890s which was designed to suck gold from the bottom of the river. It had failed miserably and ended up providing the pontoon for *Manuherikia*. Then there was the *Victoria* which started life as a current-wheel dredge but was converted to steam and sent into the gorge to battle with the currents and turbulence of the Island Basin. She failed because her ladder was too short to reach the gold-bearing gravels on the bed of the river and because of the difficulties of getting coal to her.

The power of the confined river was quickly demonstrated when the little *Manuherikia* was inadvertently allowed to swing broadside to the current, whereupon it immediately capsized. All the hard work and expense of building the vessel was gone in an instant. It took nearly a year before the dredge was refloated and back in operation. In spite of her limitations, the cheaply run dredge repaid her fortunate owners so handsomely that they began planning and building a large, modern steam-powered replacement. The success of the little dredge was duly noted by other interested parties and was no doubt a factor which led to the pegging out of every inch of the gorge during the frenetic dredging boom that began in the late 1890s.

Figure 17. 1. The first *Manuherikia* dredge was cobbled together from parts of several other dredges. It was a 'current-wheeler' driven by large paddle wheels turned by the river current. In spite of an accident which caused it to sink before it could begin work, the small dredge was eventually remarkably successful.

During 1899-1900 companies were formed and plans drawn up for at least eight dredges to work in the gorge. But the directors of the companies were faced with a major problem—how to supply coal to these dredges.

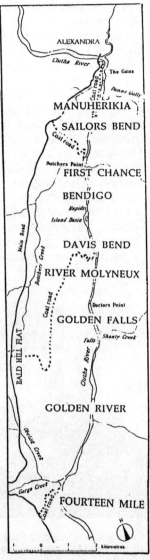

Figure 17. 2. The gorge below Alexandra and the names of dredges actually at work in 1901. Every metre of the gorge was pegged out for dredging claims during 1899 but not every company was able to put a dredge on to the river. Also shown are the 'roads' built for coaling the dredges.

Coaling the Dredges
Dredges completed over the previous 10 years, and the dozens more in

the building and planning stages, all used steam engines to drive them, and steam engines required large quantities of coal. This would have to be supplied to dredges working at the bottom of a gorge and separated from the nearest supply road by many kilometres of turbulent, swift-flowing river, complete with rapids and waterfall. And it was not just the odd bag or two of coal that was required. The dredges being planned at this time burnt a ton or more of coal each shift, which meant 40 to 60 bags had to be delivered every day. How to supply this coal at a price that would still allow the dredges to operate profitably was the problem.

Coaling the dredges on the Central Otago rivers was already a major industry. Scores of heavy wagons, each dragged by half a dozen or more horses, were constantly on the roads carting coal from newly opened coal mines to the dredges. Along most of the rivers, where the banks were gravel terraces, access to the water's edge was generally possible by rough, temporary roads which were altered and extended as the dredge changed position. The bagged coal was unloaded just upstream from the dredge and as close to the beach as possible. From here it was loaded into a coal boat. At first these boats were whale boats, dinghies or ex-sail boats, but experience showed the ideal coal boat was one with a wide beam and high, bluff bows and was not less than 6 metres long. Scores of these were built at Davis's boat yard at Alexandra.

Figure 17. 3. Scores of large wagons were constantly on the road hauling coal from mines to the dredges that required about five tons each day. This one is about to cross the Alexandra bridge during a severe hoar frost.

Dredgemen spent a lot of time in boats 'running lines'—that is, moving the mooring lines that attached the dredge to anchors on the river banks. By winding in these lines with winches on the dredge, the vessel could be moved sideways or ahead. There were generally two sidelines on each side, and one or two headlines, and all of these had frequently to be moved and re-anchored. Boat work, especially where the current was swift, was perhaps the most hazardous of all operations connected with dredging and cost many lives in the early days of the industry. And of all the boating operations, coaling the dredge was the most spectacular and the most dangerous.

Figure 17. 4. The boats used for coaling dredges were specially built, many in Davies boat-building yard in Dunorling Street, Alexandra. They tended to be broad of beam and high at the bow. This one fitted with a winch, developed by Dredgemaster Shore, designed to control the paying out of rope as the boat was backed down towards the dredge.

Almost all dredges took on coal through an opening in their starboard side, which, for those working in the gorge, was the eastern side of the dredge (dredges working in rivers always had their bow pointing upstream).If the coal had been brought to western bank of the river, as most was, a wire rope was stretched across the river from the coal landing and firmly anchored at a point downstream on the opposite bank but still upriver from the dredge. A minimum crew of three was required for the coal boat—a steersman and two men in the bow. After loading, the boat was attached by a running wire to the wire rope. The current quickly carried the heavily laden boat across the river towards the opposite shore but, just before it struck, one of the bow men leapt out with a light line attached to the end of a heavy rope coiled in the bottom of the boat. He fended the boat off the rocks, hauled the end of the rope ashore and anchored it firmly to a rock. The boat, detached from the running wire and worked back into the current, drifted slowly backwards down towards the dredge as the remaining bow man paid out the rope kept under control by a turn round the Samson post.

After unloading at the dredge, the boat was rowed to the shore on which the coal was situated and then dragged with a rope back up to the coal pile by the crew walking along the river bank path. The steersman remained in the boat to keep it clear of the banks.

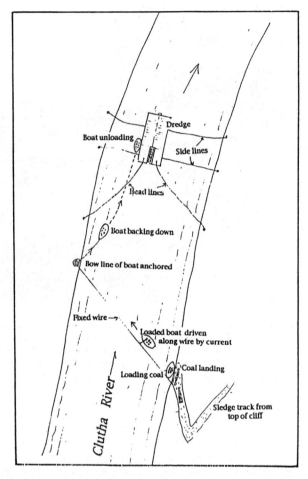

Figure 17. 5. Diagram of coaling procedure in the gorge when coal boats had to cross the river to reach their dredge. Where the dredge was some distance down river from the coal delivery point the fixed wire was dispensed with and the coal taken to the dredge by a hazardous boat journey.

It was hard, dangerous work and required experienced men. Even a minor collision with a mooring line or a floating log could upset a heavily laden boat, and once men were in the water there was little hope for them. In the early years boat crews steadfastly refused to wear life jackets, as the prevailing view was that such appurtenances were not for real men. It took years of effort on the part of inspectors, and some prosecutions, before this attitude was changed and life belts supplied and worn.

It did not take much knowledge of the gorge below Alexandra to see that extraordinary procedures would be necessary to supply coal to dredges in that isolated and dangerous place. And extraordinary procedures always cost more money, but there was no shortage of ideas.

One suggestion was that a vessel, capable of steaming at 11 knots and carrying 10 or 12 tons of coal, be used as a coal tender to supply all the dredges that were proposed for the gorge. It was said that a man and a boy could man such a boat. But, it was pointed out, their lives would not be worth much if an eddy caused the boat to sheer in the narrow parts of the gorge.[4]

A more sensible scheme suggested was to power the dredges by electricity supplied by a central generating station. In a rare show of collaboration, a meeting of the directors of four companies which had gorge dredges still in the planning stages, was held in Dunedin. It considered estimates from three well-known firms for a hydroelectric station. It would be built on the Teviot or Beaumont Streams and would supply power for a number of gorge dredges. An alternative was for a coal-fired station to be built near the coal mines at Alexandra. But preliminary estimates placed the costs of such stations beyond reach.

The scheme that was most favourably received, was for a road or tramway to be built down the western side of the gorge. There would be some difficult places but it could be done and there was every hope that the County Council would consider a subsidy—provided the dredging companies all contributed. This was where the scheme collapsed. Companies would not commit themselves to this sort of expenditure until their dredges were up and running and producing gold. So in the end it was left to each company to make its own arrangements.

How They Coped

By mid-1900 the new steam-powered dredge of the Manuherikia party, now a public company, was on its claim—the first of the modern fleet to start work in the gorge. It was fortunate that this claim, at the top end of the gorge with relatively easy access, had already proved to be a successful and sustained producer of gold. So the company was able to afford to build a road, suitable for coal wagons, from the vicinity of the Alexandra bridge down the right bank of the river for a kilometre or so. Here a landing stage was built where coal was unloaded to await the boats. With the help of a wire rope stretched across the river coaling was fairly straightforward.

Within a couple of months another dredge, the *Sailors Bend*, was completed and made ready for the hazardous trip down the gorge to her claim, which lay next downstream to that of the *Manuherikia*. Coaling this dredge was more difficult as there was no road access to the claim but an arrangement was made to use the *Manuherikia's* coal road as far as it went. From the end of the road, coal had to be boated down to the dredge.

A vivid description of this operation was given to a journalist by the

Figure 17. 6. The steam-driven second *Manuherikia* dredge replaced the earlier current-wheel model. It was the first successful steam dredge to work in the gorge and returned a fortune to its owners.

late Mr W. T. Wetherall of Naseby who was a winchman on dredges during the boom:[5]

    With four or five tons of coal aboard there is less than 6in. of freeboard as the boat is manoeuvred away from the landing stage and out into the current. The crew consists of the steersman, who is in charge; an oarsman on either side; a baler who sits in a space between the coal bags and two men in the bow. All have put on life belts. As they pull out on to the broad river the low murmuring of the river, so noticeable from the shore, dies away and the silence is eerie. There is no sensation of movement either until it is noticed how fast the rocks on the banks are flying past. Nevertheless, speed has to be increased still further by rowing in order to gain steerage way.

    Now a dredge is ahead, with its dangerous mooring lines, but the winchman sees the approaching boat and he stops the buckets and tightens the side lines so they spring clear of the water. The boat flashes past but a wave from an eddy breaks aboard and the baler is busy for a few minutes and then their own dredge appears.

    It will take the coal on its eastern side so the steersman heads over towards the western bank of the river and then, with the help of the oarsmen, swings the boat in a wide semi-circle across the river. The two bow men get ready. One stands with a coil of rope, the other has an end in his hand. "Jump" calls the steersman and the man is floundering through the shallows with the rope that he quickly ties around a pre-selected rock. The other bowman takes a turn of the rope round the Samson post as the boat is guided back out into the current and backs down the river until a line attached to the bowline of the dredge is picked up. Unloading is done a quickly as possible as the boat is probably taking water from the rough turbulence around the dredge.

An accident in October 1905, and a fortunate escape, vividly illustrated the dangers inherent in the boating operation. A boat load of coal had been brought down the gorge and was being backed down on to a dredge in the usual way, when the boat was caught in a swirl just off the bow of the dredge. The boat was swept upstream out of control and then, caught in the current, was swept back downstream. The man on shore could not hold the boat, as he had not anchored the end of the holding rope adequately. To the horror of the crew waiting on the dredge, the boat was swept under the bow of the dredge and disappeared but not before the two men in it leapt for their lives on to the dredge. The anxious crew quickly hauled them aboard. The men were wearing life belts but they would have been of little help if the men had gone under the dredge with their boat. The valuable boat appeared somewhat battered, upside down and minus its load of coal, at the stern of the dredge, and a crew set off after it in their second boat. Although they caught up with it, they could not hold the boat or bring it to the riverbank and, as they approached the falls, they were forced to give up and spend the remainder of the day slowly pulling their boat back up the river.

The long haul up the towpath was perhaps the hardest work of all. It was calculated that for every two minutes journey down the river it took an hour to pull the boat up river. The men were well paid[6] and this added to the expense of the fuel and the operation of the dredge.

Various devices and procedures were adopted to try to make coaling safer and cheaper. One example was a winch, invented by the dredgemaster of the *Alpine Consols* dredge, which took the place of the man paying out the rope, who was often pulled overboard by sudden jerks of the rope while the boat was backing down on to the dredge.

During August and September 1901, no less than four dredges were finished and making their way down to claims in the gorge. Among these was the *First Chance* whose claim lay down river from Butchers Point. To reach the claims wagons took coal across country to the edge of the gorge overlooking the mouth of Butchers Creek, where it was transferred to a horse-drawn sledge. A few bags at a time, the coal was taken down a steep zigzag track to a landing stage just upstream from the mouth of Butchers Creek. The system was very slow but worked well enough except in the winter, when coal was most in demand. Then the frozen, and sometimes snow-covered, ground made the whole operation highly dangerous. Apparently it was not uncommon for a laden sledge to get out of control and crash to the bottom of the gorge, scattering its contents far and wide. It was costly, too, as an extra 4s. a ton was charged for sledging, on top of the 8s. a ton already charged for carrying the coal from the mine to the top of the gorge.

Then someone had an idea. A wire rope was strung across the river from the top of the gorge on the western side to the terrace on the eastern side of the river at Butchers Point. Coal bags were attached to the rope and slid quickly across to the other side of the river. From the terminus of the rope a dray road was constructed along the eastern side of the river for more than a kilometre to a point where the coal could be loaded into the coal boats. The system worked well enough but was very slow and required much expensive labour. It was also costly in spilled coal.

Little wonder, then, that company directors and dredge designers cast about for alternative ways of powering dredges in the Alexandra Gorge.

Figure 17. 7. A road for coal wagons extended several kilometres down the right bank of the Clutha River from Alexandra and enabled coal to be delivered to boats and then taken to the dredges.

Electric Power

Supplying coal to the two dredges at the upper end of the gorge was hazardous and coaling the *First Chance* was expensive but still just possible financially. But what of the Fourteen-mile Beach claim? It was some 20 kilometres down the gorge from Alexandra, and with dangerous rapids and a two-metre high waterfall along the way boating coal through the long gorge was out of the question. Carting coal by wagon would mean a 20 kilometre journey over rough, hilly roads to beyond Gorge Creek to be followed by the lowering of the coal one bag at a time, down the almost vertical bluffs. The cost would be very high and was judged to be uneconomic.

The Fourteen-mile Beach Gold-dredging Company Ltd produced an elaborate and expensive solution to the question of how to power its dredge—electricity. Only once before had a dredge been run by electricity and that was the *Sandhills* dredge on the upper Shotover River. Near the Fourteen-mile Beach claim, Gorge Creek, a substantial stream which had its source in swamps on the summit of the Old Man Range, joined the Clutha River by way of a steep, rocky gorge. Water

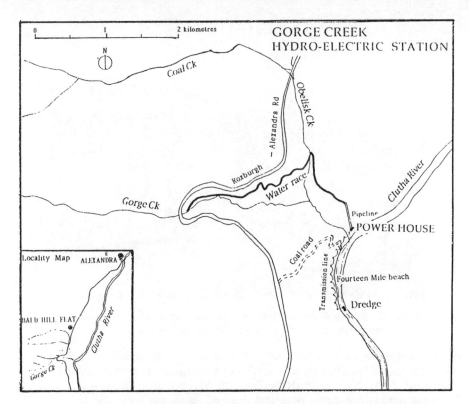

Figure 17. 8. The hydroelectric scheme at the Gorge Creek supplied power to the *Fourteen Mile* dredge. The scheme failed because of insufficient water in Gorge Creek during the winter that was the height of the dredging season in the gorge.

from both Gorge Creek and its major tributary, Obelisk Creek, would be used to generate power in a hydroelectric station on the banks of the river.

An intake was constructed in Gorge Creek just below the main road crossing, and a race, which required a great deal of fluming, carried 10 heads of water around the hillside to Obelisk Creek, where another 10 heads were picked up. The water was led to the brink of the steep slope overlooking the river and here it entered a line of pipes that took it to the power station situated on a bench just upstream from the mouth of Gorge Creek. A pelton wheel turned a 150 kw generator producing three-phase[7] current that was led, by wires supported on a line of poles, down the river to the dredge.

The *Fourteen Mile Beach* dredge was built during 1900 on the beach just below the mouth of Gorge Creek. There were difficulties, as the necessary timber and machinery had to be lowered down the steep hillside by ropes, but nevertheless, the vessel was on the claim ready to start by November of that year. But there was a holdup in finishing the electrical installation at the power station, owing to difficulties in carting materials from the railhead at Lawrence. Then, several flanges

193

Figure 17. 9. The *Fourteen Mile* dredge. Electric power wires run from the end of the pole line on the left, out to the dredge.

on the pipeline gave way, and when a trial was finally held, the race gave so much trouble that it had to be flumed over most of its length. The long delay hardly mattered as the river was now so high that the buckets would not have reached the bed anyway.

Finally everything was ready. The river had fallen, the machinery was working well and the bucket chain began to revolve in earnest. But no gold!. They were on top of a large slab of bare rock with not a flake of gold in sight. The dredge had to be shifted and a great deal of time was lost. Then there was more trouble—the generator was not producing the power required to drive the dredge. No wonder. Gorge and Obelisk Creeks were nearly dry, the swamps at their headwaters frozen solid. The company was a victim of the Central Otago paradox— the same frosts that caused the level of the Clutha River to fall and so allow dredging in the gorges also reduced the flow in the tributary streams.

The dredge had worked long enough, however, to demonstrate that it could be run for about half the cost of a steam dredge and could recover gold. In fact for the 17 weeks it had worked during 1901 and 1902 it had recovered 788 oz of gold. Nevertheless, without a reliable water supply the idea of using electricity had to be counted as a failure.

The electric dredge was sold to a Waikaia concern in 1904 but shortly after commencing its journey down the river to Millers Flat, where it was to be dismantled, it struck a rock in the gorge and was totally wrecked. The electrical generator and pelton wheel was sold to the Earnscleugh Gold-dredging Company and installed in their Fraser River power station. The Alexandra Borough Council bought the pipes and fluming for use in their Butchers Creek water supply scheme.

Figure 17. 10. The Fourteen Mile Beach was on the right bank of the Clutha River below the mouth of Gorge Creek. At one time there was an extensive settlement and much alluvial mining activity on the terrace in the middleground (with trees). This was a patch of river alluvium filling an old river channel and protected from river erosion by a rock bar. The surface of Lake Roxburgh is many metres higher than was the river level when the dredges operated here at the beginning of the century.

The company went on to acquire the *Main Lead Hercules* dredge from Roxburgh. It was dismantled and re-erected, with great difficulty, in the gorge but when it started in September 1903 it immediately began to recover large amounts of gold. By mid-1904 the company was paying dividends for the first time even though the dredgemaster had to offer 12s. a day to attract a crew to the inhospitable gorge.

The new dredge was a steam dredge and this immediately brought up the old problem of coal supply. For two years this was obtained by the hazardous practice of boating coal down from Butchers Point with laborious man-handling of the coal sacks around the falls. In 1906 a route was finally found for a long, steep, zigzagging sledge road to the bottom of the gorge just downstream from the mouth of Gorge Creek.

This dredge survived a number of company restructurings and name changes and, as the *909* dredge working at Sixteen-mile Beach, was finally closed down in November 1912 after returning fortunes to her several owners.

River Power
Even before the success or otherwise of the *Fourteen-mile Beach* electric dredge had been determined, a company with a neighbouring

195

Figure 17. 11. Gorge Creek Hydroelectric Station.
  Upper: The power house a short distance upriver from the mouth of Gorge creek, which supplied electricity to the *Fourteen Mile* dredge.
  Lower: The interior of the power house with its Swiss-made generators.

Figure 17. 12. The line of the water race supplying the Fourteen-Mile power station can still be traced from its intake just below the point where the main highway crosses Gorge Creek. In this view up Gorge Creek the remains of the old race can be seen in the foreground and at other places along the left bank of the creek. The race was difficult to maintain and eventually had to be flumed over much of its length.

claim was completing its dredge using a different power source. It was to rely on two huge paddle wheels 6 metres in diameter and 3.5 metres in width. The Golden Falls Company's claim lay between the rapids and the falls some 10 kilometres below Alexandra and it was calculated that, when turned by the current of the river, these wheels would provide adequate power to work the dredge and that she would save £50 a week in operating costs over a steam dredge.

The *Golden Falls* seemed to take an inordinate length of time to reach her claim. She left Alexandra at the end of February 1901 but four months later it was reported that she was moored at Butchers Gully. Apparently she had been tried out on the way down but the amount of drifting gravel moving along the floor of the river was too much for her so she was tied up until the river went down. Finally she reached her claim in mid-July only to find that the current was insufficient to generate enough power to work the machinery satisfactorily. What had been overlooked was the obstruction in the

197

Figure 17. 13. The electric-powered *Fourteen Mile* dredge was sold but on the way down the gorge struck a rock and was totally wrecked.

river, which gave rise to the falls, also slowed the current above the falls.

Recriminations came thick and fast. One correspondent pointed out that although the capital of the company was quoted as £5,500, it had been increased by another £2,000 during the building of the dredge. Then a loan of £1,500 had been taken out with an issue of 1,500 preference shares to repay it. So the shareholders paid £9,000 for a simple current-wheel dredge that had been condemned as impractical before it was built.

One problem was that, as the tailings built up at the stern of the dredge, they obstructed the current and so reduced the efficiency of the paddle wheels. There were also suspicions that the dredge had been damaged in passing through the rapids and that this information had not been disclosed.

What was clear, and could not be covered up, was the fact that the dredge had not recovered one flake of gold, and within two months of its arrival at the claim it was sold to Dr Hyde for £1,000. A new company, the Molyneux Falls Company, was registered on 12 February 1903, and the first thing it did was to attempt to get rid of the waterfall at the lower end of the claim. It was thought if it were removed the current would be speeded up and the dredge might then be successful. So nine hundredweight of gelignite, worth over £70, was exploded but with little effect on the waterfall.

The new company then decided to remove the paddle wheels and install a 25 horsepower oil engine. Kerosene for this was brought to the top of the gorge in cans that were opened and the oil tipped into a

Figure 17. 14. This air view, taken before Lake Roxburgh was formed, shows the road constructed down the side of the gorge to enable the parts of the dismantled *Main Lead Hercules* dredge to be reassembled at the river's edge. Later it was used to supply coal to the dredge. The Fourteen-Mile hydroelectric power station was situated on the small terrace, marked by a dark tree, immediately upstream from the mouth of Gorge Creek. The line of the race supplying the water can be faintly seen running across the hillside in the background.

tank. A 1/2 inch (12 mm) diameter pipeline, a kilometre long, conveyed the fuel down to the river's edge where it was stored in another tank. From this cans were filled and taken out to the dredge by boat.

The engine was not powerful enough and a second 41 horsepower engine was added. At last some gold was obtained in spite of the fact that the buckets were never able to reach the rock bottom of the river where most of the gold lay. In the end they did recover 110 oz, worth about £430, for the year since the company was registered. But this fell far short of the £1,191 expended over the same period and in September 1904 the dredge was advertised for sale.

In February 1905, perhaps to many people's relief, the dredge sank at its moorings and the wreck was sold for dismantling.

NOTES

1. Charles Leijon, Olaf Magnus, James Simmonds, Charles Simonsen, Thos Steele and John Mackersey. Later, after the capsize, the three McGeorge brothers collectively acquired a one third share, later increased to nearly two thirds.
2. 'Gates of the Gorge ' or 'The Gates' were dredgemen's names for the very narrow section of the river (less than 130 metres wide) just below Alexandra.

Figure 17. 15. A river dinosaur. The *Golden Falls* dredge relied on huge paddle wheels, turned by the river current, for power. As had been discovered 30 years before, the current was insufficient for the purpose. Oil engines were substituted but no gold was ever recovered. The dredge eventually sank and was dismantled.

3. See Figure 7. 2.
4. A launch fitted with an oil engine, and intended for coaling the gorge dredges, was demonstrated in June 1911. Presumably it was not successful as nothing more was heard of it. *Photographs Otago Witness* 14 June 1911.
5. Adapted from Conly, D. G. *The Weekly News* 6 December 1950 p. 8.
6. According to Moore, 1953 they were paid 1s. 6d. an hour i e £3 12s for a 48 hour week This was 3d. an hour more than regular dredgemen. There was double time on Sundays.
7. Reputed to be the first time in Australasia that 3-phase power had been transmitted over a distance.

18.

GOLD IN HIGH PLACES

Mining at Doctors Point.

Doctors Point[1], about 10 kilometres down the Clutha River from Alexandra, is not a very prominent landmark nowadays. Perhaps, before the waters of the river were impounded behind Roxburgh Dam, and rose 40 metres up the hillsides, the Point was more distinctive. But today it can be a matter of debate as to where the actual place is. Presumably it is the outermost part of the slight protuberance of the gorge wall into Lake Roxburgh just north of Shanty Creek. Nevertheless the extensive and interesting Doctors Point gold diggings remain clear enough—almost as if they had been abandoned only yesterday.

Some of the earliest miners tried their luck at Doctors Point as they passed up the gorge and one or two found sufficient encouragement to stay and peg out claims. William Blackwell was one of the few whose name has been preserved. For three years from 1864 he worked a claim on the hillside a few hundred metres up Shanty Creek, a small stream falling into the Clutha River a kilometre downstream from the Point. Then for 10 years the only mention of the locality is a newspaper note to the effect that the few miners remaining at Doctors Point 'are working with moderate success.' [2]

The First Rush

In April 1877 came the startling news that George Cameron and William Bailey had struck very rich gold high up on the side of the gorge at Doctors Point. They had taken out £100 worth of gold in three weeks from their claim which was 60 metres above the level of the river. The newspaper speculated, correctly, that the gold must have been laid down in some old high-level river bed.[2]

Within a month at least eight claims had been taken up but only that of the original prospectors, Cameron and Bailey, was producing gold. And produce gold it did. For one period of 10 days it averaged £10 worth of gold per man and in one hectic two hour period 20 oz of gold were recovered.

It was not until August that two more parties struck gold. Lewis

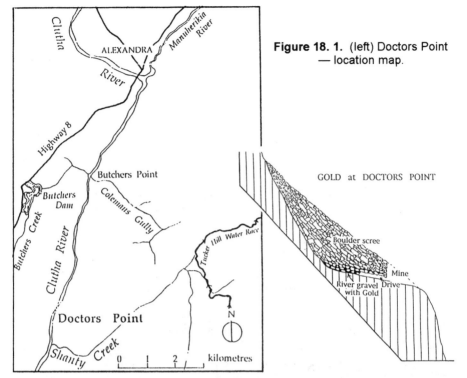

Figure 18. 1. (left) Doctors Point — location map.

GOLD at DOCTORS POINT

Figure 18. 2. (right) The gold-bearing sand at Doctors Point was deposited on the bed of the river when it was flowing at much higher level than it is at present. As the river deepened its course, part of the bed, with its gold, was left as a shelf on the hillside. Over time the shelf has been almost buried by boulders falling from the slopes above.

Cameron Snr, the father of George, was fortunate in that he had some water from the race that he had helped his son and Bailey to construct. He did quite well working into the hillside on an open face whereas his neighbours, John Dewar and party, chose to tunnel. They drove in for 60 metres along the upward sloping rock floor, with its layer of rich wash, until they had to flee before a mass of wet sand which suddenly broke into their tunnel.

One problem with the place was the old one of water shortage. Not until a few miners, led by Bailey, clubbed together to cut a high level race from Shanty Creek was water available at some of the claims. But Shanty Creek generally flowed only from May to December and for the remainder of the year, apart from storms, was dry. A second problem was the presence of countless large schist boulders. The claims were situated on a flattish rock shelf which was really a remnant of the bed of the river when it was flowing at a much higher level through the gorge. Boulders, falling from the steep sides of the gorge, had come to rest along the edge of the old river just as they do along the modern river. The spaces between the boulders had been filled with a matrix of sand and gravel deposited by the river on the inside of the bend in its course. It was at the base of this alluvium that the gold was found.

Long after the river had lowered its bed and abandoned the high level course, falling boulders continued to accumulate until almost all signs of the original shelf were hidden by a slope of coarse scree.

Two methods were used to mine this old riverbed. Those who chose to quarry directly into the hillside had to face the dangerous and laborious task of removing the ever-increasing thickness of boulders in order to reach the thin layer of washdirt. Those who chose to tunnel had to scratch the wash out from between the boulders, with the ever-present threat of large boulders collapsing on to the human moles ferreting under and around them.

In spite of the difficulties, gold continued to be won, especially from the original prospectors' claim. But all was not well with the Cameron-Bailey partnership. There had been tension between the two ever since they had teamed up to work at Doctors Point more than a year before, but the fact that they had now struck gold brought matters to a head. In the middle of May 1877, only two weeks after the announcement of their rich discovery, Cameron laid 'a plaint' against his partner, Bailey, in the Warden's Court.[3]

It had to do with money. Apparently Bailey was hard up when he had begun prospecting and had been forced to borrow money from a relative. He needed £15 for an initial payment towards the cost of cutting the water race and another £10 to buy the necessities of life. When he disclosed in Court that he had been asked to pay 50% interest on the borrowed money the warden had a few choice remarks to pass about rapacious moneylenders. He was reported as saying that

Figure 18. 3. The lower gold diggings at Doctors Point. Before Lake Roxburgh was formed these workings were about 60 metres above river level.

203

'. . . he had never heard of such a monstrously cruel thing and stigmatised the lender as anything but a Christian and a brother.' But this was only a side issue to the main one which was that Cameron insisted that his name be placed on the water race licence as a joint owner.

Cameron was sure that in March 1876 he and Bailey had entered into a mining partnership and he was able to quote the special conditions drawn up by Bailey. These included an agreement that if the mine produced £10 or more a week then Cameron would be entitled to a half-share in the race on payment of £15.

Cameron offered his £15 contribution to the race at the time the agreement was settled, and on several occasions throughout the following year, but Bailey had always refused to accept the money on one pretext or another. When it became necessary to renew the race certificate, Bailey refused to have any name on it except his own. Cameron was worried that he would lose his interest in the race and so had instituted the court proceedings to have the matter cleared up.

As his defence Bailey simply denied any such agreement existed but the warden ruled there clearly had been an agreement. Unfortunately, he said, the Court did not have the jurisdiction to deal with the matter so he dismissed the case.

It was clear that, after this disagreement, the partnership would not survive for long, although the two did continue to work together for a short time during which, for one week's work, they recovered £300 worth of gold. Although the plaint had failed, the episode apparently persuaded Bailey to accept Cameron as a full partner because in September, when Cameron finally decided to pull out, he was able to offer for sale a half share in the water race and claim.

Although it was reported that by October 1877 mining activity had quietened down, it never really stopped over the next 30 years. Names of many miners well-known in the Alexandra district, such as John Bennett, John Terry, Eugene Brady, Nicholas Anderson, Lewis Cameron jnr, Craven Paget and August Magnus appear in the records as having worked at Doctors Point at one time or another.

The Second Rush and the Magnus Story
It was late 1908 when Harry Kitto struck rich gold at Doctors Point and staked out a claim on a spur between Shanty Creek and a tributary gully to the north. What was unusual about this find was that it was very high up on the face of the gorge—far above any previous mining activities. As usual, water was critically short and Kitto had to carry his gold-bearing wash in a bag on his back some 60 metres uphill to where it could be washed in Shanty Creek. But the returns were so satisfactory that before long he was able to lay a 200 metre-length of small-diameter pipe from the creek to his claim.[4]

For more than a year Kitto worked to develop a pumping system to deliver water from the river to his claim. He had a pontoon built in Alexandra and fitted to it two current wheels from an old dredge at Lowburn. The machine was to be moored in the river at Doctors Point and was designed to pump water over 100 metres up to a dam Kitto had erected above his claim. Newspaper reports followed the design and construction of the contrivance but after it was floated down to Doctors Point, there was dead silence. It can only be assumed that it was unsuccessful.

Kitto's find was announced on 20 January 1909 and immediately the rush was on.

Figure 18. 4. Doctors Point gold diggings. The lower workings are to the left near the river and the upper workings of Magnus and party are at a higher level to the right of centre. Further to the right. at about the same level, is the mine of Kitto whose discovery sparked the second rush. Shanty Creek enters the Clutha River at the extreme right.

By 10 February, 18 or 20 alluvial claims were pegged out along the steep hillside at a height of some 140 metres above the river. Apparently the geological situation was very similar to that at the workings 60 metres lower down the hillside. This high-level wash had also been laid down on the bed of a river that was at a much higher level, and therefore much older, than the river that had deposited the gold of the lower workings. It was soon found that conditions were the same as those at the lower workings—the wash was associated with the same difficult mixture of river gravel and large schist boulders.

One of the first to peg out a claim after Kitto was John Nickander but it was not long before he took up a claim at Galloway and John and August (Gus) Magnus, Eugene Deady and Lewis Cameron jnr took over his claim. Nickander went back to live in Alexandra and, perhaps as part of the take-over deal, occupied John Magnus's house in what is

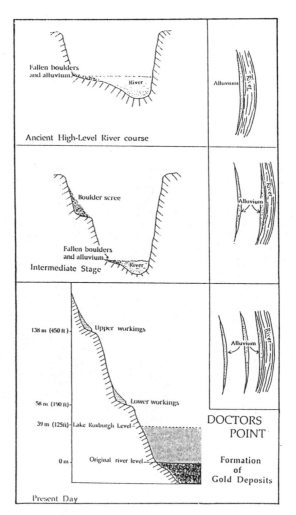

Figure 18. 5. Diagram to illustrate the formation of gold deposits at Doctors Point.

(a): Gold and alluvium deposited on inside curve (right) of a high-level course of the river.

(b): River erodes bed leaving part of old high-level course as shelf on hillside. Boulders fall on to shelf. Deposition repeated at new level.

(c): River erodes bed again leaving another fragment of its previous bed as a second shelf. Water level raised when Lake Roxburgh was formed.

now Ngapara Street. Unfortunately it was destroyed by fire in August 1909 and the Nickanders and John Magnus were heavy losers.

John and Gus Magnus were, with a third brother Olaf, well-known in gold mining circles. John himself had managed the Molyneux Hydraulic Company's mine at Alexandra; had set up a large hydraulic elevating mine at Butchers Point, and then, with his brothers, had founded the Golden Beach Company at the mouth of Chapmans Gully. Gus was a very experienced dredgemaster but with the decline of the dredging industry was looking for other opportunities. The two brothers had recently built the new reservoir on Bridge Hill for the Alexandra Borough Council.

The partners now had their claim at Doctors Point but what about water? The old race of Cameron and Bailey was still in existence and was owned by Jack O'Neill. Various miners had used it, off and on, but it was now derelict and the water right from Shanty Creek virtually abandoned. John Magnus decided to apply for this water right.

OLAF   GUS   JOHN

MAGNUS

Figure 18. 6. The Magnus brothers were experienced miners. Olaf (left) was well-known as a gold dredge owner, August (Gus) (middle) as a dredgemaster and alluvial miner and John (right) as a mine manager. Both Gus and John were involved in the upper workings at Doctors Point.

Magnus found, however, that James Rivers, the merchant/mining investor of Alexandra, who was about to open a sluicing claim on the banks of the lower Manor Burn, had forestalled him. Rivers had thought it would be easy to divert water from the upper reaches of Shanty Creek into his race which ran from Speargrass Dam (south of Little Valley) to Tucker Hill and the Manor Burn. So a month or so before the rush to Doctors Point took place he had asked for a Certificate of Abandonment to be issued against the Shanty Creek water right and then applied for it to be granted to himself. But by the time his application came before the Warden's Court Kitto's discovery at Doctors Point had brought scores of miners to the locality and his application was opposed by a number of concerned people, including Magnus. They realised that if the water were diverted from Shanty Creek the results would be disastrous for mining at Doctors Point.

The warden realised this also and, on 8 March 1909, did issue the Certificate of Abandonment but, much to Rivers's chagrin, awarded the water right of two heads to John Magnus.

Figure 18. 7. A detail of the lower workings. In the foreground is the tail-race lined with stone walls. Above, on the right, is an outcrop of solid schist rock that is part of the floor of the old high-level river bed. The tail race was cut through this. Beyond is the mine face with its large dangerous boulders. At the foot of the face is a drive which presumably marks the level of the gold-bearing wash. This tunnel may have been one of those excavated during the 1930s.

Row with Arnold Nordmeyer

It was not long before the race had been repaired and water from brought down a dry gully to the claim. Soon the partners were on ric gold but shortly afterwards, in May 1909, Arnold Nordmeyer[5] applie for, and was granted, a claim immediately below and adjoining that c the partners. This meant they could not discharge tailings from the sluicing operations down the dry gully which passed through the claim and that of Nordmeyer. Gus Magnus, on behalf of the partner applied in the following month for an 'easement' through Nordmeyer claim. He wanted the use of a strip nine metres wide, which include the gully, and this would have allowed the partners to get rid of the tailings. But the application was adjourned a number of times until it was finally overtaken by other events. Meanwhile the partners' claim was virtually unworkable without an outlet for their tailings. They decided to take a risk.

Under the Mining Act a 'water course' could be used as an outlet for tailings. The desperate partners decided they would regard the shallow dry gully as a 'water course' and so continue to send their tailings through it. Anyway they hadn't seen Nordmeyer around his claim for months. But, perversely, Nordmeyer appeared almost at once and took John Magnus to the Warden's Court to answer a 'Plaint' of trespass and to ask for an injunction to prevent the future depositing of tailings on his claim. Nordmeyer went further and accused Magnus of shifting the boundary pegs and actually mining on his claim. He demanded any gold recovered by Magnus from Nordmeyer's land be handed over.

At the November Court the warden ruled[6] that when Nordmeyer had replaced the peg, which he thought had been moved by Magnus, he put it five feet inside Magnus's claim so it was Nordmeyer himself who had shifted the boundary. The partners had not mined outside their claim after all. However, the warden ruled the shallow dry gully was not a 'water course' as defined by the Act so the partners had committed a trespass of sorts by depositing tailings in it. He refused to issue an injunction but fined Magnus £2 10s.

This added to John Magnus's woes. His personal financial affairs were going from bad to worse. The Nordmeyer affair had meant that the mine had produced little gold so far and the destruction of his house in Alexandra could not have helped. In October brother Gus tried to help him out by buying the Shanty Creek water race from him but in December John was declared bankrupt. His only asset was a quarter share in the Doctors Point claim which would, of course, be sold. And everyone thought that was the end of John Magnus's mining activities at Doctors Point.

Gus Magnus and Lewis Cameron were now the senior partners in the claim and they decided that the Nordmeyer problem had to be solved once and for all. They noted that Nordmeyer had no water right, no plant on his claim and had done no work since September when he had unexpectedly turned up to complain about the tailings. Lewis Cameron asked the Warden's Court in February 1910 to issue a Certificate of Abandonment. The Warden agreed that Nordmeyer's claim interfered with the activities of genuine miners and issued the certificate. Cameron then applied for, and was granted, Nordmeyer's claim as a Special Site for stacking tailings

Laura S. Magnus

The partners had just settled down to enjoy their new-found freedom from constraint when they found an application had been lodged, in April 1910, for three heads of water out of Shanty Creek. The new race was to start a few metres below the intake of their own race. Who had lodged this application? Someone named Laura Selma Magnus. Gus Magnus knew her well—she was his niece, the 14 year-old daughter of the bankrupt John Magnus. The girl's name was obviously being used by her father to obtain the water right which, as a bankrupt, he could

Captions next page

See previous page:

Figure 18. 8. Gold diggings at Doctors Point
  Upper: To the left of the lower course of Shanty Creek is the white scar marking Kitto's claim and further to the left on the same level is another light patch which marks a dam into which Kitto pumped water from the river. Above these landmarks the remains of the Shanty Creek water race are visible. It was flumed across the steep unstable hillside to a dam built in a dry gully (Figure 18. 9).
  Lower: The Shanty Creek race fluming was comprised of short lengths of half-round flat or corrugated iron bolted or rivetted together.

not himself own.

But worse was to come. There was also an application from the same Laura Magnus for a six-acre claim, which was, in fact, the southern part of their own claim.

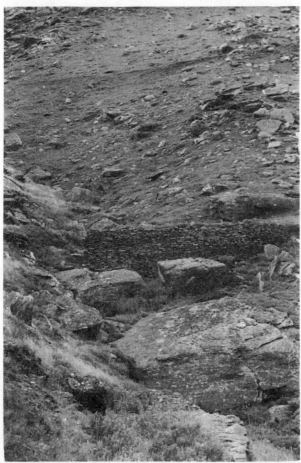

Figure 18. 9. This dam is in a dry gully high above the upper workings and received water from the Shanty Creek race. The dam was the intake to a pipeline that supplied water to the upper workings and drove a pelton wheel which powered a winch used for moving boulders.

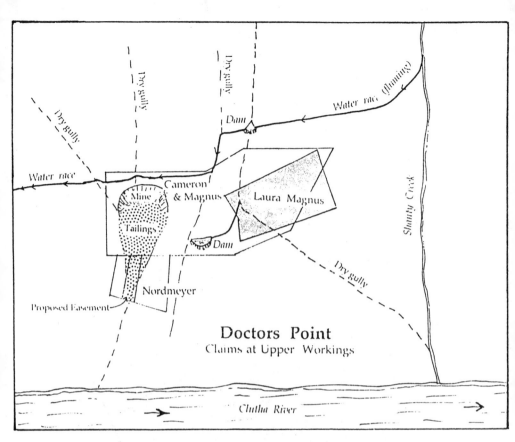

Figure 18. 10. Sketch map of claims at the upper workings at Doctors Point, with various features added. Nordmeyer's claim was taken over by Cameron and Magnus and their claim in turn became the property of the Doctors Point Mining Company Ltd.

Lewis Cameron and Gus Magnus put in strong objections to the water race application pointing out there simply wasn't sufficient water for another race except for a month or so in the spring and during storms. There was concern too that the new race, only a few metres below their own race, would make their own unstable. Indeed, as they pointed out, there had been slips already and they had had to install fluming across some of the unstable land. Nevertheless the Warden granted Laura three heads from Shanty Creek on condition the race was flumed and the sheet-iron flume mounted on trestles.[7] There is no record of any construction work ever being carried out on the new water race.

The Special Claim of six acres Laura had applied for was granted on 15 August 1910 in spite of objections from Gus Magnus and Lewis Cameron. The view was taken that Cameron and Magnus had acquired, over time, far more ground than they could possibly work. But without water no mining could be done, so the six-acre claim was never used and a Certificate of Abandonment was issued against it, at the behest of Lewis Cameron, on 9 December 1912.

The Doctors Point Mining Company Ltd

It was true that Cameron and Magnus held more ground in their claim than they could deal with in the foreseeable future. The countless boulders were a constant nightmare and dealing with these, together with the very limited and unreliable supply of water, slowed mining to the point where it barely paid. What was needed was machinery to deal with the boulders so that more washdirt could be extracted, and a larger and more reliable water supply so that more effective sluicing and processing could be carried out. All this needed more money than the partners had available. What was required was a company to provide more capital. Preparations for forming this began in late 1912 with the appointment of Daniel McDonnell as manager of the mine.

The Company, still an informal private group, was busy during 1913. A dam nearly three metres high was built across Shanty Creek at the intake to the race, and the race itself was extensively overhauled with long lengths of iron fluming installed across unstable ground. Sluicing started on 25 August 1913 using what water was available from Shanty Creek while negotiations with the Alexandra Borough Council for a much more plentiful supply were completed. This is a story in itself.

The Borough Water

The Alexandra Borough Council still owned a one tenth share of the

Figure 18. 11. The mine of the Doctors Point Mining Company Ltd (previously Cameron and Magnus) looking south. In the left foreground are two wire ropes hanging from which is gear used for lifting boulders. Centre right is the remains of a tramway with a mine trolly tipped over the end. In line with the point where the river first appears is the remains of a stone hut and immediately to its left is the massive water-powered winch.

late James Rivers's water right from the tributaries of Little Valley Creek. After Rivers's death an arrangement was made for the Borough Council to lease the whole of the water until a £90 debt to the council was cleared.

Tenders were called in July 1913 for a two-year lease of the water. The Doctors Point Mining Company submitted £38 a year but Marwood Jackson's tender of £39 was accepted. Jackson was already leasing the water from the Rivers's Estate and was overdue with his rent. However, some behind-the-scenes negotiating saw the Doctors Point Company promising to take over Jackson's outstanding debt, provided the water was made over to the Company and Council would accept the Company's promissory note. The lease was transferred a month later from Jackson to the Doctors Point Company. The Borough Council seemed quite happy about this, provided that it didn't cost it anything and that some responsible person in the Company guaranteed the rent which was fixed at £40 a year.

Figure 18. 12. The massive winch (perhaps from a dredge) is no longer in its original position but was used to pull boulders from the nearby Doctors Point Mining Company's claim. It was driven by a pelton wheel (left foreground).

The Company

The Doctors Point Mining Co Ltd[8] was incorporated on 9 August 1913. The provisional directors were Angus Campbell, bank manager; William Bodkin, solicitor and Lewis Cameron, miner, all of Alexandra. The other shareholders were Hans Olsen, dredgemaster; August Magnus, miner; Bruce Thomson, law clerk, all of Alexandra and Angus Cameron, a commercial traveller of Dunedin. Three hundred £1 shares were allocated to the shareholders.

At the first General Meeting of the shareholders, held in December 1913, the Chairman (W. A. Bodkin) outlined progress. Lewis Cameron and Gus Magnus had transferred their claim and gear to the company. The negotiations with the Alexandra Borough Council for water had been successful and the water from Mt Campbell Creek race had been diverted into the head of Shanty Creek. Mining gear, used by the recently liquidated Little Valley Sluicing Co Ltd, had been leased at 10s a week and shifted from Little Valley to the claim. The Chairman was pleased to report that, at the time of the meeting, over 53 oz of gold, worth £206, had been recovered during the four months the company had been mining. The meeting decided to install a travelling crane, worked by water power, to handle the boulders.

A substantial winch, driven by a pelton wheel, was obtained and connected to the line of pipeline which already brought water from the high level race to the claim. The crane was a simple block and tackle hanging from wire ropes suspended across the mine excavation. Chains would be fastened around a boulder and the block and tackle, worked by hand, lifted it clear of the mine floor. Then the winch pulled the block and tackle, with its suspended boulder, to a point clear of the working area of the mine where the boulder was dumped.

The six-monthly balance sheets tell the tale:

(Cumulative)	Income from Gold (Cumulative)	Expenses	Loss (Cumulative)
At 11/1/1914	£334 (86 oz)	£481	£89
At 11/7/1914	£628 (163 oz)	£836	£297

At this point the accumulated loss equalled, near enough, the £300 capital and so after only a year's operation the company called a halt. The mine was let to 'tributers' (miners who paid a percentage of their recovered gold to the company) but expenses kept climbing for another year until the mine was finally closed. The company surrendered its licences in mid-1916 and went out of business.

The balance sheet shows only one payment for 'rent of water' and that for a paltry £1 7s. It wasn't until February 1919 that the Borough Council Minutes record that the Doctors Point Mining Company's promissory note for £40 was finally written off. Councillor Murphy had asked at the Council meeting about the liability of the person who had guaranteed the rent for the water but the matter was not taken further.

Resurgence
Doctors Point was opened up again for a short time during the Depression of the early 1930s when unemployed men were subsidised[9] to hunt for gold. The race from Shanty Creek was once more repaired and brought into operation. Two men began sluicing at the old workings of The Doctors Point Mining Co's high-level claim where the pipeline and sluicing gear had been left more or less intact. Another

group of three men began tunnelling operations in the lower workings. Again large schist boulders which could not be moved proved a difficulty and the tunnels had to be diverted around them. Water for the sluice boxes for this claim was also obtained from the Shanty Creek race. These miners recovered very little gold.

Today

Today the gold workings at Doctors point are still well preserved, with the upper and lower levels clearly distinguishable. Because the river level has been raised about 40 metres, the claims are not as high above the river as they were and this makes them more accessible to visitors arriving by boat. Nevertheless, the lower workings are still about 20 metres above river level and stretch along the riverbank for about half a kilometre from a point about 750 metres north of Shanty Creek. There are fine examples of stone-walled tail races and the tunnels from which washdirt was extracted from between the boulders are clearly visible.

Eighty metres higher on the steep hillside are the upper workings and here the claim of the Doctors Point Mining Company is much as it was left over 80 years ago. The water driven winch with its pelton wheel seems in good order but lies out of its original position. The block and tackle still hangs on its wire rope and there are tramways and mine trucks scattered about. Although the pipeline that supplied the water for sluicing and driving the winch has been salvaged, the remains of the dam from which it originated are still recognisable high above the workings in a dry gully.

The high level race which supplied the water for most of the claims at Doctors Point can be followed round the hillside, with some difficulty and danger, to the intake site in Shanty Creek. All remains of the dam in the creek have long ago been washed out by floods.

No one made a fortune at Doctors Point. But it was typical of many localities throughout the goldfields where men worked for years in the most uncomfortable conditions in the hope that some day they would 'strike it rich.'

From their caves, or tents, or perhaps small stone huts if they had families, they faced a daily climb up to the mines. In the winter and spring it would be bitterly cold in the gorge with the sun reaching the mines only in the late afternoon. Working in gumboots, drenched with icy spray from the sluice nozzles and struggling to move or break heavy boulders would be most unpleasant work. In the summer, when the water race had dried up and the men spent their day lying in small stifling tunnels scratching out sand between huge boulders that threatened to collapse on them, conditions were little better.

There was little that was romantic about the search for gold at Doctors Point.

NOTES

1. No one knows who the 'Doctor' was or whether he was a qualified medical man or merely a helpful amateur. On the other hand the expression 'off to visit the doctor,' meaning to visit a sly-grog seller, was common on the goldfields and may have some relevance.

2. *Dunstan Times* 28 January 1870
3. *Dunstan Times* 27 April 1877.
3. *Dunstan Times* 14 May and 22 June 1877.
4. *Otago Witness* 20 January 1909.
5. Father of A. H. Nordmeyer, the future Labour Member of Parliament for the Oamaru Electorate 1935-49 and Island Bay Electorate 1951-69. He was Leader of the Opposition from 1963-65.
6. *Alexandra Herald* 17 November 1909
7. Much of this material is recorded in *Application for a Water-Race No 35/10* dated 13/4/1910 held by the Regional Office, National Archives, Dunedin.
8. Information about the Doctors Point Mining Company is mainly from records of companies held at the Regional Office, National Archives, Dunedin.
9. The men were paid 15 shillings per week and could keep any gold they found. Mr Ernie King of Alexandra was one of the subsidised men working at Doctors Point.

19.

THE GOLDEN BEACH

WATER PREDATOR

Olaf Magnus, a successful dredge owner and one of three mining brothers, bought the Caledonian water race in November 1895. It had had many owners since it was first constructed in 1866 to bring water from the upper reaches of Butchers Creek to Halfmile Beach near Alexandra and, at the moment, it was leased to a party of Chinese who were sluicing in Chapmans Gully. Magnus promptly cancelled the lease and bought them out for £27.

Magnus intended to use the water to sluice the gravel terraces along the western banks of the Clutha River immediately upstream from the mouth of Chapmans Creek. It was hardly surprising the miners' name for the locality, 'Poverty Beach,' was deemed inappropriate for the new company Magnus had formed. So the 'Golden Beach Hydraulic Elevating and Sluicing Company' came into being.

It was intended to make use of the hydraulic elevating equipment that Olaf's brother, John and his party had been operating at Butchers Point, a few kilometres down the Clutha River from Alexandra. But for successful elevating Magnus knew he would need much more water than the three heads he had acquired with the Caledonian race. He knew full well that, allowing for seepage and wastage, he would be lucky if half that amount arrived at the claim.

So Magnus approached Craven Paget who was already mining at Poverty Beach with his sons and his mining partner, William Noble. The negotiations were long and difficult but in the end Paget agreed to bring not only their claim but also their two water races into the new company. One of these races, the 'Mountain' race, from the south branch of Conroys Creek, had originally terminated at Frenchmans Point but was now being used by Paget in his Poverty Beach claim. Paget and Noble's other race was part of a race which originally brought water from Blackmans Gully to Frenchmans Point but now brought only water from Conroys Creek to Paget's claim.

The combined group applied to the Warden's Court for a Special Claim of 38 acres (15h), which included Paget's claim, and this was formally granted in October 1896.

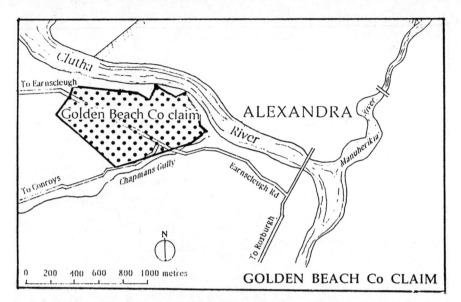

Figure 19. 1. Location of the Golden Beach claim at 'Poverty Beach.' The name 'Poverty Beach' was applied to an ill-defined stretch of the river beach at, and upriver from, the mouth of Chapmans Creek.

While all these formalities were being attended to, there was a great deal of activity on the ground. John Magnus's elevator was shifted from Butchers Point and set up in the new claim and Paget's Mountain Race was diverted into the Caledonian Race far up on the mountainside leaving the long length of the Mountain Race, below the diversion, unused. Men were employed to clean out and enlarge the Caledonian Race so it could carry the increased flow. A storage pond was formed at the site of Kett's old dam near the head of Halfmile Gully and a 37 cms-diameter pipeline was laid to convey water down to the claim.[1]

On 16 May 1896 the mine was opened with plentiful food and drink and much speechifying by town dignitaries, including the Mayor, James Kelman. Two days later sluicing and elevating was underway but immediately the company found itself in trouble. The combined Caledonian-Mountain Race water had enough pressure to work the elevator but there was insuffient water storage to run the device for the proposed three shifts.

To help remedy this, Kett's old dam was cleaned out, repaired and enlarged. After reconditioning, the new reservoir covered about 8 hectares with water up to 1.2 metres deep. This dam, which lay between the Clutha River and the main road just beyond the top of the Halfmile hill, would be referred to by the locals as the 'Halfmile Dam' or, later, as 'Lanes big dam.' Until the Manor Burn dam was built in the 1930s, Halfmile Dam attracted large crowds on moonlit winter nights for ice-skating.

Magnus's aggressive need to acquire as much water as possible to keep the elevator working soon led to strife with other owners of races

219

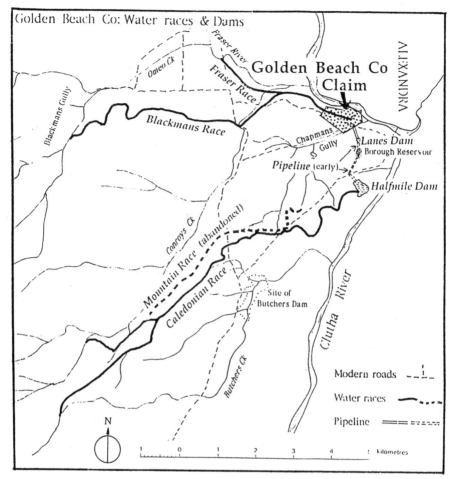

Figure 19. 2. Water races, and associated dams, supplying water to the Golden Beach claim in 1906.

drawing water from Butcher's Creek. The first to complain of Magnus's 'taking ways' was Choy Gun who, along with Lye Bow and other Chinese, lived and worked in Butchers Gully upstream from the present site of Butchers Dam. Choy accused Magnus, in June 1896, of diverting all the water from Butchers Creek in defiance of a court Order of 1888 which ruled that two heads were to be allowed to flow down the creek at all times for general use. Choy lost on a technicality. Then Lye Bow took Magnus to court on the same complaint and, in addition, demanded £5 damages.

Magnus's defence was simply that he had priority and Lye Bow could go and jump into the river. This led to what must surely be one of the most comprehensive pieces of research ever carried out by a warden. The evidence for his judgement covered a whole page of small print in the *Dunstan Times*.[2] In spite of missing documents and odd practices by previous wardens and officials, the warden traced, in great detail, the history of the water rights, now held by Magnus and by Lye Bow, over the previous 30 years. The warden's judgement was that Lye Bow's licence had priority in that it was first issued on 27 October 1864 whereas the licence for the race that Magnus now owned was first issued on 31 August 1866.

It is difficult to overlook the fact that the Magnus brothers (John was now manager of the company) were regarded by the locals as rather 'hard cases' and they apparently had little respect for the Chinese miners. It was John who was responsible for the famous hoax which involved dressing up a rather dead goat to look like a Chinese who had been reported missing. It was only during the post-mortem examination that the hoax was discovered.[3]

In spite of all its efforts to acquire additional water the company seldom had sufficient to operate its elevator satisfactorily. But when the plant was working it certainly got gold—during the last four months of 1896 it recovered 358 oz for 54 working days, an average of 6.6 oz per day. In fact in mid-October the company had been asked by a syndicate to name its price for the claim. '£20,000' was the reply, 'and find it by the end of the month.' Needless to say, there was no sale.

Still the search for more water went on. In October 1896 the company acquired the upper part of the old race which had brought water from Blackmans Gully to Frenchmans Point back in the 1860s. Now it was reinstated to bring Blackmans Gully water back into the lower part of the race where it joined water from Conroys Creek on its way to Poverty Beach.

Then it was discovered by an angry, water-deprived miner that the Mountain Race was not only drawing water from the South Branch of Conroys Creek, which it was entitled to do, but was also illegally taking water from the Middle and North Branches. In the resulting court case in March 1897 John Magnus was brought to heel.[4]

The main problem with the Golden Beach claim was that the gold-bearing wash, although 2 to 3 metres thick, lay under many metres of relatively barren gravels. This was why so much water was required to lift the wash with the elevator. Frustrated by the constant shortages of water, and no doubt noting how the Molyneux Hydraulic Company was dealing with similar problems on the opposite side of the river, the company decided to change from hydraulic elevating to dredging. The decision was made, in mid-1897, to float a public company to finance the project.

The Golden Beach Hydraulic Elevating and Dredging Co Ltd

The public company was formally registered on 20 August 1897 with a capital of £13,000 and the construction of a large, modern dredge, similar to the *Molyneux Hydraulic*, was put in hand on 15 October.[5]

In readiness for the arrival of the dredge, a number of changes were made during late 1897 and early 1898. As water at the very high pressure required to work the elevator satisfactorily was no longer needed, the pipeline intake was moved further down to a saddle between Gilberts Gully and Halfmile Gully—a location that ten years

221

Figure 19. 3. The *Golden Beach* dredge as it was when operated by steam power. The dredge is working in a pond (or 'paddock') cut off from the river in the background and is probably at a slightly higher level.

later was to become the site of the Alexandra Borough reservoir. This move enabled a kilometre or so of the pipeline to be replaced by an open race. In February 1898 the hydraulic elevator was dismantled and taken out of the mine.

Water was not the only commodity that the Golden Beach company was interested in. It needed more land as well. The claim of 15 hectares it held was more than sufficient for its sluicing and hydraulic elevating operations but was inadequate for a dredge, so, in anticipation of its arrival, another 65 acres (26 h) were acquired in September 1897. But John Magnus was still not satisfied,

The Clyde Dredging Company held a licence for 12 acres (5 h) adjoining the Golden Beach Co. claim on the riverside and Magnus coveted this block. But John Pattison, a principal member of the Clyde Company, had his house on the land and had worked a mine there until recently. On the pretext that the claim was abandoned, Magnus went on to Pattison's land, pegged it out and applied to the Warden's Court for a licence to mine it. The warden refused Magnus's application. Pattison then sued Magnus for trespass and damages. Pattison was awarded only one shilling damages but at least gained an injunction against Magnus prohibiting him from trespassing on Pattison's claim. In the end the Golden Beach Company had to purchase the claim for £700.

The Golden Beach Co's claim, now totalling about 44 hectares, included not only the low terrace flanking the Clutha River but also the intermediate terrace on both sides of the Earnscleugh road. From Chapmans Gully, where it was nearly a kilometre wide, the claim stretched along the river for nearly one and a half kilometres. It was

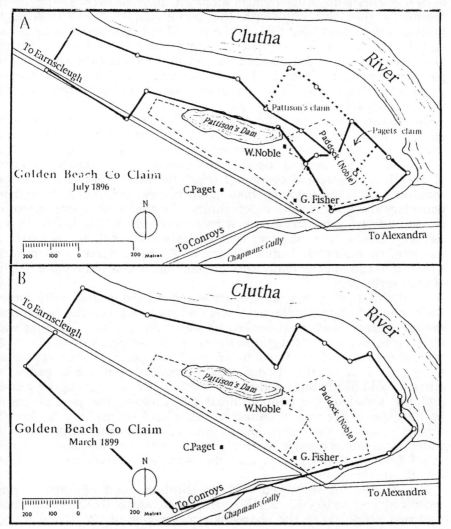

Figure 19. 4. The Golden Beach Hydraulic Elevating Co's claim.
(a): The claim as granted in October 1896. It covered 38 acres (15 h) and included Paget's claim and part of a paddock claimed by Wm Noble but did not include, at this stage, Pattison's claim.
(b): The Golden Beach Hydraulic Elevating and Dredging Co's claim as granted in 1899. This was the greatest extent of the claim. It covered over 100 acres (44 h) and included the farms of Paget, Fisher and Noble and the claim of Pattison.

different from most other dredging claims in the district at that time in that it was a 'beach and bank' claim and did not include any part of the river.

What the claim did include, however, were a number of farms and residences including those of Fisher and Paget and the pioneer orchard of William Noble. The prospect of the company being granted a licence

223

to dredge this land caused alarm amongst these settlers, as they were occupying the land only with the permission of the Earnscleugh Station and had no legal title. In the face of strong objections by Noble and Fisher the warden granted a mining licence over these occupied properties, but with conditions attached that required the company to pay compensation if it dredged any land claimed by the settlers. Twelve years later this was to lead to a tremendous legal battle that is dealt with in a separate essay.[6]

Out towards the river, the top of the intermediate terrace gravels stood some 17 metres above the river level, and the base rested on a 'bottom' of red clay lying over decomposed schist some 6 metres below river level. As the bulk of the gold was confined to the lower 3 metres of gravel, 20 metres of overlying, relatively barren gravel had to be removed before the payable wash could be reached. Along the inland boundary the gravels were much thinner, to the point where outcrops of the underlying basement schist rock were visible. The height of the terrace meant the dredge was constantly working against a dangerously high cliff of unstable gravel. Powerful sluice nozzles, with water from the hillside dam, were in constant use to reduce the height of the overburden.

For the first two years the dredge, which started in July 1898 under the command of dredgemaster Lewis Anderson, worked the beach and the low terraces and, as it worked its way inland, a bar of tailings was built up between the dredge and the river. The dredge was thus cut off from the river and confined to an enclosed pond. There was some benefit in this as the dredge was protected from the vagaries of currents and floods but, as the river level went down during the winter and the water of the pond drained out through the porous gravel barrier, the dredge was in danger of being left high and dry. To keep a dredge afloat in such a paddock required a constant large input of water from some outside source. So in 1900 the company obtained water from the Fraser River and this was led, by race and pipeline, into the dredge pond.

The dredge did very well and up until the end of 1901 it had recovered just on 6,000 oz (186 kg) of gold worth £22,807, and had returned dividends to the shareholders totalling £8,125. Then things began to go wrong.

For the first four months of 1902, under a new dredgemaster, the gold returns barely equalled running expenses and from April onwards no returns at all were reported. It was obvious if the company were to survive then either more gold had to be obtained or expenses cut. It was decided to investigate the so-called 'O'Brien' system whereby conventional steam power for driving the dredge was replaced by high-pressure water turning a pelton wheel.

With what could only be regarded as cunning foresight, the owners decided that this low period in the company's fortunes was the time for a major overhaul of the dredge. Predictably, the expenditure incurred, coupled with loss of income for nearly a year, was too much for the company and it decided on voluntary liquidation and restructuring. The initial capital of the company, £13,000, had been quite high. It meant that large amounts of gold had to be procured to give a satisfactory return on the investment. Restructuring was a device designed to make a company 'meaner and leaner.'

New Golden Beach Hydraulic Elevating and Gold-Dredging Co Ltd
Now the reason for the expensive overhaul was revealed. A new company was formed but with only £5,000 initial capital. This was sufficient to buy the dredge from the original company at a bargain price. Everyone was satisfied as the shareholders of the original company had recouped their money through dividends paid over the years and from the final sale of the dredge and claim. Shareholders in the new company (mainly the same people as were in the old company) had a cheap but newly overhauled dredge and every prospect of getting a good return on their relatively small investment.

The new company appeared in October 1903 with the cumbersome title of the 'New Golden Beach Hydraulic Elevating and Gold-dredging Co Ltd.' This did not impress the locals who, mercifully, still referred to it as the 'Golden Beach.'

The dredge started work again in October 1903 with Bill Bringans as the dredgemaster and, although gold returns were no better, averaging only 15 oz a week, at least Bringans managed to keep the dredge working regularly. There was one notable exception, however. In March 1905 the *Eureka* dredge, working on the neighbouring claim, came in too close to the boundary and caused the gravel barrier between the river and the *Golden Beach's* pond to collapse. The dredge pond drained out and the dredge was left high and dry. Money had already been borrowed and this disaster was the final straw. This time the liquidation was not voluntary.

J. P. Lane Steps in.
When the claim and dredge were put up for sale on 12 April 1905 Lane Bros, cordial manufacturers of Dunedin, bought them. The two brothers, Josiah P. Lane and William Lane, were already directors of the New Golden Beach Company and were also the mortgagees. They paid £1,200 for the dredge and claim but J. P. Lane (who was the brother who took an active interest in the dredge) admitted later that they had had to pay another £600 for the water rights from Butcher's Creek and the Fraser River which were held personally by Olaf Magnus. The company was now a private company so its affairs, including its gold returns, were no longer made public.

Lane's objective, of course, was to make the company profitable and he set out on a programme of saving money. First he surrendered all that part of the claim, comprising some 16 hectares, lying to the south-west of the Earnscleugh road. He recognised that this land, mainly Craven Paget's farm, was too shallow for successful dredging and there was no point in paying an annual rent of £20 for useless ground. Lane had the whole claim resurveyed and found that it now covered 30 hectares but still embraced the properties of Noble and others.

In an effort to save more money Lane decided to go ahead with the

Captions next page....

Figure 19. 5. The *Golden Beach* dredge was converted to water power to save money. A pelton wheel, turned by high pressure water supplied by a pipeline from the Caledonian Race, drove the machinery and water then passed on to the gold-saving table.

Upper: This view shows the arrangement of the incoming pipeline which had a number of flexible joints, one of which was mounted on a circular rail track, and these allowed the pipeline to follow the movements of the dredge.

Lower: The water-powered pelton wheel was housed in a small shed mounted on the right-hand front corner of the roof of the dredge.

proposal to convert the dredge to water power. He called on R. T. Stewart, engineer and dredgemaster of Waikaia, and who had successfully converted the *Argyll* dredge to water power, to supervise the conversion which took from November 1905 until March 1906.

A swivel arrangement involving a circular rail track was set up so that the pipes taking water out to the dredge could easily follow the movements of the vessel. The machinery was driven by a pelton wheel installed on the roof of the dredge so water, after passing round the wheel, could still be used in the screen and on the gold-saving tables situated at a lower level. A branch line of high-pressure water led to a nozzle that was used for sluicing down the high gravel bank to protect the dredge against sudden falls of gravel.

The water-powered dredge was certainly cheap to run (it was said to have saved £900 a year) and it worked well as long as the water lasted. But in the dry season that was being experienced the dams were quickly emptied and the dredge came to a halt. Little wonder that Lane cast about for every drop of water that he could conceivably entice into his dams. The campaign, begun by Olaf Magnus, to acquire as much water as possible was continued even more aggressively. It particularly irked Lane that he was forced to allow two heads of water, under the 1888 Order, to flow past his intake and on down Butcher's Creek 'for general use'—which really meant for the use of Lye Bow.

Lane went to the Warden's Court in April 1906 to seek to have the Order cancelled. Lye Bow, as was expected, objected to the proposed cancellation. Lane pointed out that when the Order was made, about 20 Chinese were mining in the lower part of Butchers Creek but now there was only one. It seemed he was wrong. In fact, the number of Chinese who turned up at Court to give evidence they were working in the creek and needed the water, was quite remarkable. The warden was evidently impressed with this show of solidarity and refused to cancel the Order so long as mining was going on in Butcher's Creek, but he did amend the requirement to one head.[7] (Lye Bow, however, retained the right to draw two heads, if he could, from lower down Butchers Creek).

Lane, however, could not bear to see even this amount of water flowing past his intake when his dredge was short of water, so a year later, in April 1907, he was back in the Warden's Court to ask that this new Order be cancelled. This time he tried a new tack. Making use of a clause in the Mining Act, which gave priority of use of water to

Figure 19. 6. Continuous sluicing helped to reduce the danger of the high gravel faces, which were being undercut by the buckets, collapsing suddenly and damaging the dredge.

mining, Lane pointed out that Lye Bow was using his two heads of water, for which he had a prior right, not for mining but for irrigating his garden. And furthermore he had never sought Court approval for this change of purpose so he was using the water illegally. The running of a large dredge with its attendant employment for 10 men was, in Lane's view, more important than any garden.

Anyway, according to Lane, the creek increased in flow through natural input between his intake and that of Lye Bow so that even if no water flowed past his intake, Lye Bow would still get an allocation. The Warden was convinced to the point where he altered the Order so Lane need only allow one half-head to flow past his intake.

Lye Bow's Water
Lye Bow's was so concerned about this harassment that he decided to offer his water right to the Alexandra Borough Council. The grateful council, disappointed and exasperated over the failure of its very expensive waterworks installed only four years before, acted immediately to buy this valuable, first-priority water right of two heads. The agreement was signed on 19 November, 1907 but the 'change of purpose' from 'mining' to 'domestic use' still had to be

approved by the Wardens Court.

Now it was Lane's turn to be worried. Taking on an old Chinese was one thing but fighting a borough council was another. He saw the water slipping from his grasp, so he objected to the 'change of purpose.' In his evidence he again went through the arguments that must by now have been very familiar to the court. He pointed out once more that he needed water to run his dredge—an important industry in the district—and that there simply wasn't enough water in Butcher's Creek, apart from a short period in spring, to supply both his requirements and those of other people. The constant shortages of water seriously interfered with the operations of his dredge. He generously conceded that the borough was entitled to water, but not at the expense of the mining industry. Anyway, he pointed out, the borough really only needed one head of water and that was all the Warden should think about granting to it. In spite of Lane's eloquence the Warden granted the change of purpose.

Mr Lane still had a card to play. He came back to the Warden's Court in December, apparently somewhat humbly, asking that the warden fix the price of the water Lane was entitled to take from Butcher's Creek. He explained to the Court that, though the borough now held a prior right to two heads of water, they were using it for domestic purposes. The Mining Act, he pointed out, provided that an inferior right holder who wanted water for mining, as did Lane, was permitted to apply for half of a superior right if the water under that right was not being used for mining. The price was to be fixed by the Court so would the warden please get on and fix the price of the head of water that Lane was entitled to. But the warden wasn't going to be bustled. He pointed out that that this was the first time such a case had come up in the district and he intended to defer his decision until had gone into the matter thoroughly. Meanwhile Lane could go ahead and use the water provided the borough did not want it. And the borough was certainly not in a position at the moment to use the water. It first had to build a race which had to traverse the sheer cliffs of Butchers Creek gorge, then a reservoir had to be constructed and a pipeline laid to connect the scheme with the town reticulation.

Meanwhile, Lane was glad that he had retained the boiler and steam engine on his dredge when he converted it to water power. It meant he was able go back to steam power as the drought of 1907 took hold and water supplies failed. For some time he operated a dual power system—for the short period in the spring, when ample water was available, he used water power and for the remainder of the year the dredge was driven by steam. Finally the dredge was fully converted back to steam. But water was still required for sluicing the overburden, and even more importantly, to replenish the pond in which the dredge floated.

So when the Borough Council wanted the site occupied by Lane's pipeline intake for its new reservoir, it was fairly easy to persuade him to move the intake down to the brow of the escarpment overlooking his claim. Here a small dam was built in 1909 and the water led into a 15 inches (375 mm) pipeline that conveyed it to the dredge pond and to

Figure 19. 7. Lanes Dam is a relic of the gold dredging era. It was built in 1909 as the intake to the pipeline that supplied water to the *Golden Beach* dredge working at river level 80 metres below. The small reservoir now makes a pleasant centrepiece to Blackmore Park on Bridge Hill.

the nozzles used for sluicing overburden. This dam, known as 'Lanes Dam' by the locals, is still in existence. Lane benefited by moving the intake, not only in having a shorter pipeline to maintain but also, as part of the deal, in gaining the overflow water from the newly built borough reservoir.

In March 1909 Lane bought the *Perseverance* dredge for £1,100, which after extensive alterations, was renamed *Golden Beach No 2* and set it to work in the shallower ground in Dry Gully (the lower end of Chapmans Gully). It was to became notorious as the destroyer of Noble's orchard, one of the earliest stone fruit orchards of the district.[8]

In one of his last attempts to acquire water Lane negotiated, in 1911 to buy water from the Last Chance Mining Company at Bald Hill Flat (Fruitlands). But the necessary connecting water race would have had to be at a level far below the intake of his race in Butchers Creek and it would need a long and very expensive siphon across Butchers Creek to connect the new race with the Caledonian race. So Lane asked the Borough Council to temporarily swap races—the borough could have his race and water from upper Butchers Creek (the Caledonian race) and then he could run the Last Chance water into Butchers Creek and pick it up in the borough race at Lye Bow's intake. The two races ran parallel and only a metre or so apart over the last few kilometres so there was no problem sorting out the water at the termination of the races. But the council declined to discuss the proposition.[9]

By this time Lane was losing interest in water as he was engrossed

Figure 19. 8. The *Perseverance* dredge was bought in 1909 from the Perseverance Gold Dredging Company, given a longer elevator, and renamed *Golden Beach No 2* before beginning work in Dry Gully. This was the dredge that ruined Noble's orchard (Chapter 23).

in the long-running confrontation with William Noble whose orchard stood in the way of his dredges.

The last *Golden Beach* dredge closed down in November 1914, ostensibly through shortage of manpower but mainly because it had run out of suitable ground. The council bought Lane's big dam at the top of the Halfmile hill, the Caledonian Race and the Butchers Creek water rights.

Today the most tangible evidence of the Golden Beach Company's activities, apart from an extensive wasteland of dredge tailings at the mouth of Chapmans Gully, is Lanes Dam, which is the centrepiece of the small Blackmore Park. Parts of the water races are now used for irrigation but the big Halfmile dam is long empty, its enclosing walls still visible but its floor ploughed and supporting crops of lucerne.

NOTES

1. The water was first piped directly from an intake on the Caledonian race at the site of the old dam built by Michael Kett at the top of Halfmile Gully. Then Kett's dam was reinstated. Later the intake was moved to a saddle between Halfmile and Gilbert Gullies (later to be the site of the Borough reservoir). In 1909 the intake was shifted down to the brow of the hill overlooking Dry Gully. This intake pond still exists as Lanes Dam.
2. 23 October 1896.
3. This tale has been retold in many publications. The incident was first reported by the *Dunstan Times* 18 October 1895 and published as an article by the perpetrator, J

Magnus in *Alexandra Herald* 22 August 1928 and subsequently as a booklet *The Lost Chinaman.*

4. *Dunstan Times* 26 March 1897.

5. The hull was 27 metres long by 8 metres wide with a depth ranging from 1.5 to 2 metres. The 18 metre-long ladder, which allowed dredging to a depth of 20.5 metres, was fitted with 33 buckets each of 4.5 cubic feet capacity. The buckets delivered 120 cubic yards of gravel an hour. The waste material was carried away in an elevator which stacked the tailings 9m high.

6. Chapter 24.

7. *Alexandra Herald* 11 April 1906.

8. Chapter 24.

9. *Alexandra Herald* 5 April 1911.

20.

THE ANTIMONY MINE

There was excitement in Alexandra in early 1882 when John Bennett, a well-known miner of Conroys Gully, announced that he had discovered antimony ore on the bank of the Clutha River opposite Alexandra and about quarter of a mile above the bridge. Bennett, and his old mates Stephen Foxwell and Richard Dawson, formed a group to work the lode, much to the delight of the local newspaper which commented that the future of the town depended on this project. However, the paper should have noted also that, within a month, Dawson had sold his third share in the enterprise for £20.

During the detailed exploration and prospecting of Central Otago by miners in the years following the gold rushes, a wide variety of minerals was discovered. Cinnabar (ore of mercury) at Nevis and Waipori, malachite (ore of copper) at Moke creek, scheelite (ore of tungsten) at Glenorchy and Macraes, and various others. In spite of initial enthusiasm about the discoveries, often followed by the formation of companies to mine the ore, none, with the exception of scheelite, proved in the end to be commercially viable.

Stibnite, the ore of antimony, was also in the list of mineral discoveries and there were reports[1] of its occurrence at Hindon, Waipori, Nevis Bluff and Carrick Range.

Antimony is a silvery-grey, brittle metal, a little lighter than iron and has the valuable property of expanding slightly when it cools after melting. This makes it most useful for making small, intricate castings. The fact that it retained this property when alloyed with lead led to its extensive use in the printing trade as type metal. Antimony-lead alloys are still widely used in industry for storage battery plates, electric cable sheathings, collapsible tubes such as for toothpaste and so on.

Stibnite, when pure, theoretically contains 71% antimony but in nature there are almost always impurities and smelters buy the mineral on the basis of 45% antimony metal. Higher metal content attracts a bonus and lower content is discounted.

Antimony Ore at Alexandra
At Alexandra the stibnite is in the form of small needles, lead-grey in colour, arranged in rosettes often smeared with yellow antimony oxide. Shortly after his discovery, John Bennett sent samples to the Colonial

Laboratory for analyses[2] which showed that the mineral was 73% stibnite which, in turn, contained 52.41% antimony. This result was sufficiently encouraging for the Director of the Geological Survey to instruct one of his young geologists, James Park, to carry out an investigation of the occurrence of the mineral.

Figure 20. 1. Stibnite, an ore of antimony, from the mine site, Alexandra. The specimen is about 25 mm long.

Park reported[3] that the mineral occurred in irregular bands 50-150 mm wide set in rusty, broken quartz in a lode 30 cms wide. He saw the original outcrop near the edge of the river—so close, in fact, that Bennett had to excavate the river mud to expose the mineral and he also saw another outcrop about 100 metres higher up the bank. There was yet another small outcrop about 300 metres along the Earnscleugh Road. Park took samples which, when analysed, showed 64% antimony together with 11 oz of silver to the ton. Nevertheless, in Park's judgement, the cost of exploiting the mineral, taking into account the cost of transport to the coast would be uneconomic and he therefore recommended no further development at the time.

In spite of this warning, three men from Bannockburn, Messrs Pryde, James Horn and John McKersie, formed[4] a small group in 1891 to work the lode but after excavating a shallow shaft and bringing out a few tons of ore nothing further was heard of the enterprise.

Antimony Exploration Syndicate
Mining the lode was not taken seriously until Robert Blair, a quartz-miner from Thames, arrived in Alexandra early in 1901 and prospected the site,[5] Samples were taken and sent to various analytical laboratories who returned results showing about 50% antimony.[6]

Blair and his two partners formed the Alexandra Antimony Exploration Syndicate and took out a licence over 16 hectares. With the help of three employed men they set up a windlass and bucket and, working in two shifts, began to clean out the old shaft. But at a depth of 11 metres it began to collapse and was abandoned.

Two more shafts were sunk and the lode was proved to range in width from 15 cms to 90 cms at depths of 14 to 23 metres. Trenching showed that the lode was continuous between the two shafts. Several

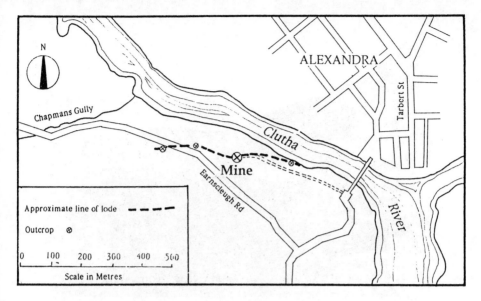

Figure 20. 2. Location of the antimony mine with known outcrops of stibnite.

tons of ore were taken out and bulk samples sent to Dunedin for shipping to England for assessment. There was talk of setting up a crushing plant that would cost £350-£400, but the Syndicate had already spent about £700 and production and transport costs were just too much when antimony was fetching only £35 a ton. An inrush of water into the shaft was the final straw and in 1904 the mine was abandoned.

When James Park carried out his geological survey[7] in the summer of 1905-1906 he re-examined the lode and noted that the ore was in irregular bands 50 mm to 300 mm wide set in rusty, crumbly quartz. He pointed out that the ore would need to be at least a continuous 300 mm wide in this inland locality to be profitable.

Alexandra Antimony Co Ltd
Early in 1907 a group of Wellington businessmen, encouraged by a rise in the price of antimony and the fact that the railway had at last reached Alexandra, decided to reopen the mine. James McQueen of Alexandra, on behalf of the syndicate, was granted a Mineral Licence for a claim of 130 hectares. During the course of the hearing[8] in the Warden's Court, McQueen explained that he had traced the lode for three kilometres, hence the rather peculiar dimensions of the claim which was 3.5 kilometres long but only 400 metres wide. Charles Rillstone, late manager of the OPQ quartz mine at Waipori, was employed to supervise the excavation and timbering work.

Soon eight men were at work clearing out old shafts and erecting winding and pumping gear. In mid-1908 the syndicate formed a public company registered as the Alexandra Antimony Co Ltd with a capital of £100,000. The work force was increased to 20 men and a new shaft

Figure 20. 3. Shaft being sunk by the Alexandra Antimony Syndicate in 1901. The group consists of three members of the syndicate and three employees.

Figure 20. 4. The antimony mine in 1906. A steam engine has been installed to pump water from the shaft which is being sunk, under cover, in the building. Later the Alexandra Antimony Company Ltd would be formed and a brick smelter erected.

was sunk to a depth of 50 metres and then a drive excavated along the lode.

Although the price of antimony had risen markedly during the last five years, it was apparently still insufficient to cover the cost of sending ore to Australia or Britain for refining, so the decision was made to process the ore at Alexandra. This meant building a smelter.

The Smelter
New Zealand patent rights for a new process of refining, developed in Australia by Frank Cotton, were secured and a Mr Kingdon who was

familiar with the process, was brought over to supervise the erection of the smelter.

It was claimed that the ore could be processed to 'star' antimony[9] in two and a half hours by this 'oxyhydro' method. Furthermore it was claimed to be a very cheap process in that one ton of local lignite could smelt up to 10 tons of ore. Although the newspaper article[10] does not explain the process, it was likely to be one in which air and steam were passed over the heated ore. Antimony oxide condensed from the resulting fumes on the walls of cooling chambers. The oxide was then collected and reheated along with fluxes in a crucible. Soon molten antimony metal would begin to collect under the layer of flux and, when it cooled, it solidified to 'star' antimony.

Meanwhile ore was being extracted from the mine and stockpiled ready for the smelter. By October 1908, 40 tons of ore had been extracted and the company was encouraged when it was found that there was an appreciable amount of gold in the lode.

By the end of March 1909 the concrete foundations had been laid for the smelter and bricks for its erection were arriving from Wingatui. The company let it be known that it would accept antimony ore from all parts of Otago for smelting. By June the smelter was finished and undergoing trials but in spite of the expert supervision of Mr Kingdon, difficulties were encountered in the operation and it was decided that alterations were necessary. Finally they seemed to get it right and the smelter began to work and ore to be processed.

Disaster

Then on 7 August 1909, disaster.[11] An explosion ripped through the smelter blowing out part of the brickwork of the cooling chambers and bringing refining to a standstill. The mine had to be closed down and men laid off. There was some hope for a revival when word was received from the company in October that the smelters were to be rebuilt. But it was not to be.

The mine lay idle through 1910, and in March 1911 a meeting of the shareholders resolved on liquidation and in August the gear was sold by auction.[12]

The final act took place in the Warden's Court in December,[12] when the surrender of the company's mining licence was accepted.

NOTES
1. P. G. Morgan 1927: p. 97.
2. 16th Report Colonial Museum and Laboratory 1882: p. 43.
3. J Park 1888: p. 33.
4. *Dunstan Times* 13 March 1891.
5. *NZ Mines Records* Vol IV 1900-01: p. 111.
6. The full results were:
   Government Analyst: sample contained 73.5% ore which gave 52.8% antimony.
   Thames School Mines: sample contained 69.7% ore which gave 50% antimony.
7. J. Park 1906.
8. *Alexandra Herald* 17 April 1907.
9. 'Star' antimony was so named because of the characteristic star pattern developed on the surface as the molten metal solidified.
10. *Alexandra Herald* 25 March 1908.

11. *Alexandra Herald* 11 August 1909.

12, Many of the bricks from the smelter were used in construction of the Alexandra Bowling Club's pavilion acco rding to Mr E. V. King (personal communication).

13. *Alexandra Herald* 13 December 1911.

21.

LYE BOW'S TWO HEADS

Lye Bow was worried. After all, he was an old man and a foreigner and he was up against a powerful and influential dredgeowner who could afford lawyers versed in the intricacies of mining law. They would probably get their way, and Lye Bow's water, in the end.

Lye Bow,[1] an orchardist and market gardener of Butchers Gully, had a most valuable possession. He had a prior right to two heads of water from Butchers Creek. For several years the Golden Beach Company had been trying to get hold of his water right. First it was the founder of the company, Olaf Magnus, who disputed Lye Bow's priority but the Warden's Court had confirmed that Lye had the prior right. Then, when J. P. Lane took over the Golden Beach Company, he tried to obtain Lye Bow's water by attempting to show that he was no longer using it for legitimate mining. So far Lye Bow had managed to hold Lane off, but it was becoming more difficult.

Remembering an approach by the Alexandra Borough Council nearly 10 years before, Lye Bow let it be known to the mayor (Henry Schaumann) in March 1907, that he might now be prepared to sell his two heads of water to the borough.

The council, at it wit's end over the disastrous water scheme of Rivers, immediately appointed a subcommittee, with power to act, to interview Lye Bow through an interpreter, with a view to buying his water right. The committee was able to report to the council meeting of 10 June 1907, it had agreed to buy the water right, and about a kilometre of race, for £500.[2] An agreement was prepared by the Town Clerk stipulating that the council would pay the money at the rate of £100 a year completing the payments in 1912. The agreement was signed on 19 November 1907.

With the lesson of the Rivers scheme fiasco fresh in mind, the mayor and council were determined that new proposals for a water supply would be fully investigated and have the full support of the townspeople before public money was spent. So George Campbell, an experienced miner and raceman, was asked for a report on the scheme. Campbell's report was all such a document should be. He said that, in his opinion, the scheme was a good one and then he proceeded to set out the route of the race needed with details of the earthworks, flumes, siphons and so on, which would be required. Water would be

Figure 21. 1. The two men who ensured that Alexandra got its first reliable water supply.

Upper: Lye Bow who sold his valuable water right to the Borough Council. This photo is believed to show Lye Bow in his vegetable cart, with employees, in Alexandra.

Lower: Henry Schaumann (1851-1938) was Mayor of Alexandra and negotiated a deal satisfactory to both sides when Lye Bow offered the Council his water right.

conveyed mainly by an open race but there would be some 200 metres of pipes required to cross gullies and another 200 metres of iron fluming to take the water across swamps and around cliffs. For more than half of its length the race would make use of the abandoned part of the old Mountain race from Conroys Creek. It would be renovated and enlarged. In total the race would be about 8.5 kilometres from intake to a dam overlooking the town.

Next the mayor called a public meeting at which he explained the history of the negotiations and presented Campbell's report. The scheme was overwhelmingly endorsed by the large crowd present, especially when the mayor pointed out that the scheme would be paid for out of present income and would not require an increase in rates.

There was, however, one curious facet of this meeting. A motion was proposed heartily approving of the action of council in purchasing Lye Bow's water right and authorising it to hold a poll sanctioning the borrowing of sufficient money to complete the project. This was seconded enthusiastically. Then an amendment was proposed by Archie Ashworth who, at the next election, would begin what was to become a 25-year colourful career as a borough councillor and mayor. The amendment almost negated the motion and was simply 'That the scheme be not gone on with.' The seconder of the amendment must have occasioned some surprise by his action—it was none other than George Campbell, the man who had drawn up the excellent report on the scheme and shown it to be perfectly feasible, cheap to construct and to maintain. But the amendment received only five votes whereas an overwhelming majority passed the original motion.

What were Campbell's reasons for opposing the scheme? One possibility is that, because Campbell still worked for James Rivers as his manager, and Rivers still supplied the town with water, his stand may have had something to do with loyalty to his employer and perhaps even job security.

As a result of the favourable response at the public meeting, it was agreed that £1,200 be borrowed at 3.5% for a term of 41 years for the new water works scheme. Council discovered that, in spite of its assurances to the public, it was required by law to strike a rate as security for the loan. So a special rate of 3d. in the £ was struck but it was agreed that it would not be levied as the loan charges would be paid out of the general rate.

There was still a lot of red tape to be dealt with. First, council had to apply to the Warden's Court to make use of part of the Mountain race. This was an early race that had brought water from the south branch of Conroys Creek to Frenchmans Point. In its lower reaches it ran parallel to, and only a few metres away from, the Caledonian race from Butchers Creek.

When Paget and Noble had joined the Golden Beach Company in 1896 the water from their Mountain race was diverted into Magnus's Caledonian race. This diversion took place far up the mountainside leaving many kilometres of the lower course of the Mountain race as an abandoned race. Strictly speaking this abandoned section still belonged to the Lane brothers who had taken over the Mountain race

Figure 21. 2. The abandoned Mountain race and Golden Beach race after crossing the main highway. A few hundred metres further along the Mountain race was taken over by the Alexandra Borough Council, renovated and put into service to carry the borough water supply.

with the Golden Beach Company in 1905 but it is doubtful whether the Lanes were even aware that they were still the owners. In fact it had been assumed that this old abandoned race had no owner until the Borough Council discovered that it was actually owned by the Lanes.

The Borough Council smartly applied to the Warden's Court for a Certificate of Forfeiture over the part of the race that it wanted to use. Lane was taken by surprise and the best he could do was to ask that a fine be imposed instead of forfeiture. But the warden was having none of that and issued the certificate. So the abandoned section of the Mountain race passed into the Borough Council's hands.

Next, the council had to apply to the Warden's Court to extend Lye Bow's race to the proposed borough dam at Halfmile Gully, and then a poll of ratepayers had to be held to approve the loan. The result of the poll was a measure of the desperate situation of the town regarding water supply—84 voted for the loan and only 4 against.

The mayor, on his own initiative, bought secondhand pipes and iron fluming from the New Fourteen-Mile Beach Gold-Dredging Company which had abandoned a proposal to run its dredge by hydro-electric power. He was anticipating their use along the proposed race and, luckily for him, council approved his action in spending the £200 involved.

The mayor's action was an indication of the financial state of the town after the extravagances of the Rivers' scheme. There is no doubt that the Butchers Creek scheme, through necessity, had to be built on

Figure 21. 3. **Left:** L. D. Macgeorge (1854-1939) had been engineer for Vincent County from 1877 until 1902 when he resigned to take up private practice in Dunedin. He was hired to carry out the survey of the proposed new race from the Butchers Creek intake to the new reservoir.

Right: George Campbell (1863-1924) mine manager for James Rivers and master race builder. He reported favourably on the proposed Butchers Creek scheme and selected a route for the race. He won the contract for construction and, in spite of engineering difficulties, finished the job in record time.

the cheap, but the chickens came home to roost in the form of the heavy maintenance bills which had to be met in later years.

L. D. Macgeorge, a civil engineer, at this time living in Dunedin but well-known in Central Otago after 25 years service as engineer to Vincent County, was given the job of surveying the route of the proposed new race, and completed the work in September 1908.

Word came through in early November that the loan had been approved by Treasury and immediately the council called tenders for three contracts:

1. Cleaning out and reconstructing Lye Bow's old race together with about 23 chains (470 m) of new race construction and some short flumes.

2. Construction of a section of a race, including siphons and about 10 chains (200 m) of fluming, starting at Butchers Creek and terminating at the main road.

3. Cleaning out and reconstructing about 3 miles (5 km) of the old

Mountain race together with about 20 chains (400 m) of new race and about 4 chains (80 m) of fluming.

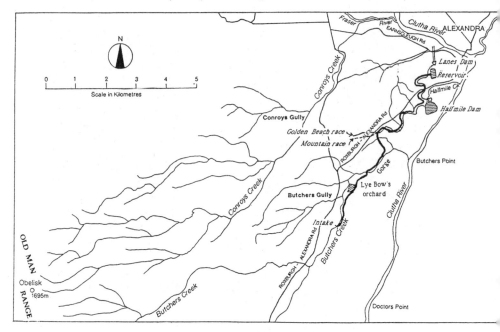

Figure 21. 4. The Butchers Creek race was completed in 1909. The map shows, in addition, part of the Golden Beach race, the new reservoir and the repositioned intake to the Golden Beach pipeline.

George Campbell, the man who had drawn up the report (and opposed the scheme at the public meeting) was awarded all three contracts on 2 December 1908, with a tender of £550, and the same day tenders were called for building the reservoir that was to mark the termination of the race at the town end. It was to be sited on a saddle at the head of a branch of Halfmile Gully on the northern side of the main road. The tender of Magnus Bros for £196 was accepted early in January 1909.

Speed was all-important. A newspaper reporter was shown over the scheme in March and gave a graphic description of the work in progress.[3] He noted the contractor was 'taking the water with him' as he built the race. By this method any defects in the race would be evident and it also ensured the race was not going uphill—a situation often only discovered when water was first turned into a new race!

The intake was in the gorge upstream from what is now Butchers reservoir and the water then flowed along about a kilometre of existing race used by Lye Bow. This required only cleaning out and widening. Then 400 metres of new race, including several short lengths of iron fluming to take the water across small gullies, had to be constructed to reach the edge of the deep and precipitous gorge of Butcher's Creek.

244

Figure 21. 5. The intake to the race was in a rough gorge about a kilometre up Butchers Creek from Lye Bow's orchard. Today the valley is so overgrown with briar and other vegetation as to be virtually impassable.

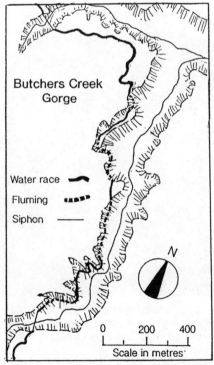

Figure 21. 6. Plan showing details of the route of the borough water race as it first crossed the formidable gorge of Butchers Creek, and then traversed the, in places, vertical Western Wall of the gorge.

Figure 21. 7. A damaged photograph showing the fluming carrying the Alexandra water supply. It was constructed along the vertical wall of the Butchers Creek gorge by men suspended from ropes.

Figure 21. 8. There is sufficient fluming remaining in place today to give a good idea of the engineering difficulties encountered in bringing the race through the gorge of Butchers Creek.

An 'inverted siphon,' consisting of a 100 metre-line of 15 inch (37.5 cm) pipes, carrying the water across the 25 metre-deep gorge was completed by 3 February 1909. The pipes descended one steep wall, crossed the gorge on a bridge supported on three 10 metre high trestles and then climbed the other side where the water discharged into an open race 1.5 metres lower than the inlet. The race then followed along the wall of the gorge, but high up on the western side, for another 550 metres before it ran into difficult country. For the next 450 metres the race had to be carried around steep bluffs on stone walls, or on shelves blasted out of the rock and where it crossed vertical guts in the rock or ran along sheer cliffs, it was carried in iron fluming supported on long lengths of timber.

The fluming was shaped from 2.4 metre-long sheets of flat galvanised-iron. Each sheet was riveted to its neighbours, with liberal quantities of tar used to seal the joints. At intervals of about 1.2 metres were wooden supporting frames with a piece of timber across the top which was bolted to the edges of the sheet iron and so prevented the fluming spreading under the weight of water it was carrying. Mostly these timber supports were bedded on a firm earth or rock base but where the flume crossed a gap in the cliff face the wooden frames rested on a pair of heavy timber stringers lying parallel to the fluming. In some places, to save fluming, the race was taken through ridges of solid rock by cuttings that were as much as 3 metres deep.

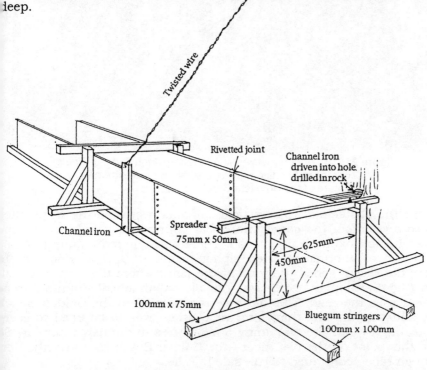

Figure 21. 9. Open fluming was constructed from sheets of galvanised iron bent and rivetted together and sealed with tar. The flume was supported by timber frames. Around cliffs the frames lay on heavy timber stringers which, in turn, lay on channel iron supports which had one end inserted into holes drilled in the cliff face and their outer ends held up by heavy wires fastened to the cliff above.

The most difficult and spectacular construction was at the last bluff where men had to cling to the vertical cliff face while drilling holes into the rock. Into these holes channel-iron beams were driven and fixed with iron wedges, and then the upturned, outer ends of the beams were tied back to the cliff with heavy-gauge, twisted-wire supports Bluegum timber stringers laid across these channel-iron beams supported the wooden frames that in turn carried the fluming. All this construction was done over a sheer drop to the creek bed far below with men and materials lowered down the cliff face on ropes.

Figure 21. 10. Another view of the remains of the fluming (much damaged by falling rocks) also shows the extremely rugged nature of the Butchers Creek gorge.

Once the obstacle of this vertical cliff was overcome the water race turned away from the gorge into easier country as it approached the Alexandra to Roxburgh main road. There was one more gully to cross by means of another inverted siphon, some 100 metres in length before the race reached the road at the point where the Golden Beach race (the Caledonian race) and the old, abandoned Mountain race came across the road. This old race ran parallel to the Golden Beach race and was the one that, after renovation, was to be used to carry the borough water the remaining 5 kilometres to the new reservoir. So from this point on the two races—the Golden Beach race and the new borough race—continued to run side by side.

The New Reservoir

Owing to the continual shortage of water, the Golden Beach dredge had reverted to steam power, and no longer required water under high pressure. Water was now needed only for sluicing off overburden and for keeping the dredge afloat in its pond. So Lane was quite willing to

248

Figure 21. 11. A closer view of the remains of the fluming shows the iron supports inserted in the rock wall and, in turn, held up by twisted wire.

move the intake to his pipes further down the hill and away from the site of the proposed new borough reservoir because the move considerably shortened his pipeline and reduced maintenance. Lane built a substantial dam at the new intake in 1909 and the resulting pond, still called 'Lanes Dam,' forms the centrepiece of a very pleasant, small park.

Meanwhile the Magnus brothers began working on the new reservoir, which was being constructed on the flat saddle between a branch of Halfmile Gully, and another gully running to the north. This rather peculiar location, which was similar to that of the Halfmile dam, meant a wall about 80 metres long and more than three metres high, had to be built across the head of each gully to create the reservoir. Each wall was formed of rammed earth with a stone retaining wall on the outside. The reservoir was estimated to hold about 5.75 million gallons (26,800 cubic metres). A deep cutting through one of the natural walls of the reservoir allowed a short race to lead water into a pipeline

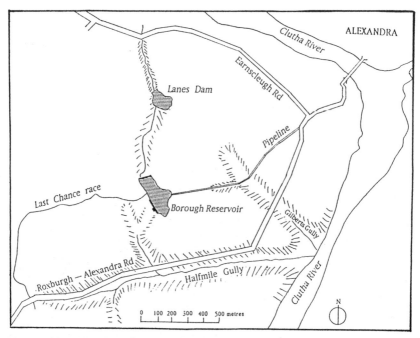

Figure 21. 12. The Borough Reservoir was built in 1909 on a saddle between two shallow gullies necessitating a dam across each gully. At the same time the Golden Beach Company moved the penstock for its pipeline further down the northern gully and built a small dam which is still known as Lanes Dam.

supplying the town. An offer by Magnus to 'scrub the walls of the reservoir' did not mean the council was paying scrupulous attention to hygiene but referred to laying scrub against the inside earth walls to prevent erosion and discolouration of the water.

The newspaper stressed that all the contractors were doing an excellent job and the work was well up to schedule. In fact, water first flowed into the new reservoir on 1 June—less than six months after the work began. But there was still a lot to do.

Final Stages

Tenders were called near the end of May for dismantling the pipelines that connected the 'white elephant' tank on the ridge behind Tucker Hill, and also the Chatto Creek race, to the mains. Using the old pipes, a 1.3 kilometre pipeline was to be laid connecting the new reservoir to the town mains. Again George Campbell was the successful tenderer, even though his price, £147, was some £12 more than the lowest tender. There was some criticism of this but the council obviously recognised in Campbell a man who could do a job quickly and reliably and judged this was worth the extra money. There was some discussion as to whether the pipeline should cross the Clutha River under the bridge as was originally planned, but after consulting the engineers it was decided to run it along the bearers outside the rails where it was far more accessible

Figure 21. 13. This visitor, posed against the big suspension bridge crossing the Clutha River at Alexandra, did not realise that the photograph would also show the Borough pipeline running along the outside of the main span, around the left hand column of the masonary arch then dropping down from the bridge (on the right) and dividing. One branch went to the left round the river bank to the foot of the main street and the other went straight ahead into Ennis and Limerick Streets.

Finally the townspeople were called upon to face their last period of inconvenience—or so they hoped. Once more the barrels for carting water from the river were brought out as water from both the old reservoir and the Chatto Creek race was turned off to allow the old pipes to be removed and the pipeline from the new dam laid and connected to the town supply. Council promised that when the water was again turned on it would be from the new supply and, sure enough, the new water works were opened on 28 July with much toasting and self-congratulation.[4]

The mayor pointed out that the whole scheme had cost £125 less than they had paid James Rivers in 1902 for one head of water. In spite of this rather pointed remark, Rivers accepted an invitation to speak and added his congratulations. Then there was another nice touch, as the newspaper reported:

> The Mayor here introduced Lye Bow whose grin bore sufficient evidence of his delight at seeing the scheme completed and the honour conferred on him by the Mayor.

It is probable that his grin faded and his delight was much subdued when he later returned home to his extensive garden and realised that he no longer had a water supply. Meanwhile it was all festivities and

251

Figure 21. 14. There was near panic when the Western Wall of the new reservoir began to bulge a year after completion. Smart work by the borough staff built a buttress that has been effective in stabilising the wall for nearly 90 years.

Figure 21. 15. The Borough reservoir, no longer used for town water supply, today makes a pleasant, small lake in an arid landscape.

bonhomie as the mayor opened a hydrant and produced a very satisfactory flow. Although, as he pointed out, the new reservoir was 10 metres lower than the concrete tank of the Rivers' scheme, the mayor was able to demonstrate that the pressure in the mains was more than adequate.

Minor Problems

Water troubles for the borough were not, however, over by any means. Before the end of the year an ominous bulge began to appear in the western wall of the newly built dam and the borough dayman and a workman began excavations to build a buttress to reinforce the wall. Worse still, a particularly dry season meant that by December the borough was again short of water and the council was threatening to turn off the valve into the pipeline between 8 pm and 8 am.[5]

To add to the Council's troubles, Lye Bow applied to the Warden's Court for a quarter-head of water from Butchers Creek. The council and Lane both felt obliged to formally object but the borough's lawyer stated at the outset that they 'weren't exactly objecting' although he didn't explain further. The Warden ruled that the Borough Council was to allow half a head to flow past its intake and Lye Bow was to take his quarter-head from this. A couple of councillors were sent out to Butchers Gully to have a quiet word with Lye Bow about his water supply. If they could persuade him to make do with less, then the borough could divert more into the town supply. No doubt they were treated to Lye Bow's famous grin.

For ten years or so the scheme worked well, so well, in fact, that water was used in a liberal fashion. The constant changing of the water in the swimming pool was a drain on the system and an increasing number of people were using the high pressure water of the mains for generating electricity or for running machines of various kinds. The Borough Council set the pattern itself in setting up water-driven generators to light the Town Hall and Library, and the hotels and a number of businesses followed its example. O'Kane, the dentist, for example, not only lit his premises with electricity generated by a pelton wheel but used another to drive his workshop machinery.[6] In 1920 council had to curb this use of water because weaknesses in the water supply system were beginning to show up. The first problem was recurring shortages of water during the summer and the second was the increasingly heavy maintenance of the race owing to the widespread use of secondhand materials during construction.

Lane's Dams

It was the familiar Central Otago stream pattern—plenty of water in the spring and then decreasing amounts for the remainder of the year—that caused the water shortage. The answer, as always, was more storage. But how was this to be achieved? Council cast envious eyes on Lane's Halfmile Dam that probably had a storage capacity of about 9 million gallons (40,800 cubic metres).

The *Golden Beach* dredge closed down in November 1914, mainly because it had run out of suitable ground and in 1917 Lane offered his

Figure 21. 15. Lane's Big Dam or the Halfmile Dam was acquired by the Borough in 1920 and became the principal storage reservoir for the town. In this recent air view what appears to be water filling the dam is actually a crop of lucerne on the floor of the dam.

water rights, dams and races to the Alexandra Borough Council for £1,500. The council was certainly interested in acquiring the Halfmile Dam, but at the price suggested, treated the offer as a joke. So Lane decided to bide his time. He turned his attention, in a half-hearted way, to sluicing not only at the dredge site but also at a 50-acre (22 h) claim he held in Halfmile Gully. Dredgemaster Livingston had been kept on to supervise these enterprises but they were apparently very much part-time affairs. Finally, there came a time when the water races were neglected and the dams lay unused.

The Borough Council, by this time becoming increasingly anxious about lack of water storage, saw its chance. It applied, in August 1919, to the Warden's Court for a Decree of Forfeiture. The warden could cancel Lane's licence for the dams, so making them available for sale, or he might simply fine the miscreant and warn him to start bone fide mining operations forthwith or forfeiture would follow.

Lane saw the writing on the wall and before the reserved verdict was finally given, again offered the Borough Council the Butchers Creek water rights with race and dams, this time for £350. Council again turned down the offer.

Meanwhile the warden delivered his verdict.[7] Lane was fined £30 and the warden warned him he must either apply to the Court for protection of his dams or he must start using them again immediately for mining purposes. Apparently Lane had grown tired of the whole business and arranged a meeting between the Borough Council and

Figure 21. 16. The Halfmile Dam
> **Upper:** The northern wall of the Halfmile dam probably began as part of the intake for the pipeline that served the elevator of the Golden Beach Hydraulic Company at Poverty Beach on the Clutha River.
> **Lower:** The long southern wall of the dam was far from watertight and required constant attention. In both of these photos the floor of the dam is being used for a crop of lucerne which, to some extent, gives an impression of what the reservoir looked like when it held water.

Figure 21. 17. After the height of the dam walls was increased in 1928, stones were placed against the inside of the walls to prevent erosion by wave-lap.

settlers from Earnscleugh district. The meeting agreed to buy all c Lanes' water assets for £900 of which £250 was put in by the counc: for the dams, the Butchers Creek water rights and the Golden Beach race.

There was a last minute hitch when the application for 'change c purpose' (i.e. from mining to domestic use), after going through th Warden's Court, was sent to the Minister for the required approval. I was turned down. The reason given was that it was the Minister' intention to set up a commission to investigate the whole subject c water conservation on the goldfields. This greatly alarmed the Boroug. Council, which from firsthand knowledge of such inquiries, saw th matter dragging on for years, so the mayor promptly lodged a stron protest with the minister. His representation was successful and th mayor was able to announce within a fortnight that the 'change c purpose' had been approved.

As a result of all this manoeuvring the borough became the owner c Lane's big dam at the top of the Halfmile hill. It was hoped that th would solve the problem that plagued all water schemes in Centr Otago—the lack of sufficient storage to even out the season fluctuations in the stream flow.

Council had also acquired, as part of the deal, the long Golde Beach (Caledonian) race, and the water right to three heads that wer with it, from an intake far up Butchers Creek. As the borough alread owned the prior right it was immaterial that the new right was inferic to the first. This race made much use of natural water courses as came down the mountain side but, as it had not been used for som time, the race, and the siphons and flumes in particular, were out

256

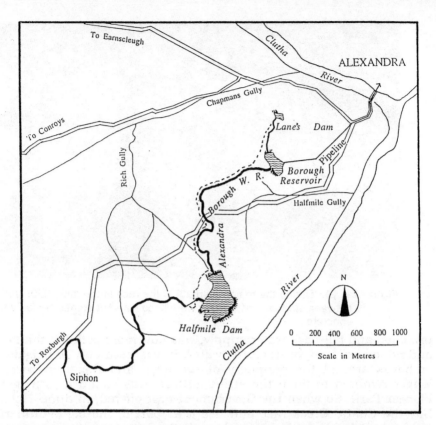

Figure 21. 18. The arrangement of races after the Halfmile Dam was taken over as Alexandra's main storage reservoir. The dam walls were increased in height and the area of the reservoir enlarged. In order to make use of the dam, parts of the old Golden Beach race were used as the borough race.

repair. Thrown in with the deal also, was Lane's small dam sited in a narrow gully overlooking Earnscleugh. It was of little use to the town supply as it was small and much lower than the borough reservoir.

A lot of work was required by council to make the Halfmile dam watertight. At the same time, the walls were raised by 18 inches (450 mm) which increased the area of the reservoir from 10 acres (4h) to 16 acres (6.5h) and the storage capacity by about 260,000 gallons (1,212 cubic metres). Unfortunately wave erosion threatened the newly heightened walls, and stones, placed on the inner side of the wall to offer protection, were not completely successful in preventing this.

In the midst of all this wheeling and dealing councillors minds were suddenly diverted back to matters concerning the old Chatto Creek race.

Chatto Creek Race Sold
The Chatto Creek race which had served the borough faithfully both as

257

Figure 21. 19. During the major overhaul of the race in the mid-1920s parts between stretches of fluming were lined with flat stones sealed with concrete.

principal and fall-back water supply, was now more polluted than ever, and no longer used for domestic water. It was used only to irrigate the orchards around the periphery of the town and the town race, no longer required to flush the street gutters, was confined to irrigating Pioneer Park. So when the Government first offered, in June 1921, to buy the Chatto Creek race and use it as part of the big Manuherikia Irrigation Scheme the Borough Council showed immediate interest.

Council asked for £5,000 and a guarantee that Government would deliver two heads of water to the town boundary for all time. The Government accepted the council's conditions and the mayor, Mr Black, and Councillor Bringans, after a quick trip to Wellington to sort out details, returned in triumph to receive the congratulations of councillors and citizens alike. They were able to report that Government would pay £1,000 in cash (which would wipe out most of the Borough's overdraft) together with £4,000 of Government debentures. The yearly income from these, £220, more than replaced the income the borough had received from the sale of water from the race. Furthermore the council would no longer have the £180 or so annual expenditure for upkeep of the race. Even the orchardists were happy as they still had a guaranteed water supply and it was to cost them less than they paid the Borough Council. No wonder councillors were pleased with their deal.[8]

Maintenance Problems
Councillors were not so pleased with their Butchers Creek water scheme, however. Chickens were coming home to roost in that the secondhand pipes[9] and fluming, which the council of the time had been forced to use because of the expense of the ill-fated Rivers scheme, were now giving constant trouble.

258

There was a discussion as to whether it might be better to renovate the newly acquired Golden Beach race and use it for the main supply. But Council was convinced that it would cost more to put it in order than it would the borough race. Apart from short lengths near the Halfmile Dam, the borough never used the Golden Beach race.

Secondhand pipes bought from a mine at Matakanui were used, in 1923, to replace the pipeline and there were long and earnest discussions about the rapidly deteriorating siphon across Butchers Creek. Should it be replaced as it was or was there another route which might do away with the long fluming round the cliffs? In spite of many inspections and much levelling, no one could find a practical way to bypass the gorge. One scheme that was looked at seriously was to run a pipeline along the bed of the stream in the bottom of the gorge and bring it up when the cliffs were passed. In the end it was decided that the present siphon and fluming would have to be repaired.

Annual expenditure on the whole race had risen from £125 for 1919-20 to £301 for 1923-24 and still the whole race was leaking badly. Measurements showed that of the five heads entering the race at the intake, only one and a half heads reached the dam. Little wonder the dam could not be kept full.

Fluming was patched with liberal amounts of tar and many short lengths of race between the stretches of fluming were sealed with flat stones set in concrete. These repairs made some improvement but it was the deal made with the Public Works Department on 4 February 1925 that saved the situation. In return for the use of the Golden Beach race, water would be supplied to the borough race from the Last Chance Irrigation Scheme.

Meanwhile the Halfmile Dam became the town's favourite skating venue and led the council to worry about pollution of the town's water supply. Debris left by crowds of people found its way into the water when the ice melted. So notices went up telling people not to spit ('expectorate' was the word), or drop cigarette butts and to keep dogs off the ice. If they didn't, well, council would prohibit skating on the dam.

NOTES

1. There was a story that Lye Bow was smuggled out of China and into New Zealand by his well-to-do family after he had been condemned to death for killing a man in a duel (personal communication: late Mrs G. McArthur, Alexandra). According to Ng, Vol 1 p 342 and Vol 4 p. 288, Lye Bow came from the county of Dungguan (Tungkoon) near Canton. In the Electoral Rolls Lye Bow's occupation is given as 'storekeeper.' He may have bought supplies in bulk from Dunedin and supplied the local Chinese miners. The remains of his storeroom are still in the trees on the shore of Butchers Dam reservoir.
2. *Alexandra Herald,* 12 June 1907.
3. *Alexandra Herald* 7 March 1909.
4. *Alexandra Herald,* 28 July 1909.
5. Apparently this practice was adopted on a regular basis. There is a report that Mrs Williams' house and shop caught fire at 2.30 am on 1 March 1911. There was a considerable delay in beginning fire fighting while waiting for the water to be turned on.
6. This system was still in operation during the 1950s.
7. *Alexandra Herald* 17 September 1919.

8. *Alexandra Herald* 19 October 1921

Someone recognised pipes in the Butchers Creek siphon that had once been part of the Molyneux Hydraulic pipeline laid in 1893 from secondhand pipes purchased from the Commissioners Flat Company at Roxburgh East when that company went into liquidation.

22.

MANOR BURN "FALLS"

"I would hate to say whether they are man made or natural," was the reply of one 'long-time Central Otago resident.' He had been asked by the editor of the *Central Otago News* for his opinion about the origin of the Manorburn 'Falls' featured in a photograph published by the newspaper on 19 October 1990. This uncertainty was rather surprising, as there were people alive who could have given a definite answer at the time the photograph was published.

The Manor Burn enters the Manuherikia River two kilometres upstream from Alexandra and many older people remember a small dam across the stream as a favourite picnic spot. No one, however, seems able to recall when or why it was built. It was covered by the waters of the reservoir behind the Lower Manorburn Dam in 1934 and has not been visible since, but there are a number of photographs in existence. The one published in the *Central Otago News* shows that the face of the structure was a series of steps made from blocks of schist rock. Comparison with the height of people standing on top of the steps in the photograph, and even allowing for foreshortening, gives the impression that the finished structure may have been somewhat higher than the estimate of 12 feet (3.7m) given in the Application (by 'His Majesty the King' no less) to the Warden's Court.

'Coolgardie'
The Manor Burn was always an important place for gold miners. At first, it was the flat low-lying, gravelly delta between the stream and the Manuherikia River that attracted attention. Great works were undertaken by groups of miners who diverted the streams so they could ground-sluice their exposed beds. As early as 1863 there was the Manuherikia Ground Sluicing Company and the Grand Junction Company, which made itself unpopular by building a dam across the river which flooded out its neighbours and made their claims unworkable. And there were many others.

Then gold was discovered in the shallow dry gullies that abound between the rocky outcrops on either side of the Manor Burn. But the difficulty was to get water on to the ground. The Manor Burn flowed in a very deep, narrow, rock-bound gorge and building water races to divert the water was a major undertaking. Until this was done, the

Figure 22. 1. The Manor Burn 'steps' taken in 1928. Comparing the height of the weir with the people standing on the face it seems that the finished structure was considerably higher that the 12 feet (3.7 m) mentioned in the Application to the Warden's Court. The reservoir behind the weir seems to be filled with detritus which is supporting a strong growth of rushes. The weir was about 20 metres upstream from the wall of the present Lower Manor Burn dam.

gold-rich dirt was carried down to the river in sacks, in wheelbarrows, on sledges or in small trucks running on tramlines.

Then came the dredges which reworked the delta and poked far up into the Manor Burn itself. Even the building of the railway bridge across the creek in 1905 did not put a stop to such activity.[1] All the time miners were trying to work the undoubtedly rich ground on the dry ridges and gullies on both sides of the creek. There was something of a rush to the place in the early 1890s and it became known as 'Coolgardie' after the rich gold mining district of Western Australia

Richmond Hill

James Rivers, an early pioneer of Alexandra and by the turn of the century a well-established merchant and inveterate investor in gold mines, was one who was interested in the Manorburn field. After mining for some time at Tucker Hill, further down the Manuherikia River, he opened a mine near the Manor Burn in a hill of white 'granite wash'—in fact, quartz gravel. He called it 'Richmond Hill' after his birthplace in Middlesex in England. This mine later became a source of builders' sand for Alexandra and has been steadily enlarged into what is now the large sandpit on Tucker Hill Road.

Manor Burn Sluicing Company

But Rivers was not the only one interested in investing in the mining

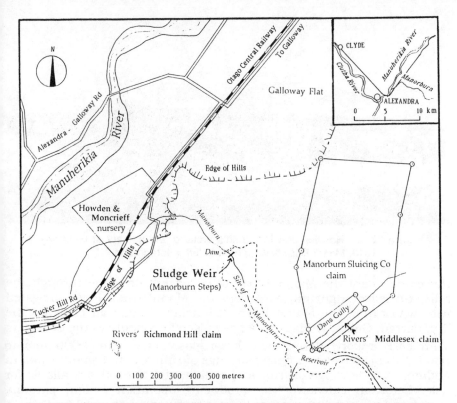

Figure 22. 2. The map shows the location of various mining claims near the Manor Burn and of the sludge weir built in 1908 to contain the expected tailings from the Manor Burn Sluicing Co's claim. The weir was designed to prevent tailings flooding over the orchard and nursery of Howden and Moncrieff. The site of the future Lower Manor Burn Dam is shown.

at this locality. In 1903 several Dunedin businessmen applied[2] for, and were later granted, extensive claims. Although the claims were adjacent, they were separate, and held under individual's names. It was the intention, apparently, to work as a syndicate. The claims covered over 300 acres (120 h) of the low hills on the northern side of the Manor Burn adjacent to Galloway Flat.

It took a long time to organise the enterprise. First, water had to be obtained from the Bonanza Water Race Company, and midway through arrangements this company was taken over by the Government and negotiations had to begin again. By June 1908, when it was decided to form a public company, no mining had been carried out.

Howden and Moncrieff's Nursery

Now a new problem arose. In 1895 Messrs Howden and Moncrieff, the well-known Dunedin seedsmen, had established a very successful nursery and orchard on the fertile soils of the terraces bordering the Manuherikia River. Their 34 acre (14 h) property was directly opposite

263

Figure 22. 3. Howden and Moncrieff's orchard and nursery at Galloway in 1913. Manor Burn flowing right to left in foreground.

the point where the Manor Burn, after leaving its gorge through the hills, turned at right angles to join the Manuherikia River. Irrigated with water from the Manor Burn, it quickly became an oasis on the dry, barren, Galloway Flat and a showplace for visitors to the district.

An early report[3] describes a large glasshouse with 3,000 tomato plants, and extensive outdoor plantings of rhubarb and small fruits. In addition a wide range of fruit and ornamental trees was available for sale. Later an extensive seed-producing operation (onion, parsnip, carrot and various flower seeds were mentioned)[4] was developed which covered more than 20 acres (8 h) of the property. The remainder was devoted to the nursery and to a permanent stone fruit orchard.

Howden and Moncrieff were concerned that the activities of the Manor Burn Sluicing Company would cause the Manor Burn, already choked with tailings, to overflow and spill into their nursery at the point where the stream turned sharply southwards. So they and other nearby settlers opposed the granting of a mining licence to the Manor Burn Sluicing Company.

The Government decided, in the public interest, it would build a 'sludge weir' across the Manor Burn. The site selected was 20 metres upstream from the stock bridge which spanned the Manor Burn at the spot later occupied by the wall of the Lower Manorburn dam. The weir was to be 190 ft (60 m) long and 12 ft (3.7 m) high comprised of large selected schist blocks arranged in a series of steps on the downstream side which meant that the base of the weir was some 50 ft (15 m) thick. It was calculated that the reservoir behind the weir would be about 60 metres wide and 120 metres long.

The structure was designed to hold back the tailings and so protect the low-lying ground at the mouth of the stream but at the same time allowing mining to go ahead. Having received this assurance from the Mines Department and, after inspecting the site, the Warden granted the company a licence on condition that mining had to start within six months, that is by 8 December 1908.

Figure 22. 4. This photograph was probably taken during construction of the weir. We are looking down the Manor Burn with the upstream face of the weir visible on the left. Water, brought across the gully in a pipe, is being used to make mortar from the sand stored in the hopper. Beyond the hopper is a tent with a chimney. The stream bed below the weir is filled with tailings raising the level of the stream so that a flood could threaten the nursery (buildings in background). These tailings have now been washed away by floods revealing, today, a deep, narrow, rocky chasm.

Howden and Moncrieff made it clear that if the company dared to start mining before the weir was built they would slap an injunction on it, so the company had no option but to wait until the weir was erected.

The weir was built by the Public Works Department at a cost of £448[5] and was completed during February 1909. The Manor Burn Sluicing Co. geared itself up for a start to its mining operations at the beginning of March. But it had overlooked something—the six months grace granted by the warden had expired and the company no longer had a licence to mine.

The Middlesex Mine

James Rivers, ever one with an eye on the main chance, forthwith pegged out a 10 acre (4 h) block along the floor of 'Dan's Gully' which ran through Norman's claim (a member of the Manor Burn Sluicing Co). Rivers applied to the Warden's Court for a Certificate of Abandonment for the ground.

It was granted on 19 April 1909[6] and Rivers was given one month to start mining on the property. The Manor Burn Sluicing Company appealed to the Supreme Court on the grounds that a fine was the appropriate penalty—not the issue of a Certificate of Abandonment. But the learned Judge did not see it that way and the appeal was dismissed in August 1909.[6] So Rivers got his claim and the Manor Burn Sluicing Company went into liquidation.

Rivers called his new claim 'The Middlesex Claim' and his manager, George Campbell, began to open it out with water brought across the Manor Burn in a pipeline from an extension of the Tucker Hill race. Unfortunately, James Rivers died in early 1910 and the Middlesex claim, which had been left to his daughter and daughters-in-law, was

Figure 22. 5. By 1913 the sludge weir had become filled with debris — not mining tailing which it was designed to hold, but silt washed from the hillsides depleted of vegetation by grazing animals and by fire. The wall of the Lower Manor Burn Dam now spans the gorge at the site of the stock bridge.

carried on for a few years but gradually fizzled out amidst court cases over ownership of the water that was being used.

With the demise of the Manor Burn Sluicing Co Ltd, the weir, built at public expense, became unnecessary. It remained standing for 25 years as a picturesque monument to yet another failed mining enterprise. If it held back any tailings, it would be only the small quantity from Rivers's Middlesex mine. But before it was submerged in 1934 beneath the rising waters of the newly built Lower Manorburn Dam the reservoir behind the weir had completely filled with silt[7]—an indication of the amount of soil eroded from the vegetation-depleted hillsides of the lower catchment of the Manor Burn.

Howden and Moncrieff's business also underwent changes. George Howden left the partnership and the seed production was abandoned. By 1912 the property, now wholly owned by Moncrieff and managed by

Gadd, was entirely devoted to fruitgrowing. In September 1914 the homestead was destroyed by fire and shortly afterwards the orchard was taken over by R. Kinraid. But by this time the gradual raising of the bed of the Manuherikia River by the influx of mining tailings, coupled with the increasing irrigation of the surrounding land, had caused a substantial rise in the water table so that fruitgrowing was no longer possible. The once fine orchard reverted to the lush grassland we see today.

NOTES

1. The small *Blacks Flat* dredge was dismantled and re-erected as the *Old Man* dredge above the railway bridge. It was unsuccessful.

2. For the record the names of the applicants were:- J. C. Thomson, Robert Lee, Henry Fletcher Norman and Robert Thomas Wheeler. Eventually the Manor Burn Sluicing Company held mining licences over:-

          Sections 1 Block VIII: Tiger Hill Survey District.

          Sections 51 & 52, Block IX: Leaning Rock Survey District.

                Total 207 acres.

3. *Dunstan Times* 1 September 1895.

4. D'Esterre, E 1903 p. 14.

5. AJHR 1909, D1. Like the height of the weir, the price increased somewhat from the original estimate of £250.

6 *Alexandra Herald* 21 April 1909.

7. *Alexandra Herald* 30 June 1909 and 25 August 1909.

8. According to the late Mr George Govan (Personal communication).

23.
CONFLICT OF INTEREST
The Battle for Noble's Orchard

When the Golden Beach Company decided to change from hydraulic elevating to dredging, it applied to the Warden's Court for an extra area of 26 hectares and this was granted in September 1897. Included in this enlarged claim were adjoining properties occupied by Fisher and by William Noble—the same William Noble who was a partner in the company.

The properties lay on the northern side of the road to Earnscleugh, just beyond the crossing of Chapmans Creek (or Dry Gully as this crossing was, and is, often called). Fisher's place was a nearly square block of about 1.5 hectares, but the more extensive Noble property stretched along the Earnscleugh road for nearly a kilometre and covered 7 hectares. The somewhat oblong-shaped farm was mainly in rough grass but at the eastern end, where it widened considerably, there were two blocks of fruit trees. One, close to the road, had been planted soon after Noble settled on the property and was called the 'old orchard' and the other, near the house, and planted more recently, was the 'new orchard.' A long narrow mining dam, fed by a water race from the Fraser River, lay along the northern boundary of the property and was a favourite swimming spot for Alexandra school children.

Noble, one of the pioneer fruitgrowers of Central Otago, had occupied the land since the early 1870s and had developed it into a veritable showpiece of the district. One of the attractions of Alexandra was to walk out to Noble's, in the season, and partake of strawberries and cream.

With the granting of the mining licence to the Golden Beach Company, both Noble and Fisher realised they could be facing a serious situation because neither had legal titles to their holdings.

Squatters
In the early days they had simply settled on the land, with nothing more than the permission of Earnscleugh Station within whose boundaries it lay. Later, at one of the many court hearings, Noble was to claim that he had legitimately acquired four 'Residence Areas' of one

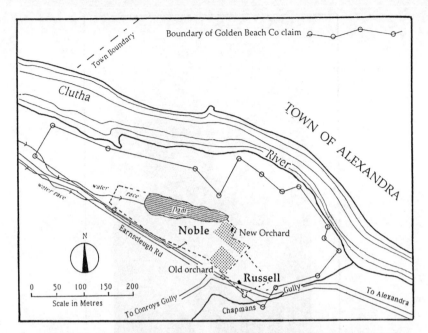

Figure 23. 1. Plan of the Golden Beach claim as it was in 1910 at the time of the confrontation with William Noble and Mrs Russell. The area of the claim was 30 h (74 acres). The boundaries of Noble's and Russell's properties are dotted as they were not legal boundaries.

ιcre each but could no longer produce any documentary evidence to ƨupport his claim. For the bulk of his orchard and paddocks, however, ιe had no title whatever. He was not alone in this. Many other well-ϲnown orchards and small holdings began in a similar way. There was ιothing secret about the situation and Noble's circumstances had, in ϝact, been highlighted in the Warden's Court two years before.

In November 1895, when Craven Paget, a local miner,[1] had applied ϝor a 4 hectare claim at Poverty Beach, William Noble objected on the ϝrounds that the claim was part of rich agricultural land from which ιe had made his living for over 20 years. It came out in evidence that Ϡoble had occupied the land with the permission of William Fraser, the ιicensee of Earnscleugh Station, but had no other right to it. But worse ʋas to come. It was pointed out by the Court that Fraser himself had ιo right to assign any part of his run to some other person without the ϸermission of the Land Board and certainly he could not give anyone ϊhe right to cultivate land when he himself only had a licence to ϸasturage.

It was made clear at that time that Noble was actually trespassing ϧn Crown Land and so had no status to object if a miner, with a Ϡiners Right, applied for a claim on the land. The fact that Noble had ϸeen in occupation for more than 20 years made no difference ʋhatever to his status. Needless to say, his objection failed.[2]

Nevertheless, the warden, in granting the licence two years later[3] to ϊhe Golden Beach Company to mine the land, was sympathetic to the

Figure 23. 2. William Noble established an orchard and farm that was one of the showpieces of the district but he did not have a title for the land so it was available for mining. Official and public pressure resulted in special sections being added to three separate Acts of Parliament before adequate compensation was paid to Noble and his wife for the loss of their orchard.

settlers' situation. He imposed conditions which required that Noble's land could not be worked or interfered with unless:

> . . . and until the full surface value of the land with all improvements thereon be fully paid to the said William Noble; the value to be arrived at under the 'Arbitration Act, 1890. . .

This meant compensation had to be paid if and when the land was actually mined. It could be taken piecemeal and compensation paid accordingly. The same conditions were imposed regarding Fisher's land (now occupied by Asquith.)

At this stage the imposed conditions did not worry the company as it had plenty of other land to work and later it had more pressing problems of a financial nature. But by 1901 the dredge had begun to work its way into a paddock used by William Noble, so Noble asked for compensation. This was to be the first test of the conditions attached to the licence. The warden appointed assessors but they failed to agree, so he himself ruled that compensation of £42 be paid to Noble and that fences were to be reinstated and made rabbit-proof.

These court negotiations were conducted in the gentlemanly and civilised manner expected amongst friends but in April 1905 the mortgagees, Josiah and William Lane of Dunedin bought the Golden Beach company. Outsiders, city businessmen indeed, had entered the arena.

Enter J. P. Lane

Josiah Pierce Lane proved to be an energetic dredge owner and was determined nothing would stand in the way of his making the Golden Beach dredge a financial success. He quickly took the company in hand and straightened out its affairs. For the next 10 years hardly a month went by when he was not represented in the Warden's Court battling for some advantage to the company.

Figure 23.3. Josiah Pearce Lane (1861-1941) was a partner in Lane's Cordials Ltd of Dunedin. He and his brother held the mortgage on the Golden Beach Company and in 1905 took it over. J. P. Lane began an agressive policy to make the company profitable. His vigorous water acquisition policy led to disputes with neighbours and his determination to dredge the properties of Noble and Russell estranged him from local people.

Lane soon gained a reputation for not having too much concern for people when profit was at stake, and this aspect of his character is still remembered, and spoken of with some feeling, by older townspeople.

As part of his constant vigilance and reassessment of company affairs, Lane decided that the part of the claim that lay to the southwest of the Earnscleugh road, was undredgable owing to the presence of rock at shallow depth. So in 1906, to reduce his rent, he surrendered his licence and was granted[4] a new one covering only 30 hectares, surveyed off as Section 52.

The new licence was for land which still included Noble's orchard and farmlands and, at the behest of Noble and Mrs Ellen Russell, who had taken over Asquith's property, and to the chagrin of Lane, the warden imposed the original conditions on the new licence.

For the next three years Lane was busy keeping the dredge at work and battling to acquire more water to keep it afloat. But by the middle of 1910 his dredges (he now had two[5]) had reached the boundary of the occupied properties and he wanted to begin dredging parts of them. The time had arrived to determine compensation.

Assessors were appointed to assist the warden in the task. John Ewing, a well-known and very experienced miner, was appointed by Lane and George Rivers, a local valuer, represented Noble. The panel eventually fixed compensation at £400 for Noble, comprising £125 for the 1.7 hectares of paddock and £275 for the 0.7 hectare block of orchard that was to be destroyed. Mrs Russell was awarded £100 for the whole of her property. The figures were based on the value of the land and improvements, less a sum because of the lack of titles.

Lane was dissatisfied not only with the amount of compensation he was asked to pay but with the whole business of his having a licence with conditions attached. Instead of paying compensation he decided on a new tack to get rid of the conditions. He once again surrendered his licence and lodged an application for a new one, this time for only 20 hectares which were surveyed off as Section 62. This new section excluded all the ground that the company had already dredged but still included Noble's and Russell's properties. This move again reduced Lane's rent but he also hoped that this time he could persuade the warden not to impose conditions on the new licence. Noble and Mrs Russell were equally determined that the conditions would remain on any new licence issued.

At the hearing[6] in the Warden's Court it was admitted that Lane had the right under the Mining Act to mine the land. But, said Noble's lawyer, his client had spent a lifetime cultivating and improving the property. Had the land been taken and compensation paid 14 years ago when the conditions were first imposed, the lawyer said, Noble could have gone elsewhere and started again but he had been lulled into a sense of false security by the long delay in settling the matter. Mrs Russell, too, had bought her property and made many improvements since the previous warden had imposed the conditions, which should not now be set aside lightly.

Lane's lawyer took the hard line. Noble and Mrs Russell were simply intruders and were occupying the land illegally, he said. Here was a block of unalienated Crown land in a Mining District open for mining and Lane must be granted his licence without any conditions for compensation. In fact, he pointed out, there was no provision in the Mining Act for any compensation, so the conditions imposed by the previous wardens were actually invalid.

The warden pointed out, in passing, that the conditions had been agreed to by the original Golden Beach Company but as this was an application for a new licence he did not see any profit in reviewing th decisions of previous wardens. He did rather doubt the validity of the conditions imposed on previous licences but, nevertheless, he made it clear that he was sympathetic to imposing similar conditions on any new licence. The whole question was complex and accordingly he would refer the matter to the Supreme Court for a decision on the validity of any conditions he might impose on the new licence that was being applied for.

Figure 23. 4. The Golden Beach Company bought their second dredge from the liquidated Perseverance Dredging Company and renamed it *Golden Beach No 2*. It was smaller than *Golden Beach No 1* so was used to dredge the shallower ground in Dry Gully and to dredge through Noble's orchard. Here, with lengthened elevator and other alterations, it is heading into Dry Gully (Chapmans Gully) with Noble's orchard behind.

Public Sympathy

There was a great deal of sympathy for Noble's case. It was probably generated partly by the David and Goliath situation, and partly because the day of the gold dredge was fading and fruitgrowing, now that the railway had arrived, was seen as the coming industry of the district. There was also a measure of dislike among the ordinary townspeople towards Lane himself—the rich man from the city pushing them about.

The *Alexandra Herald* felt strongly that if the orchard were to be destroyed then Noble should be adequately compensated. A public petition was organised.

273

Meanwhile, at the instigation of Noble's lawyer, the mining Registrar had carried out a search and had discovered two titles for 'Residence Areas,' one issued in 1868 and the other in 1871. It appeared that Noble had, indeed, taken out one Residence Area in his own name and had bought others. The importance of this discovery was that Residence Areas could not be mined unless they had been cancelled. This information was of value to the warden who was 'stating a case' for the Supreme Court.

Supreme Court Hearing

At the Supreme Court hearing[7] held on 27 March, 1911 the questions to be resolved were essentially:

— Can those who occupy, without a licence, unalienated Crown Lands in a Mining District, expect compensation either for the value of the land or for improvements?

— In this present case have the occupiers, through their occupation, acquired the right to compensation?

— Were the conditions imposed on previous licences valid?

— If all, or some of the conditions are valid, are the occupiers entitled to compensation for improvements?

Figure 23. 5. The *Golden Beach No 2* dredge cutting into Noble's orchard.

In his judgement, given a couple of months later, Mr Justice Williams pointed out that, as with all applications for claims of over 30 acres (12 h), the previous applications had received the consent of the Minister of Mines. Because the Minister had the absolute right to grant or refuse licences he could also grant licences with conditions. If the applicant didn't like the conditions he didn't have to accept the licence.

274

Furthermore any new licence issued in substitution for the existing licence must be issued subject to the conditions on the original licence.

Finally the judge gave the answers to the questions set out for the Court's resolution:

1. Those who occupy Crown land without a licence are not generally entitled to compensation.

2. Because of the conditions on Lane's licence, Noble and Mrs Russell are entitled to compensation.

3. The conditions on Lane's licence are valid.

4. Noble and Russell are entitled to compensation for improvements in existence at the time their possession is disturbed. They could not expect to be compensated for the destruction of the land as it belonged to the Crown

It was clear from the judgement that, as the Crown had approved the conditions with their promise of compensation, so the Crown had some responsibility for the compensation.

Special Legislation

As compensation could not be paid under the Mining Act, special legislation was necessary and a Clause was included in a 'washing-up' Bill passed late in October 1911.[8] The Clause contained two sections:

1. The said conditions are hereby declared valid except so far as they apply to the payment of compensation to the said William Noble for the surface value of the land.

2. If at any time hereafter the said Josiah Pierce Lane . . . desires to surrender or exchange his licence . . . it shall be lawful for the Warden . . . to insert in any licence which comprises the land of the said William Noble the conditions contained in said licence No 1068A as declared valid by this section.

The passing of this Act effectively finished Lane's attempts to get a licence without attached conditions.

Destruction Begins

Impatient with these delays and anxious to keep his dredges working at all costs, Lane had already started dredging both Noble's and Russell's land but without handing over any compensation. Noble and Russell promptly sued Lane for damages. There was confusion as to whether the promised compensation covered only the area that was to be dredged or was for the whole property, so Noble claimed £125 for the portion that had been dredged so far. But Lane held that the agreed £500 (£400 for Noble and £100 for Russell) was meant as compensation for the whole of the two properties and the warden had to agree there was nothing in writing to suggest otherwise. Noble was non-suited and, in addition had to pay £3 3s. costs.[9] However, at the same time the warden granted Mrs Russell £15 damages for the destruction of part of her property, although she had asked for £50.

Back in Court again in October to belatedly obtain permission to take 0.5 hectares of Noble's land, Lane was now prepared to pay the value of that particular piece. The warden gave permission provided

Figure 23. 6. Another view of *Golden Beach No 2* working into Noble's orchard. Earnscleugh Road is in the foreground. The pipeline is from Lanes Dam (high up on a hillside to the left) and is supplying water to the dredge pond which at this stage is several metres above the level of the Clutha River.

Lane first paid £100 into the Court. All this was rather academic as the land had already been destroyed.

The Warden's Court in December[10] 1911, dealt with two aspects of this long drawn-out saga. The first was Mrs Russell's claim for compensation for her whole property which by this time had been almost totally destroyed. She was successful in that she was awarded £100—the amount agreed upon earlier. The second was yet another move by Lane to get his hands on the whole of the Noble property and avoid paying rent on the land that he had already dredged. He offered to surrender his complete dredging claim (most of which was already worked out) in return for a new claim of only 8 hectares of unworked ground which was, in effect, the undredged remnant of Noble's property.

The warden was getting tired of the whole business and he told Lane, in no uncertain terms, what he thought about his machinations. He pointed out that Lane had deliberately damaged Noble's land and still would not pay compensation. Lane would get no more titles, he said, until he had treated Noble fairly and paid up. Lane's lawyer tried to remonstrate and play the injured innocent but, as the newspaper reporter put it, 'In spite of further argument the warden remained unmoved.'

In February 1912 the warden decided that the only fair way to settle the matter once and for all was to award Noble compensation for the improvements over the whole of his property so he recommended[11]

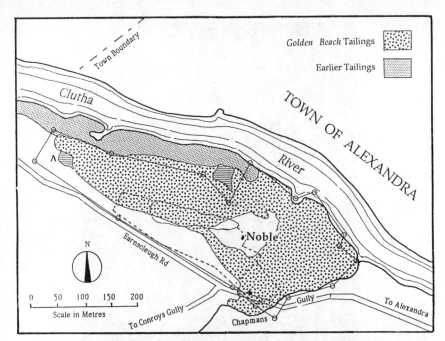

Figure 23. 7. Plan of the Golden Beach claim as it when dredging in stopped in 1914. It shows how Noble's orchard was cut off from the remainder of the property. The pond 'A' marks the spot where the *Golden Beach No 12* dredge was dismantled in 1916.

that the issue once more go to arbitration. This time Mr McPhail of Roxburgh acted for Lane and George Rivers once again for Noble. As these could not reach agreement it was the warden who made the decision which he announced on 23 April 1912. William Noble would be awarded £675 in full payment for all improvements on his whole property, the arbiters were to get £15 15s. each and costs would be £7 7s. bringing the total amount payable by Lane to £698 2s. This amount was to be paid by 29 April and Noble was to give possession within 14 days of that date.[12]

By this time the Noble and Russell properties had been ruined. Mrs Russell's land had been completely dredged; Noble's 'old orchard,' apart from a few trees hard up against the Earnscleugh road, had gone.

His 'new orchard' and house together with a few hectares of adjoining, unoccupied land that for some reason were left undredged, had been separated from the rest of the property by a wide dredged channel. This effectively cut off access and irrigation water and drastically lowered the water table so fruitgrowing became virtually impossible.

The house and remaining orchard were now on an island bounded on all sides by gravel cliffs and surrounded by a sea of dredge tailings. Lane would no doubt have excused this action on the grounds that the dredge was following a 'lead' of gold but it is impossible to escape the conclusion that it was an act of vindictiveness designed to force Noble to abandon the property.

Figure 23. 8. An air photo, taken in March 1949. Alexandra is at lower right and Earnscleugh Road at left. The remnant of Noble's orchard—the darker 'island' surrounded by lighter coloured dredge tailings, stands out clearly in the centre of the photograph.

More Public Sympathy

William Noble was, by this time, a man of 80 and the general feeling about the way he was being treated was summed up by the Alexandra correspondent of the *Evening Star*.-

> It was one of the choice spots of the district, the earliest orchard in the place, and Mr Noble has grown from a young man to venerable old age in that little picturesque corner—a corner he transformed from tussock into its present condition. The case all along has been a peculiar one, but one thing is certain: the compensation paid was totally inadequate. Another feature is that in a district like this, where fruit-growing is more precious than mining land, it is a thousand pities to see a corner that would keep a family in comfort for all time and a corner, too, that would yield in the form of produce wealth for ever, destroyed for the sake of the gold that lies on the bottom. It is a veritable outstanding example of killing the goose that lays the golden

egg. You will not meet a single person in Alexandra who is unbiased and qualified to judge who does not assert that Mr Noble got just about half the value of his improvements, and general sympathy is felt for him in the matter.[13]

It was pointed out by the local newspaper that the property yielded over £200 a year profit and, furthermore, that bare land around Alexandra had recently fetched £50 an acre. Perhaps, it suggested with heavy sarcasm, Mr Lane should make a country home of this choice little corner.

The Government would certainly have noted the Supreme Court judgement which pointed out the Crown responsibility for compensation. No doubt the publicity and public outcry was a factor too in persuading Government to add a clause[14] to another wash-up Bill which passed into law in 1913. It said:

113 Whereas it is desired to grant compensation to William Noble, of Alexandra, Otago, for the loss suffered by him by reason of the issue of a licence under the Mining Act for a dredging claim over the land occupied by the said William Noble as an orchard; Be it therefore enacted as follows:-

The Minister of Finance is hereby authorized, without further appropriation than this Act, to pay out of the Consolidated Fund to the said William Noble, of Alexandra, Otago, the sum of thirty shillings a week during the remainder of his life, in compensation for loss suffered by him, as hereinafter recited.

Lane had at last achieved his objective of getting control of Noble's property, although at considerable cost, and with the matter finally settled the warden granted him Section 62, Block I Fraser Survey District of 49 acres as a Special Dredging Claim with no conditions attached to the licence.

Hollow Victory

No sooner had Lane gained possession of Noble's property than he decided to lease it. Why did he not go ahead and dredge the whole property after taking so much trouble to get rid of Noble?

The answer probably is, that as the dredges could not be laid up awaiting the outcome of the court battle, they had to bypass the orchard and continue working the western part of the claim. By the time the matter was resolved the No 2 dredge[15] was well beyond the orchard and only the dam and paddock that made up the western part of Noble's property could be easily dredged.

When the dredge reached the end of the dam it presumably could have turned round and worked its way back to the orchard through the remainder of the property. Instead, because of falling returns, increasing maintenance and difficulties with manning because of the War, it came to a final stop at the western end of Noble's property and was eventually dismantled in the pond that still marks the end of the Golden Beach tailings.

So after all his effort and expense, and after all the worry his actions had caused, Lane did not succeed in his objective of completely dredging Noble's property.

Figure 23. 9. The only original building of the Noble farm still standing.

Pension for Mrs Noble

On 3 February 1915 the *Alexandra Herald* reported the death of William Noble and commented that whereas he had received 30 shillings a week compensation for the loss of his orchard, his wife was not included in the arrangement and now she had nothing. And the editor was apparently not content to leave it there, as a note appeared in the same paper on 16 August 1916 which said:-

> For some time several Alexandra gentlemen, including ourselves, have been trying to have the pension granted to William Noble continued to his wife as being his joint helper in the matter of the fine orchard which he lost. We are now in receipt of information from our Wellington correspondent that it has been decided by Parliament to grant Mrs Noble 30 shillings a week for the rest of her life.

The editor was referring to the Reserves Act for 1916 in which the following clause appeared:[16]

> **67** Whereas. . . it was provided that a pension of thirty shillings per week be paid to William Noble . . .And whereas the said William Noble is now deceased, and it is desirable that the pension should be continued to his widow: Be it enacted as follows:-
>
> > The Minister of Finance is authorized . . . to pay . . . to Mrs Ann Noble, widow of the said William Noble, deceased, of Alexandra, Otago, the sum of one pound ten shillings a week during the remainder of her life.

Mrs Noble at least had the satisfaction of living to see J. P. Lane surrender his dredging licence at the end of 1915 and his dredges dismantled during the following year. In late 1916[17] Lane offered the remnants of the orchard for sale as he tried to realise what he could from the remains of the Golden Beach mining venture. It was

280

noticeable too that Lane left the business of disposing of the property to D. Livingston, who had been Dredgemaster of the *Golden Beach* dredge. Lane had washed his hands of this particular venture and had moved on to others.

A succession of owners have improved and replanted the property through to the present day. Bulldozers have filled in the dredged channel to provide access to the 'island' from the 'mainland' and irrigation water from the Last Chance Scheme ensures that the small orchard not only survives but flourishes like an oasis overlooking a desert of old dredge tailings.[18]

NOTES

1. Craven Paget had been a neighbour and mining partner of Noble for many years. They had mined together at Frenchmans Point and Chapmans Gully, had jointly owned the Mountain race and Lower Conroys race and both became partners in the Golden Beach Company. Under these circumstances, which were quite common, it is difficult to believe that much of the litigation that took place in the Wardens Court between friends was taken seriously.

2. *Otago Witness* 5 December, 1895.

3 The licence for the Special Claim of 65 acres (26 h) was granted on 18 September 1897.

4. *Dunstan Times* 19 March and 19 June 1906.

5. J. P. Lane bought the *Perseverance* dredge from the liquidator of the New Perseverance Gold Dredging Company in March 1909 (*Alexandra Herald* 17 March 1909) and, after alterations and overhaul, it started work as *Golden Beach No 2* in late April 1909 (*Dunstan Times* 28 April, 1909).

6. *Alexandra Herald* 20 July 1910.

7. *New Zealand Law Reports* Vol XXX, 1911: p. 73.

8. Clause 17, Reserves and other Lands Disposal and Public Bodies Empowering Act, 1911.

9. *Dunstan Times* 4 September 1911.

10. *Alexandra Herald* 6 December 1911.

11. *Alexandra Herald* 14 February 1912.

12. *Alexandra Herald* 8 May 1912.

13. reprinted in *Alexandra Herald* 22 May 1912.

14. Reserves and other Lands Disposal and Public Bodies Empowering Act, 1913.

15. It is believed that one was dismantled in the pond at the western end of Noble's property and that dredge remains in a pond in the tailings north of Noble's property may be the remains of the other.

16. *Alexandra Herald* 1 November 1916.

17. Reserves and other Lands Disposal and Public Bodies Empowering Act, 1916.

18. At least one building from the Noble era survives.

24.

LINGER AND DIE

Most residents of Alexandra think they know what and where the 'Linger and Die' is—"It's that river flat down by the baths" some will say. Others will tell you that it was the name of a mine, but they are not sure exactly where it was located. There is probably no one left now who knows for certain the origin of the colourful name.

The Setting

Less than a kilometre above its junction with the Clutha River, the Manuherikia River has, in time past, swung in against the terrace on which the town is located and eroded a deep embayment. The river has now partly retreated from the embayment leaving behind a flood plain in the form of a low terrace a metre or so above normal water level. The low terrace, about 200 metres long, 100 metres wide, and covering an area of more than a hectare, is now protected from river erosion by an artificial barrier of broken rock. At the downstream end the terrace is cut off by a steep, rocky hillside. Upstream it abuts against a sheer rock cliff and along its landward side it is bounded by the high scarp of the town terrace.

An Old River Course

The site of the embayment is the only place where there is a break in the otherwise continuous ridge of schist rock which extends up the western bank of the Manuherikia River for two kilometres from its junction with the Clutha River. In the 200 metre-gap in the ridge, the gravels of the town terrace form the bank of the river and it is because these gravels offer less resistance to river erosion than the solid rock of the ridge that the embayment has formed. But what formed the gap in the ridge?

It was first pointed out by Professor Park[1] that the break in the ridge marked an ancient course of the Clutha River and what little evidence there is, tends to confirm his thinking. For one thing the gap itself is most likely to have been formed by erosion and the most powerful agent of erosion available is a river. Then there is the fact that the course of the Manuherikia River above the gap is confined to a narrow, rocky gorge but below the gap it is much wider, though still rock bound. It is very likely that this widening of the course was caused by a much larger flow of water. Finally the borings done by the Golden

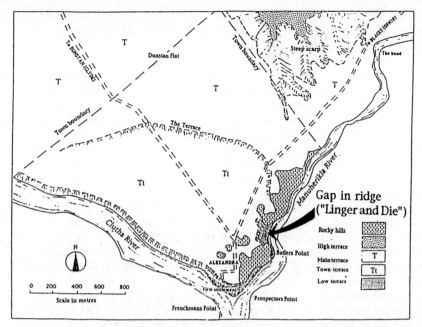

Figure 24. 1. A prominent physical feature of Alexandra is the break in the rocky ridge which runs up the western side of the Manuherikia River for two kilometres. It was almost certainly occupied by an ancient course of the Clutha River.

Bend Company in 1904 showed that the rock bottom in the gap is 10 metres below the present bed of the Manuherikia River.

Mention of old river courses is guaranteed to excite miners into a frenzy of activity as they visualise the beds of ancient rivers paved with gold. The fact that the *Golden Link* dredge struck a rich patch in the embayment was taken as evidence that she had struck the buried treasure and much effort was expended in later years in trying to reach and follow this elusive 'deep lead.'

Although the embayment seems to mark the junction of an old course of the Clutha River with the Manuherikia, it is impossible to trace the course of the old river above this junction. The present course of the Clutha River is a recent feature and has no relationship to the old one, so it is useless trying to speculate where the old course left the present one.

The fact that the old course is now completely filled with the gravels that make up the main terrace, means the old river bed is very ancient and was probably formed several hundreds of thousands of years ago when the river was cutting down from the level of the high terrace on which the airport lies.

Ground sluicing of the terrace scarp facing the embayment during the 1860s left shallow gullies[2] and remnants of some of these still persist. The small area sluiced indicates returns were not good and the claims were soon abandoned because it had been discovered that the uppermost gravels of the town terrace are only marginally auriferous.

It was found later by boring, that rich wash, overlying bedrock, lies some 10 metres below the flood plain of the Manuherikia River—20 metres or so below the surface of the town terrace.

The most extensive mine was at the southern end of the embayment where the workings covered the site of the present Centennial Swimming Pool and extended across Thompson St into the section now occupied by the Community Centre theatre. The upper end of this sluiced chasm was used as a town rubbish tip[3]for many years and in the mid-1940s the whole gully was filled with rock debris from excavations at the Bank of New Zealand site on the corner of Skird and Tarbert Streets, and from the neighbouring shop sections. The area so reclaimed was used first as a Ministry of Works yard and then for the swimming pool.

Another sluicing claim formed a chasm running up from the flood plain parallel to and including part of the present Walton Street. The upper end of this gully, which was close to Tarbert Street, formed a convenient depression in which to build the Coronation baths in 1911 and, in fact, part of the gully had to be filled to form the floor of the baths. Below the baths the gully was opened out as a quarry to obtain gravel for Borough works and when it was no longer required for this the sides were smoothed down and the site used for a Borough Council works yard. It is now the site of the Museum. Rock excavated during the widening of Skird Street in the late 1940s was used to fill this gully where it crossed Thompson St.

Much of the gully formed by the third sluicing claim still exists. From the northern corner of the embayment a deep gully was sluiced almost up to Tarbert Street. At the bottom end of this gully a number of futile attempts were made over the next 80 years to reach the elusive 'deep lead' which was believed to run back under the gravels of the town terrace.

The *Golden Link*

During the dredging boom at the turn of the century, a dredging claim, covering a one mile length of the Manuherikia River, was taken up by the Golden Link Gold Dredging Company. The claim, which covered 40 acres (16h), stretched from just upstream of the mouth of the river to beyond the site of the railway bridge. The Company was registered in July 1899 and the dredge, built by A. & T. Burt during 1900 at the mouth of Stockyard Gully, started work in February 1901.

The *Golden Link* met with moderate success as she quickly dredged her way up the river. Her directors, who were pleased when she recovered 34 oz of gold for six days' work, were quite ecstatic when she suddenly struck a rich patch while dredging the low terrace in the embayment. From one spot, close under the town terrace, she recovered 70 oz of gold in the course of two shifts. In their excitement the crew overlooked the danger of the steadily increasing height of the vertical gravel face as the buckets dug further and further into the terrace. Suddenly, the inevitable fall occurred and tons of gravel landed on the bow of the dredge, causing some damage. The dredge withdrew to lick its wounds and did not renew the attack.

The *Golden Link's* total for 1901 of 598 oz was worth £2,300 but, unfortunately, the company had expended more than £8,000 in recovering it. Worse still, the dredge had covered all the easily worked ground. The result was inevitable. In March 1902 just 13 months after starting, she was closed down. The company was liquidated the following month and the dredge sold in May for £1,230. Later in the year it was dismantled by Jeremiah Drummey and sent to Nelson.

The bend in the river where the *Golden Link* had made her rich strike became known as the 'golden bend,' and the search to rediscover and follow the elusive lead continued off and on for the next 30 years.

Figure 24. 2. The *Golden Link* dredge was built at the mouth of Stockyard Gully and began dredging in the Manuherkia River in February 1901. Its main success was to strike a patch of rich gold in the embayment later to be called the 'Linger and Die.' The dredge closed down inn March 1902.

The Golden Bend Mining Company

The Golden Bend Mining Co, a syndicate of local men, was formed in early 1904 and made two fruitless attempts to open up a 'paddock' and reach the bottom where the rich gold was reputed to lie. Little wonder they had difficulty—borings showed the rock bottom was 30 ft (9m) below the surface and the intervening gravels were saturated with water. Nevertheless they persisted. They installed a steam engine which was used to haul trucks of gravel up an inclined tramline from the mine and also work a Californian pump.[4] But it could not cope with the inrush of water and for some time the mine was abandoned while the partners gave some thought to their next move.

In early 1905 they installed a more powerful steam boiler to work a 10 inch pump and it was soon lifting a head of water 20 ft and pushing it up a further 12 ft into the sluice box where it was used for washing the gravels. Then the partners decided to scrap the tramline and trucks and install what was, in effect, a land dredge. It consisted of a ladder and line of buckets with about the same capacity for shifting material as a more conventional river dredge. It apparently worked well enough although the men found it extremely difficult to move forwards when required. But they still could not get down to the gold in the face of the tremendous quantities of water. The enthusiasm of the group for the project lingered on for some time and, finally, in 1908, died.

It is believed that it was the experiences of this company that gave rise to the phrase 'linger and die.'

No doubt, over the years, individuals and small groups pottered about at the site in the hope of striking gold but, if so, their efforts are unrecorded.

Alexandra Deep Lead Gold-mining Company Ltd

It was not until 1925 that another serious effort was made. A public company,[6] registered in September with a capital of £6,000, received a good deal of local support. A Mr Hammer was appointed manager. The company's main effort was directed to opening up the 'paddock' where the old *Golden Link* had struck its gold and the directors anticipated the water that they knew they would encounter by installing a 5 inch electrically-driven pump. But it was not sufficient and the pump had to be doubled in size.[7]

All through 1926 the workmen concentrated on sinking a huge pit or shaft 18 ft by 11 ft 6 in (5.4 m by 3.4 m) by means of an hydraulic elevator worked by a pump driven by an electric motor. This was a massive undertaking considering that the hole had to be 30 ft (9 m) deep and the walls of loose gravel had to be supported by heavy timbers. Finally they reached bedrock and commenced driving a tunnel in the supposed direction of the lead of gold. But the flow of water was too much. It came through a layer of open, porous gravel about 10 ft (3 m) above the main bottom and its control proved too costly. This company died too, in October 1927.[8]

The local power board inherited much of the equipment as part payment for the large power bill that the company had run up during its short existence.

Mining House (NZ) Ltd

A company called Mining House (NZ) Ltd employed several men during the Great Depression in another attempt to reach the elusive 'deep lead.' This time, instead of sinking a vertical shaft, it was planned to drive twin tunnels down at an angle of 45,° but again the influx of water and loose gravels pouring into the tunnels made work very difficult. Finally, after a flood in the nearby river, the water level rose uncontrollably in the tunnels and they collapsed and that was the end of that venture.[9]

Left behind was the usual debris of an abandoned gold mine including rusting pipes, tramrails, trucks and other gear which, over the years, gradually disappeared. Finally all that was left was a large evil-looking, slime-covered pond, hiding within its depths more than 30 years of fruitless endeavour. During the 1950s a contractor, who lived close by and was concerned for the safety of his and other

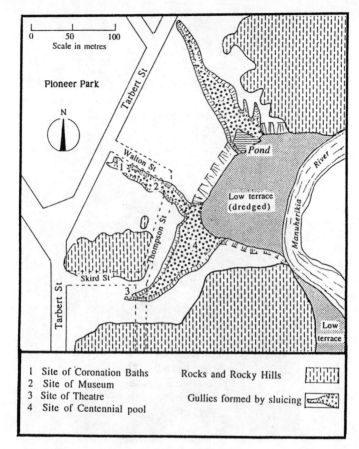

Figure 24. 3. Map of 'Linger and Die' vicinity. The pond shown occupied the mine workings called the "Linger and Die."

children, used his bulldozer to fill in the pond.

But this was not the end of activity in the area. It was widely believed the embayment would be permanently flooded when the lake rose behind the Roxburgh Dam. It was hoped that a pleasant recreational area would be formed within a short distance of the main street of the town. These hopes were boosted when tree-felling gangs appeared in the mid-1950s and cleared the willows from the area. Anticipating a substantial depth of water over the low terrace, enthusiasts spent a lot of labour and cement in constructing a concrete boat-launching ramp at the southern end of the embayment.

Unfortunately, presumably through some misunderstanding about the new water levels, the new lake did not flow into the embayment at other than flood times and the concrete boat ramp stood high and dry for many years until finally buried by the formation of a new road.

The low terrace was the scene of other activity during the construction of the Roxburgh Dam. The site was selected for the building of two substantial steel caissons that were later floated down the lake to the dam to be used for holding back the lake waters when it

Figure 24. 4. A 1949 air photo shows the pond occupying the old mine workings. It was filled in a few years later as a safety measure.

was necessary to remove the sluice gates for maintenance or repair
The work of constructing these continued day and night for month
accompanied by the chatter of riveting and whine of pneumatic tools
The noise stopped only when the whole project was covered by floo
water through an unexpected rise in the river and construction wor
had to give way to salvage and several week's work of clearing awa
silt.

Since then the 'Linger and Die' has remained a wilderness, wit
periodic flooding preventing any worthwhile attempts at landscaping o
development.

The Name
So far as can be ascertained the first appearance of the name 'Linge
and Die' is on an Application,[10] made by Lewis Cameron in 1912, for
claim of 4.5 acres covering most of the flood plain embayment. Th
Application says it is for the area 'formerly worked by the Linger an
Die party.' This is the only reference to such a 'party' but no forma
reference to a 'Linger and Die' company, syndicate or claim has bee

found in the records. Presumably it was a nickname coined by locals for the unfortunate claim. The expression must have been in common use by 1925 as the *Alexandra Herald*, in its report[11] of the setting up of the Alexandra Deep Lead Company referred to the proposed mine 'formerly known as the Linger and Die claim.' It apparently did not think it necessary to offer any explanation for the unusual name. It is likely that the name was first used in reference to the persistent but futile attempts of the Golden Bend company to reach gold during the 1904 -1908 period.

The fact that the expression, which was obviously intended to apply to the claim itself, is now popularly applied to the whole embayment is unimportant. What is important is that the name be preserved to take its place alongside other colourful names that expressed the hardship and uncertainties of life on the goldfields.

NOTES

1. J. Park, 1906 p. 26.
2. The gullies are clearly seen in a photograph taken from the hills to the east of the town by G. F. Griffiths and published in J. Park, 1906 p. 8.
3. During excavations for the rifle range, which is under the stage of the theatre, all sorts of relics were recovered including several lemonade bottles with glass marbles as stoppers.
4. *Alexandra Herald* 29 September 1904.
5. *Alexandra Herald* 7 February 1906.
6. *NZ Gazette* 1927 p. 3460.
7. AJHR C2 1927 p. 281.
8. AJHR C2 1928 p. 25.
9. Pers. comm. Mr E. V. King of Alexandra who worked for the company.
10 Application 24/12 of 22 September 1912 to Alexandra Warden's Court. Application held in National Archives, Dunedin Regional Office.
11. *Alexandra Herald* 5 August 1925.

25.

LAST CHANCE

For more than 20 years, James Hesson and party successfully mined their claim on Obelisk Creek at Bald Hill Flat (later called Fruitlands). During this period, they acquired the rights to a large quantity of water from a number of sources. First, in 1891, they constructed a 12-kilometre race to bring in eight heads from Gorge Creek and with this they recovered sufficient gold to justify installing a hydraulic elevator. But to work this satisfactorily required even more water. So they bought the liquidated Commissioners Flat Company's water right for 20 heads from Shingle Creek and another from the Quayle brothers for the same creek. To bring all this water to their claim, they extended their race to a total of 27 kilometres in length, employing three men constantly to keep it in order. In spite of the large quantity of water that they now owned, it was still very difficult, because of the dry weather and the nature of the country through which the long race passed, to deliver more than 4 heads to the claim.

Last Chance Companies

In 1895 Hesson and Simmonds formed the Last Chance Hydraulic Elevating Company as a private company and then, in 1899,[1] they converted it to a public company, the Last Chance Sluicing, Elevating and Gold-Dredging Co Ltd, with capital of £12,000 and 103 shareholders.

Probably the company's most successful year was 1903 and from then on it was all downhill. The company was liquidated in 1907 and sold off to a much smaller concern called the Last Chance Mining Co Ltd. which struggled on for a few years and finally petered out in 1911.

At this point Charles Weaver, well known dredgeowner and master of the *Earnscleugh* dredges, stepped in and bought the Last Chance claim, plant and water rights for £1,000. He immediately resold the races and water rights to the Government for £1,200. He was criticised for this and felt obliged to make a public statement in which he explained that it was a chance to ensure that the land between Shingle Creek and Earnscleugh was brought under irrigation. He admitted that he had made £200 from the deal but regarded that as his commission for his work in making the arrangements.

Because of the First World War, and the fact that the Manuherikia Irrigation Scheme had priority for manpower and materials, it was

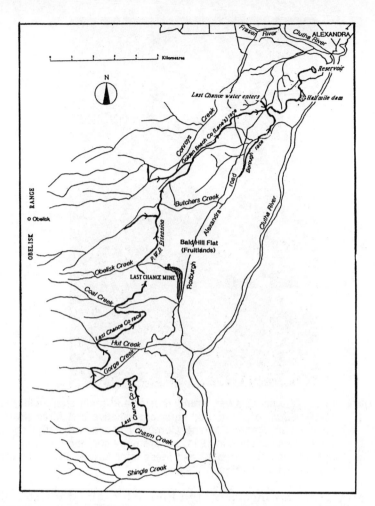

Figure 25. 1. During 1923-24 the Public Works Department developed the Last Chance Irrigation Scheme. The Last Chance Mining Company's race from Shingle Creek to Obelisk Creek was renovated and extended to meet up with the old Golden Beach race which was then upgraded and connected to the Alexandra Borough water race. For many years extra water was, in this way, supplied to the borough.

1922 before the Public Works Department was able to turn its attention to the Last Chance Scheme, as it was called. The Department began by renovating and extending the old races of the Last Chance Company and was able to supply six settlers at Fruitlands with irrigation water the following year. It was then decided to extend the scheme northwards to Butchers Creek and beyond. So in 1924 negotiations were begun with the Alexandra Borough Council to take over the Golden Beach race, and the water right from Butchers Creek that went with it, which the council had bought from J. P. Lane a few years before.

Figure 25. 2. Charles Weaver, dredgemaster and main shareholder in the *Earnscleugh* dredges, had sufficient initiative and foresight to buy up the Last Chance Mining Company assets when the company went into liquidation in 1911. He promptly sold the races and water rights to the Government and these later formed the foundation of the Last Chance Irrigation Scheme.

As an interim arrangement, the Borough Council insisted that some water be delivered into the borough race, and this was accepted. Then the Public Works Department began to renovate and realign the old race so that it commanded much of the easy country between Conroys and Butchers Creeks. The end of the race was led into the borough race at the point where it came close to the main road.

At this point the Borough Council suggested that the Government should swap about 1,000 acres (400h) of Crown Land in exchange for the race. The block that the council had its eye on lay between the Roxburgh road and the Clutha River and stretched from the Halfmile Dam to Butchers Gully. Unfortunately, this land was already firmly leased to runholders, so there were difficulties in the proposed arrangement and instead, at the end of 1925, the council accepted the Government's offer of £75 cash for the race, but excluding the water rights.

So for the next 12 years Alexandra's water supply from Butchers Creek received a supplement from the Last Chance irrigation scheme by way of the old Golden Beach race.

292

Figure 25. 3. The old Caledonian race, first constructed in 1864, has had many owners including the Golden Beach Company, the Alexandra Borough Council, the Public Works Department and finally, today, as part of the Last Chance Scheme, it is controlled by the irrigators themselves. Here the race approaches the Butchers Gully-Conroys Road.

Perhaps this additional water was more than the borough reservoir could stand, because at 6.30 pm on 3 February 1930, an orchardist who lived near the mouth of Chapmans Gully was disturbed by the sound of a large quantity of water flowing past his house. As there was no rain, he reasoned the water must be coming from the reservoir and accordingly notified the authorities. Workmen, the mayor, Town Clerk and some councillors assembled with commendable speed to inspect a scene of imminent disaster. Strong winds had whipped up waves in the brimming reservoir and these had eroded the clay backfill of the northern wall and allowed water to reach the outer stone wall.

Up to 20 heads of water were pouring through the stone work and down a steep gully leading into Chapmans Gully. The clay liner sealing the reservoir was being quickly eroded and a gap, already several metres wide, was growing wider by the second. The stone wall was in imminent danger of collapse which would allow the whole reservoir to

Figure 25. 4. W. A. Bodkin (later Sir William) (1885-1964). First elected to Parliament in 1928, he represented Central Otago as the candidate for United, United Coalition and National Parties and, until he retired in 1954, was a tireless protagonist for the development of his electorate. He was largely responsible for persuading Government to start the programme of dam building during the Depression.

drain catastrophically.

Willing workers hurriedly gathered rocks and earth and dumped them into the hole until the leak was reduced to a trickle and the danger of wall collapse was over. Next day permanent repairs were carried out.

Butchers Dam

It was realised early in the development of Central Otago irrigation schemes that the same pattern of stream flow which had plagued the miners was going to detract from the benefits of irrigation. Only in the spring when snow was melting on the hills, was there a surplus of water, but it so happened that this was the time when there was also a surplus of moisture in the farmers' soils and irrigation was unnecessary. The dry summer and autumn that brought a large demand for irrigation water also caused a shortage of water in the streams supplying the races. 'Run of the river' irrigation schemes, as they were called, were mainly unsuccessful. The answer, as the miners well knew, lay in large storage dams.

The first dam to be constructed and the largest of all, the Upper Manorburn Dam, had been built before the Great War. It wasn't until the Depression of the early 1930s, however, with its abundance of unemployed men, that the Government, prodded by the Member for Central Otago, W. A. Bodkin, began a flurry of dam construction. First, came the Poolburn Dam in 1930 to boost the southern Ida Valley Scheme and then Idaburn Dam for the northern part. Falls Dam on the upper Manuherikia River to supply the Manuherikia Scheme came next, followed, in 1932, by the Lower Manorburn Dam for the Galloway flats.

Conroys Dam, to service part of Earnscleugh, was completed in 1935 and a year before it was finished, Cabinet approved[2] a dam across the upper entrance to Butchers Creek gorge, with work to be put in hand as soon as possible. The purpose of this new dam was to enable the Public Works Department to supply Alexandra, and the fairly small area of land between the dam and Alexandra, with water stored during the spring thaw. This meant that, during the summer, when every drop of water was precious, all of the water in the high-level Last Chance race could be used to irrigate the extensive area of land between Butchers and Conroys Creeks.

Although there was universal satisfaction over the decision to build the dam, not everyone was prepared to go along with the agreement the Public Works Department proposed for supplying water to the borough. It was, that in exchange for the council's water rights to Butchers Creek, the Department would deliver into the borough reservoir an average flow of one and a half heads throughout the year with a maximum of three heads at any one time. For this water the department was to charge £200 a year for the first 10 years and £225 a year thereafter which was about the standard charge for irrigation water for the district. The arrangement was for all time and the borough was, of course, relieved of all upkeep charges on the race and dam.

It looked like a good deal. It would deliver more water into the reservoir than the overloaded and shaky borough race was capable of doing, and one particularly attractive aspect was the plan to have the outlet from the dam through a long tunnel. This would cut out the siphons and flumes of the Butchers Creek gorge with their high upkeep and vulnerability to rock falls and slips.

Bill Bringans, the mayor, called a public meeting and pointed out that if the council were to enter into any sort of agreement to last for more than 21 years, then either a poll or special legislation would be necessary. After explaining the proposed agreement and having the Town Clerk quote the cost per year for upkeep and the amount of water actually received through the race, the mayor opened up the meeting for discussion. The theme of many speakers, including some councillors, was that they were giving away a very valuable asset in their water right and then having to buy the water back. The tone of the meeting seemed unfavourable to the agreement and the mayor wisely suggested that they adjourn for a week to let people think about the proposition.

An editorial, and letters to the editor all strongly in favour of the agreement, appeared in the interval. The second meeting was marked by an attendance twice that of the first. The arguments marshalled by the mayor and backed by reports from engineers, were hard to fault. As much as one and a half heads of water were lost from the present race through leakage and there was no way that the Halfmile Dam could be raised safely to provide extra storage. If the borough itself were forced to build Butchers Dam it would cost £500 a year in charges alone without upkeep. Here was the Government offering to spend £20,000, almost entirely for the borough's benefit and giving it a guaranteed supply of more water that they had ever had, for £200 a year.

This time the audience was more sympathetic. One man pointed out the concern seemed to be they were giving away their water rights but, he said, it was not rights they wanted—it was water. Father Daniel O'Connell, who would go on to become one of the town's characters, made a speech which must have been the highlight of the evening. Amongst other things he said:

> I had not realised that men could talk so eloquently on water alone. It has been said that water was good if taken in the right spirit and I hope that the argument tonight will be taken in the right spirit. The argument about the value of rights is not sound, as the value of the rights is over-estimated. The argument is similar to the position of a man who had a horse worth £5000 but cannot catch it. If we get sufficient water over an enduring future I cannot see any value in 'rights' This is the long-term view. The short term view is that many wage earners need the wages that work on the dam will bring. Taking the long or short term view it is a good scheme. It will relieve the borough of all future anxiety and responsibility and expense. I think the ratepayers would be unwise not to accept the scheme.[3]

Father Dan's speech swayed the meeting and a series of motions and amendments resulted in a resolution being passed requesting council to hold a poll of ratepayers. The poll was held and it was reported on 14 November 1934 that 134 were in favour of council entering the agreement and only 22 against.

Butchers Dam

Conroys Dam was finished in late March 1935 and the men were moved over to begin work on Butchers Dam. The site, already surveyed, was a few metres upstream from where the siphon on the borough race crossed the narrow gorge. Work began at once on excavating the foundations and on the outlet tunnel which, by July was one third finished. Concrete work on the dam started soon afterwards and proceeded steadily until the completion in late 1937 The dam is a concrete arch 27 metres high and 32 metres round the top. A noteworthy feature is that water leaves the reservoir by means of a tunnel more than 700 metres long, cut through solid schist rock before continuing in a race which, although following closely the route of the old borough race, entailed much renovation and new construction.

Alexandra Borough Council and the Government agreed on 1 April 1937, that the borough water right to Butchers Creek should be surrendered to the Crown in return for a supply of 550 dayheads (that

Figure 25. 5. Butchers Dam was completed in 1937 and solved the problem of lack of water storage both for local irrigators and Alexandra borough for a number of years. This air view shows the dam and reservoir and, in the centre, old gold workings. Beyond these are the trees surrounding the orchard and garden established by Lye Bow.

is, a flow of one and a half heads for 365 days) of water for a term of 999 years. The new water supply came just in time, as the fluming and siphon in Butchers Creek gorge were at the end of their life. Certainly, much of the fluming had been relined, but there was a limit to this sort of expediency and nothing could be done, short of complete renewal, to prolong the life of the worn out pipes of the main siphons.

So after the agreement was signed, it was with thankfulness that the council gave up responsibility for the race. Nor was there any longer need for the council to provide storage, so the Halfmile Dam, with its constant leaks and shaky walls, was also abandoned without regret. The skating fraternity had already found much more reliable ice on the Lower Manorburn reservoir completed a few years before. Water from Butchers Dam was first turned into the borough race in January 1938.

Irrigation

Although supplying Alexandra with water was the main function of Butchers Dam and the race leading to the reservoir, both were part of the Last Chance Irrigation Scheme and irrigation from the race was always an important aspect. There are many controlled openings along the race and these feed water into distributary ditches. From these water was allowed to trickle, more or less at will, down slopes, a procedure known as 'wild flooding.' It is not regarded as a particularly efficient use of water but is the only practical method (apart from very expensive spray irrigation) for covering this rocky terrain and, with a certain amount of hand labour, results in a high proportion of the land below the races being irrigated.

Figure 25. 6. An unusual feature of Butchers Dam is the 700 metre tunnel, driven through solid rock, which provides an outlet for the stored water and does away with the need for a water race through the precipitous gorge below the dam. The photograph is of the outlet of the tunnel.

Shortages and Pollution

Future shortage of water was something not envisaged in 1938 when the water from Butchers Dam began to flow along the borough race. There was so much water, in fact, that those with orchards in the residential part of the town were encouraged to draw water from the town mains so that the remaining races distributing water from the Chatto Creek race could be closed down. It was reasoned that if the town did grow, it would be at the expense of orchard and farmland within the borough and houses would use less water per acre than horticultural land.

It did not work out that way. When Alexandra's population began to increase rapidly after the Second World War, water consumption went up alarmingly.

Water use increased to the point where the street mains, many of them the small-diameter pipes laid for the waterworks scheme of 1903, were simply not large enough to handle the draw-off. No doubt adequate when first laid, they could not be expected to handle the requirements of whole new suburbs of modern houses with modern water requirements, including almost constant irrigation of gardens and lawns for six months of the year. In addition, summer saw thousands of visitors descend on the town.

The climax came in the summer of 1955-56 when, in spite of rationing, the available stored water in the Butchers Dam was, for the first time, completely exhausted. There was insufficient water to keep

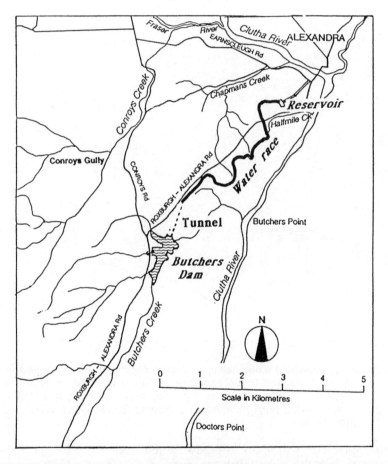

Figure 25. 7. The final configuration of the Butchers Creek water supply. The race through Butchers Gorge was abandoned when water from Butchers Dam became available, as also was the Halfmile Dam.

the town mains full and people on the Terrace were without water. A large fire would have been a calamity.

The catchment of Butcher's Creek was open run-country stocked with sheep and accessible to the public. People lived on the banks of

Butcher's Dam; the main highway ran across several of its arms and it was also a favourite fishing spot. Furthermore, the race connecting the dam to the borough reservoir ran for some kilometres through farmlands and, in places, ran alongside and crossed under the main highway.

Many of the water samples regularly tested by the Health Department showed that there was an increasing amount of pollution in the water. Much of it was vegetable matter which, though relatively

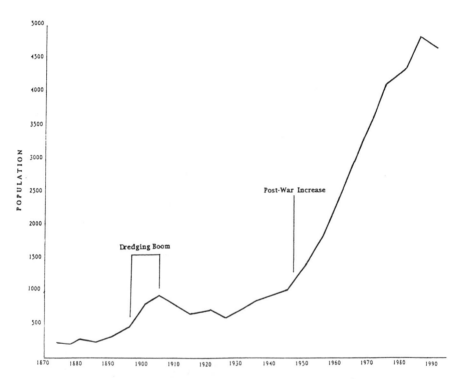

Figure 25. 8. Alexandra's population increased rapidly during the dredging boom of the late 1890s and then fell away with the reduction in dredging. It did not equal its 1906 population until the mid-1940s. About 1948 a rapid increase in population began which continued until recently.

harmless, gave the water an offensive smell and a distinctive colour. More serious was the increasing presence of *E. coli*, an easily identified bacterium used as an indicator of the presence of other, possibly dangerous, bugs. Other things came through the pipes too—there was the occasion when, at a practice session, the fire brigade pump coughed and spat out the macerated remains of a large fish that had passed through it from the mains.

So water supply, and its problems, was once more back on the council's monthly agenda. There were some obvious things that could be done to save water. A bore was put down and water pumped into he baths. Everyone was delighted with the clear, sparkling, but very old water. Onlookers could even see the rather cracked bottom of the pool—something that had not been possible when the baths were filled with water from the borough mains. But, what was this? Within two days the clear water had turned a brilliant green colour and was a thick as soup. Apparently algae in the water had proliferated mightily as the nutrient-rich water warmed up. It was a good idea that didn't work but the pumped water was not wasted—it was diverted to spray-irrigate Pioneer Park, another prolific user of the borough water.

The pipeline from the reservoir down to the bridge was showing its

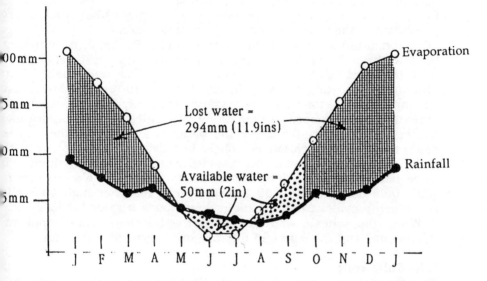

Figure 25. 9. About 90% of Alexandra's water supply is used for irrigation of gardens and lawns. The need for irrigation is explained by the diagram that shows that only during the months of May through to October does the soil contain sufficient moisture to sustain plants. For the remainder of the year water is lost from the soil by evaporation and must be replaced by irrigation.

age. The secondhand pipes, bought in the 1920s, were rusting and developing small holes. As the pipeline was laid on the surface, these leaks were fully visible and gave rise to spectacular small fountains, which in days of hard frost, formed wondrous formations of icicles. The standard cure for these leaks was to drive a small, shaped, wooden peg into the hole and borough workmen carried a ready supply of these in their truck. The net result was to convert the pipes into porcupine-like objects which were a curiosity to strangers and a source of interest to local children who delighted in removing the pegs to reinstate the fountains. This could not go on indefinitely and the worst pipes were replaced in one long, non-stop, 24-hour effort during which time the town was without mains water.

There was talk of water-meters to restrict water use but this was regarded as too radical for a town which, without adequate water would quickly revert to a dust bowl. Several meters were, however installed in volunteers' properties and the results were startling. They showed that the highest water consumption was about 1,000 gallons (about 4,500 litres) a day for each person, with normal daily summer consumption about 500 gallons (2,200 litres) per person and normal winter use 130 gallons (600 litres).[2] Irrigation, holiday visitors and the requirements of the swimming baths accounted for much of the difference between summer and winter use.

It was the great amount of water expended on very necessary irrigation that made the council hesitate when it was clear that the obvious solution to the pollution problem was to treat the water. Council was loath to introduce expensive treatment when such a large proportion of the town's water was used for irrigation.

On consultants' advice, large trunk mains were laid directly through the town from the bridge to serve the outskirts and a test well installed near the river bank to carry out prolonged flow and quality tests. Although this testing proved satisfactory it proved very difficult to have an application for the necessary loan approved. Wellington bureaucrats, ensconced in their rainy city, ruled that Alexandra used far too much water—far above the national average. So they turned down the loan application not once, but twice. It was not until the early 1970s that a system was installed which included pumping from three bores sunk deep into the riverbank gravels. It also included 1,000,000 gallon (4,500,000 litres) covered reservoir high on Bridge Hill which provides water for about three hours' serious fire fighting.

When the scheme was completed the Butchers Dam supply was abandoned and the dam and the race used solely for irrigation.

The Full Circle

The present scheme is almost exactly the same as that drawn up Postlethwaite 100 years ago. His plan (Chapter 14) was to use electric pumps to lift water from wells sunk into the gravels beside the river pipe it to a holding reservoir on a hill and from there feed water in the town's mains.

All through the 130 odd years that the town has been battling with succession of schemes to provide itself with water, the great river has been gliding serenely on its way not far below the main street. The first settlers drew their water directly from the river and, although it has taken more than 110 years for the wheel to make a full turn, the townspeople of today again draw their water from the river—though a much more complicated and expensive way. The prediction made the editor of the *Dunstan Times* 95 years ago has come to pass:

> A scheme that commends itself is lifting water from the river. . . T
> is no doubt the best water and will eventually be the scheme by wh
> the people of Alexandra will obtain their water.[5]

NOTES

1. The company was registered on 27/7/99.
2. *Alexandra Herald* 29 August 1934.
3. *Alexandra Herald* 10 and 17 October, 1934 Reports of public meetings, editorial and correspondence.
4. It is interesting to compare these figures with those for Ngaruawahia, a town of similar size when these readings were made, but with an annual rainfall four and a half times as great (1500 mm v 330 mm)

	NGARUAWAHIA	ALEXANDRA
Annual rainfall	1500 mm	330 mm
Normal summer daily consumption per head	147 galls(667L)	500 galls(2,200L)
Normal winter daily consumption per head	55 galls(250L)	130 galls(600L)

(Ngaruawahia information from Latta 1963 and 1980).

Alexandra's summer consumption is 3.4 times as much as that of Ngaruawahia.
The high winter consumption in Alexandra is attributed to the fact that taps are left running to prevent pipes from freezing.
5. *Dunstan Times* 26 February 1901.

INDEX